Russian–American relations in the post-Cold War world

James W. Peterson

Manchester University Press

Published by Manchester University Press
Altrincham Street, Manchester M1 7JA
www.manchesteruniversitypress.co.uk

British Library Cataloguing-in-Publication Data
A catalogue record for this book is available from the British Library

ISBN   978 1 5261 0579 0   paperback
ISBN   978 1 5261 0578 3   hardback

First published 2017

Typeset
by Toppan Best-set Premedia Limited
Printed in Great Britain
by CPI Group (UK) Ltd, Croydon CR0 4YY

Russian-American relations in the post-Cold War world

Manchester University Press

This book is dedicated to Bonnie, Jesse, Jenna, Azeez, and Ayan

Contents

Acknowledgements

The author would like to acknowledge the strong support from the members of the Department of Political Science at Valdosta State University. There has been mutual appreciation for the research projects of each other as well as readiness on the part of many to interact in a meaningful way with faculty members at institutions in the former communist bloc. He also acknowledges our vital connections with faculty members in the partner Department of Politics and European Studies at Palacký University in Olomouc, Czech Republic. Each of them has shared the memories and experiences of what life was like in the period under communist control as well as in the period after its ending. The positive interactions of the faculty members in these two departments are particularly important to the author, who spent several years as a translator on the old West German–Czechoslovak border in an effort to defend against the threat that emanated from the communist bloc. It is important to remember and celebrate the positive changes that have taken place in recent decades.

The author would also like to acknowledge the excellent work of the editorial staff at Manchester University Press, in particular Tony Mason, Rob Byron, Alun Richards, and David Appleyard, and of copy-editor Judith Oppenheimer.

Two anthems

Russian State Anthem (Verses 1 and 2, translated by Fabio Lazzati)

Russia, you are our sacred Power!
Russia, you are our beloved land!
The mighty will and the immense glory –
Here is your heritage in any predicament.

Our woods and our fields extend
From the southern seas as far as the North Pole.
You are a one in the world! You are quite a one,
Native land protected by God.

The Star Spangled Banner (Verse 4, Francis Scott Key, 1814)

Oh! thus be it ever, when freemen shall stand
Between their loved home and the war's desolation!
Blest with victory and peace, may the heav'n rescued land
Praise the Power that hath made and preserved us a nation.
Then conquer we must, when our cause it is just,
And this be our motto: "In God is our trust."
And the star-spangled banner in triumph shall wave
O'er the land of the free and the home of the brave!

Abbreviations

ABM	anti-ballistic missile
APEC	Asia-Pacific Economic Community
CFE	Conventional Forces Europe
CIA	Central Intelligence Agency
CIS	Commonwealth of Independent States
CPSU	Communist Party of the Soviet Union
CSTO	Collective Security Treaty Organization
EU	European Union
G8	Group of Eight
ICBM	intercontinental ballistic missiles
INF	Intermediate Nuclear Forces
ISIS	Islamic State in Iraq and Syria
NAC	North Atlantic Council
NATO	North Atlantic Treaty Organization
NRC	NATO–Russia Council
OSCE	Organization for Security and Co-operation in Europe
PfP	Partners for Peace
SALT	Strategic Arms Limitation Treaty / Strategic Arms Limitation Talks
SCO	Shanghai Cooperation Organization
START	Strategic Arms Reduction Treaty
TPP	Trans-Pacific Partnership
WMD	Weapons of Mass Destruction

Introduction: from the Cold War to the Crimea: a bumpy road

Russia and America are two large and powerful eagles that share the perspective that their destiny in the world is a very special one. Both celebrate that unique status in the anthems that they integrate into special events such as presidential inaugurations. Each anthem emerged at a unique and parallel time in the history of the nation. For Russia, its current anthem became official a decade after the implosion of the Soviet Union and the emergence of the modern state. In the American case, the anthem has been in place for two full centuries and emerged in the midst of a war in which the new nation defeated its former colonial power for a second time, several decades after the first victory. Both nations and peoples draw inspiration from a much deeper well of historical experiences that the two anthems evoke. For Russia, there is a striking parallel between the soaring words of the current state hymn and the original one written in 1791 to commemorate the outreach of Catherine the Great into the former Polish kingdom as well as the far-off Black Sea region. For America, its anthem evokes memories of an expansive nation that once huddled on the shores of the Atlantic but eventually incorporated all the territory to the Pacific Ocean and beyond. In their official anthems, both nations have essentially created hymns of religious intensity to the God that opened these doors and bestowed his blessing on the results.

It is time to take a careful look at the road that these two nations have traveled in the first quarter-century of the post-Cold War era. There is no question but that it has been a bumpy one.

In fact, the ambiguity and misperceptions of the period have roots in the late-Cold War period. Pursuit of détente agreements coincided with both tough actions by the Brezhnev regime near the Soviet border and a significant build-up of military capabilities by the Reagan administration. It should be no surprise that this potent mixture of contradictory expectations exploded once more with the crisis over Crimea and the Ukraine in 2014 and after. Once again, there was concrete evidence of both Russian aggressive outreach and a stiffening of American/NATO (North Atlantic Treaty Organization) resolve to stand up and put a stop to those purposeful moves from the East. It is important for both scholars and practitioners to develop models and action plans that can guide and nudge this turbulent relationship into predictable channels that can calm the waters. This Prologue will outline a book that will clarify some of these questions and offer hope for a more predictable relationship.

Chapter 1 will outline important theories of great-power conflicts that can illuminate certain features of the complicated Russian–American relationship. Key concepts that will receive attention include those theories that center on the balance of power, bipolarity, unipolarity, multi-polarity, and continuous chaos. It is possible to notice elements of each theory in the relationship between the two powers at different points in the period after 1991. The mutual search for allies through NATO expansion by the West and through the creation of structures such as the Commonwealth of Independent States (CIS) and the Eurasian Economic Community by the East conjure up images of at least the possibility for an equitable position between Moscow and Washington. Their unrelated pivots toward Asia provide another picture of potential balance between the two. Bipolarity may be an accurate way of depicting the mutual understanding between the two nations and sets of leaders after the 9/11 attacks in 2001. Russian leaders then hoped that their American counterparts would now understand what they had been facing with the terrorist attacks that had their origins in the Caucasus. This may explain in part the Russian willingness to permit American access to two military bases in Central Asian countries that had been part of the old Soviet Union.

Unipolarity occasionally helps to clarify the picture at key points in time. For instance, the American free hand during the Gulf War of 1990–91 suggested that the only remaining superpower had no real rival in shaping a "New World Order." Similarly, after fourteen years at the top, in 2014 President Putin took actions toward the Ukraine that were not really checked or countered by the concerned nations that made up the "West." In other regions it would be difficult to escape the conclusion that both strong nations realized that new centers of global and regional power were emerging over which they had little influence. That emerging multi-polarity included the rise of powerful Asian states, the resurgence of Islamism that was part of the Arab Spring upheavals, and the outbreak of civil wars in Libya, Syria, Egypt, Iraq, Yemen, and the Ukraine. Finally, chaos theorists might throw up their hands at the "bumpy road" between Russia and America and conclude that there really has been no pattern after the end of Cold War predictabilities.

There are five secondary theories that will assist in the overall analysis of this complicated relationship. One is the traditional Systems Theory that can be useful in examining the kind of symbiotic relationship between the two, as the topic of Russian–American relations involves more than two separate nations acting exclusively in their own worlds. Second, Legacy Theory helps to delineate the carry-over of traditions and practices from previous historical periods and regimes or governments. Third is an informal theory of Critical Junctures that can be very helpful in delineating watershed points in time when the relationship between the two moved in a new and different direction. Fourth, Realist Theory can help to scratch beneath the surface of the idealistic anthems presented at the beginning. Leaders in each nation used both hard and soft power to protect their national interests and extend the reach of their national units. Fifth and finally, national elites of both nations became aware of the limits of state-centered realism and began to make policy initiative and adjustments in the light of Revised Realist Theory that gave much greater play and space to the torrent of globalization streams that have been so characteristic of the twenty-first century.

Chapter 2 will explore the ambiguities of the later Cold War in the 1972–91 time frame. The spirit of détente in part animates the period, for the Cuban Missile Crisis put a scare into both superpowers about what crises were like in the nuclear age. Meetings in the decade before 1972 paved the way for the meaningful agreements of the 1972–79 period. In 1972, the United States and the Soviet Union signed the SALT (Strategic Arms Limitation Treaty) I Agreement that froze the numbers of nuclear warheads and limited the number of anti-ballistic missile (ABM) sites to two in each country. Later diplomacy reduced the number of ABM sites to one each in the Vladivostok Agreement between President Ford and First Secretary Brezhnev in 1974. The next step entailed a cut-back in the number of offensive warheads in an equitable way as the SALT II Agreement neared its final phase in 1977. The outcome of the Helsinki meetings and agreement in 1975 was also promising, with implications for greater protection of human rights and increased economic connections among nations both East and West. Such talks and agreements set a different tone than the one that had characterized the first quarter-century of the Cold War. They were possible in part because the United States had completed its involvement in the War in Southeast Asia, while the Soviet Union at the time did not face any sharp challenges from its East European partners.

However, there was another side to the story of détente. Many critics within the United States wanted stricter verification of the agreements, for they doubted that Soviet leaders were actually implementing them. Differences between an open and a closed society accounted for that kind of skepticism. In 1977 the new Carter administration wanted to take a fresh look at the details of the SALT II Agreement, and the incoming U.S. president also initiated sharp criticism of the Soviet leadership for its human rights record with respect to dissidents. This postponed ratification of the Agreement from 1977 to 1979, and by then it was too late. The Soviet invasion of Afghanistan at the end of 1979 prompted President Carter to withdraw the Treaty from the Senate just as that body was considering ratification. A grain embargo and boycott of the 1980 Moscow Olympics followed soon thereafter. Eventually, in the 1980s President Reagan embarked upon a major arms build-up that strengthened all components of the American nuclear arsenal, with hostile reactions from a series of leaders on the other side. Thus, the door that had opened in the early period of détente closed in the following decade. These experiences suggest a duality that clearly carried over into post-communist times.

In Chapter 3 the break-up of the Soviet Union and its impact on Russian–American relations will receive attention. The collapse of the huge federation occurred at the end of 1991, but the rise to power of reform leader Mikhail Gorbachev in 1985 was the precipitating factor. His reforms relaxed internal controls, reallocated power from the Communist Party of the Soviet Union (CPSU) to the government, and led to considerable retrenchment in foreign policy. His willingness to withdraw from Afghanistan, to reduce the Soviet military presence along the Chinese border as well as in Europe, and to sign the INF Agreement in 1987 led to better relations with the United States.

However, by 1990 Gorbachev was in a much weaker position domestically within the Soviet political system. When Iraq invaded and took over Kuwait in August 1990 a partial global leadership vacuum permitted the United States to take the lead in coordinating the response through a series of UN resolutions. Although the Soviet Union had earlier sold weapons to Iraq, it did not stand in the way of the western military effort that led to Iraq's defeat and pull-out from Kuwait by early 1991. A coup temporarily deposed Gorbachev in late summer, and by the end of the year both he and the Soviet Union were gone from the political scene. These developments gave a huge advantage to the United States and invited the George H.W. Bush administration to embrace concepts such as New World Order in which America would take the lead in attempting to resolve global crises. Obviously, there were political forces and personalities within the new Russia that regretted the profound imbalance of power and hoped for restored greatness in the future.

Chapter 4 will include coverage of Russian–American tensions and differences over the Balkan Wars of the 1990s. In western eyes, the Serbian leader Slobodan Milošević was the provocative player who engaged in wars in Slovenia, Croatia, Bosnia, and Kosovo. The first three had been republics in the larger Yugoslavia that collapsed in 1991, while the fourth was at the time still a republic in the much shrunken Yugoslavia. Both the Bosnian and Kosovan conflicts eventually led to American-orchestrated NATO operations. After considerable passage of time and loss of life in the Bosnia War of 1992–95, NATO finally carried out military strikes on Serbian positions that eventually brought all parties to the bargaining table and resulted in the Dayton Agreement of 1995. The western military alliance reacted much more quickly in 1999, once the Serbian military went into Kosovo in an operation against the overwhelmingly Muslim population. The result was a pull-out of Serbian forces from the Muslim sectors of that republic.

However, Russian leaders had very different perceptions of those wars in Southeast Europe. Russians and Serbs had been close historically, and this led President Boris Yeltsin in Russia to react in protective ways toward Milošević. From the Russian point of view, the Serbs in the new Yugoslavia were simply looking out for and protecting the now Serbian minority in all four locations. When there was a larger Yugoslavia, the Serbs in the four territories were part of the group that had a plurality of the population and enjoyed predominant advantages. Now the tables were turned and the Serbs found themselves in a minority position in each area. Kosovo was an outlier, in the sense that it was not a nation but continued to have a special status in Yugoslavia as a republic. However, nearly a decade of war in the region awakened the aspirations of the 90% Muslim majority in Kosovo to what its new political status might be. The Russians also drew parallels between the situation of the Serbian minorities in the four new political units and the plight of Russian minorities in new countries such as those in the Baltic region. Fears of discrimination against those Russian minorities in Estonia, Latvia, and Lithuania heightened the natural sympathy of the Russian State for the situation of the Serbs and even the decisions of their president. The different choices that the American and Russian leaders made in the Balkans had grave implications later on in their application to Georgia and Ukraine.

In Chapter 5 readers will learn how the expansion of the NATO alliance acted as a wedge that pushed Russia and America even further apart. When the Cold War officially ended in 1991 there were many who anticipated and even predicted the collapse of both military alliances. Some expected that East–West organizations like the Organization for Security and Co-operation in Europe (OSCE) might be the alliance of the future. Indeed, the Warsaw Treaty Organization or Warsaw Pact dissolved rapidly, and many expected that the same outcome would occur for the western alliance. However, new challenges such as those in the Balkans underlined the value and utility of a military organization whose original design had been for a force that could halt Soviet probes across the Iron Curtain. Indeed, American leaders began to set up the Partners for Peace (PfP) program that would establish candidate status for former communist nations that sought additional measures of security. As a result, the alliance added new members in three stages across a decade. In 1999, NATO admitted Poland, the Czech Republic, and Hungary. The Class of 2004 included Estonia, Latvia, Lithuania, Slovenia, Slovakia, Bulgaria, and Romania. The last stage in the process of incorporation granted membership to both Croatia and Albania in 2009. The admission of the three

Baltic states particularly angered Russia, for all three had actually been republics in the Soviet Union, and so the admission process hit particularly close to home. Russian leaders protested that NATO was marching to their very doorstep and encircling them in a way that had characterized the Cold War. Bitterness percolated through every statement about the NATO expansion process.

The attacks on American territory on September 11, 2001, had the result of pulling Russia and America back to a point of some common understandings. In Chapter 6 there will be a focus on the reasons and extent of that common understanding. It is of crucial importance that the West was critical of Russian military actions during the first (1994–96) and second (1999–2001) wars against violent forces in the Republic of Chechnya. That republic had actually declared independence in 1991 and asserted its intention to become an Islamic state. The Russian military engaged in two wars against the militant forces in Chechnya, in an effort to stop the terrorist actions that sporadically occurred. Western leaders were quite critical of Russia's overreaction and excessive use of force by its military. Of course, the terrorist actions that stemmed from the Caucasus would continue through the first years of the new century, with Chechen attacks on public institutions such as a theater and school.

Once America felt the pain and shock of the 9/11 attacks by Islamists committed to violence, there was new common ground between the two global players. President Putin expected that the George W. Bush administration would now comprehend what the Russians had been going through. In the wake of that attack there was no serious Russian protest against arrangements that America worked out with both Kyrgyzstan and Uzbekistan for rights to use local military bases. Thus, Manas became available in the former state and Khanabad in the latter. The ensuing presence of American military forces on the territory of former Soviet republics was indeed a new development that characterized temporary harmony between Moscow and Washington. Ironically, the turbulence in the Caucasus also produced the terrorists who took so many casualties during the running of the Boston Marathon in 2013. Even that attack added a few building blocks to a small but definite foundation of understanding.

The American wars in Afghanistan and Iraq as well as the brief Russian war in Georgia consumed the entire first decade of the twenty-first century, and they provided plenty of fuel for Russian–American misunderstanding. This topic will form the centerpiece of Chapter 7. After all, Russia had fought its own war in Afghanistan in the 1979–88 period, and now America was battling in the same location and quite close to the Russian border and sphere of influence. At the same time, Russian leaders shared the doubts that many European leaders had about the decision of the Bush administration to invade Iraq with the goal of regime change. While Russia shared America's interest in preventing the spread of nuclear weapons into unpredictable and dangerous hands, over the years, the duration and course of the war gave rise to serious Russian doubts.

It is also the case that NATO's involvement in both wars compounded the Russian anxiety. By 2009 the military alliance was fully in control of the Afghanistan operation, while it also played a key role in Iraq in training local military and police forces. Many troops from former communist states and Soviet/Yugoslav republics were active in those efforts. As members of the "new" Europe, they were more willing to follow American leadership than were traditional allies of the U.S. such as France and Germany.

Russia's war in Georgia and the resulting inclusion of two of its enclaves into Russia in 2008 was a major divisive issue between America and Russia. President Saakashvili of Georgia had initiated the attacks against the enclaves of Abkhazia and South Ossetia, but the Russian response appeared to be an overreaction to western powers. If misperceptions between East and West had deepened over Afghanistan and Iraq, they sharpened considerably during and after the Georgia War.

In the midst of these wars, America proposed a Missile Shield project that sought to protect Europe from a potential nuclear attack by Iran or by another rogue state that developed such weapons, and this project will receive attention in Chapter 8. The Missile Shield proposal itself included radar-detection sites in the Czech Republic as well as anti-missile interceptors in Poland, plans that were controversial in both countries but that their leadership accepted. Even though parts of western Russia would receive protection under the Shield, its leaders in the diplomatic and military areas saw it as renewal of the Cold War and possibly directed against Russia. Their response was the announcement of plans to build up their own military capabilities in the exclave of Kaliningrad, a Russian republic that was located between two NATO partners. The project culminated in summer 2008 as American leaders traveled to the Czech Republic and Poland to sign the key documents. Even though President Obama cancelled the plan in fall 2009, it had revealed sharply differing priorities between Russia and America.

In Chapter 8 also, the Arab Spring of 2011 moves to center stage, for it turned out to be a series of revolutions that poked and pricked at the Russian–American relationship in manifold ways. Contrasting priorities between the two were very evident throughout the international discussions. The civil wars in Libya and Syria probably pushed the U.S. and Russia furthest apart. In mid-2011, after a series of demonstrations and leader replacements in Egypt and Tunisia, a military conflict broke out in Libya. Decades of simmering resentment against Colonel Muammar Gadhafi resulted in polarization between the eastern and western parts of the country. NATO air strikes protected the opposition in the east from the attacks by Gadhafi's military forces stationed in the west, and associated countries such as Qatar offered assistance as well.

The Russian leadership envisioned the NATO operations as intrusive and another sign of the alliance's overreach in the post-Cold War period.

More bitter tensions between Russia and America occurred as the prolonged civil war in Syria continued to grow in complexity and casualties. Western military involvement proved impossible, due to the divided opposition to Assad that included democratic activists but also al Qaeda elements. However, there were points at which the western powers were willing to pass resolutions that called for the resignation of the Syrian leader, Bashir Assad. Both Russia and China vetoed such resolutions on several occasions. When evidence pointed toward use of chemical weapons by the Assad military against the opposition, President Obama called for a selective military strike on those capabilities. Eventually, President Putin offered another way out by presenting a plan for supervised removal of the weapons. While this proposal removed the risk of deepened military involvement by the West, it contributed to the increased political rivalry between presidents Putin and Obama.

In spite of all the contention between the two over America's wars, the aftermath of the Arab Spring, and Russian manipulation of various exclaves, both President Putin and President Obama officially announced similar foreign policy pivots toward Asia. Chapter 9 will explore both the motivations and prospects for success in these endeavors, and a key question will be the impact on Russian–American relations. Foreign policy frustrations actually had much to do with the outreach of both countries toward Asia. For President Obama, increased emphasis on Asia was partly related to the American desire to move past the decade of frustrations connected with the wars in Afghanistan and Iraq. For President Putin, an opening to Asia provided welcome relief from the heightened western criticism of Russian policies toward the exclaves, especially the Crimea and eastern Ukraine. At the same time, both nations understood the economic boom of East Asian nations such as China, Japan, and South Korea. China's thirst for Russian oil and the interest of all three Asian nations in markets for their exports acted as magnets for both America and Russia.

Complicating the picture was evidence of Chinese restlessness in the South China Sea, moves that rattled American allies such as Japan, South Korea, and the Philippines. Russia would not be as worried about that Chinese aggressiveness, but it did begin to put together a new Eurasian Economic Community in the first half of 2014. It is likely that the mutual pivots toward Asia would bring a new dimension of competition in both economic and military strategy between Russia and the United States. Hopefully, that enhanced competitiveness would not result in outright confrontation, but it is undeniable that there would be increased strain on their connections. In light of the rogue-state threat of North Korea and its unpredictable leader, Kim Jong-un, the price of continued American–Russian animosity in the region would be very high.

Chapter 10 will deal with the Ukrainian crisis as a culmination of the Putin factor that has loomed so powerfully over the American–Russian relationship since 2000. The emergence of the new president on January 1, 2000, was a surprise for much of the world. The ailing President Yeltsin had not been expected to step down so suddenly. Vladimir Putin had moved through appointment into the office of Prime Minister in that late fall of 1999, and prior to that he had been a key part of the Security Services. It was clear that there was a thirst in Russia to get beyond the stagnation of the 1990s and to move back to a more dynamic global role. This was a mission for which Putin turned out to be perfectly suited. In his first year in office he won the regular election that the constitution mandated for prime ministers who took over the presidency after the resignation of the former leader. In that year he also endorsed the writing of a new, more patriotic state anthem that was sung to music composed for the 1943 World War II anthem that celebrated the motherland rather than the international proletariat. He continued to build on those themes and to create an aura around his personality even during the four years (2008–12) in which he served as prime minister with President Dmitry Medvedev.

As the immediate aftermath of the 9/11 attacks began to fade, Putin's willingness to assert Russia's national interests against American objectives accelerated. When Russia won the right to host the 2014 Winter Olympics, the president resolved to make the Olympic events at Sochi into a symbol of the revived Russia.

In 2014, Ukraine's ethnically Russian President, Viktor Janukovych, reached out to Russia for considerable financial assistance. His move led to the Euromaidan protests in Kiev, which called for greater ties with the West and the European Union (EU). The new caretaker leadership in Kiev took provocative steps such as declaring Ukrainian the sole official language. The Crimean Peninsula, which was part of Ukraine but 60% ethnically Russian rebelled and passed a referendum that called for breaking away from Ukraine and becoming part of Russia. The continuing presence of a major Russian naval base in Sevastopol made the revolt more possible. The intrusion of military forces from Russia itself tilted the balance, and President Putin moved swiftly to make the annexation an officially established fact. Obviously, Russian aggressiveness towards Ukraine strained Russian–American ties considerably, and fears about the fate of ethnically Russian eastern Ukraine led to increasing casualties and kept the diplomatic pot boiling. The resulting tension between Russia and America threatened to take on world-shaking proportions.

The Conclusion will consist of an integration of themes, with an emphasis on erosion and convergence, in the light of the empirical analysis in the ten chapters themselves. Over the quarter-century since the end of the Cold War, there has at times been a considerable erosion of the good will that characterized conversations between the leaders of the two nations during the late 1980s. At that time, American leaders welcomed the Gorbachev reforms and drew hope from the Soviet leader's new foreign policy that called for a drawdown of military forces in a number of key locations. One symbol of that newfound late-Cold War amity was the willingness of the Soviet leadership to permit the United States to take the exclusive lead in developing a coalition to drive Iraqi forces out of Kuwait in 1990–91. In the light of that high-water mark of mutual understanding, the bitter discussions over NATO expansion in the 1990s were signs of a budding partnership in decline. Advocates of the democratic peace theory, who posited that the embrace of democracy by previously authoritarian regimes would result in a safer world, were disappointed.

Contention over the role of the Clinton administration in seeking to contain the aggressive moves of Serbia in the Balkans continued to embitter the more positive American–Russian relationship that had emerged at the end of the Cold War. Inevitably, the emergence of President Putin on the Russian scene would eventually compound the misperceptions and misunderstandings between the two states. America would have difficulty understanding the efforts of the strong Russian leader to build a sense of nationalism in a population that had fallen off the ledge of the superpower status that it maintained during most of the Cold War. In that sense, the Western consternation over Russian moves during the Georgia War in 2008, and again during the Ukrainian crisis that began in 2014, was more than understandable. From the point of view of key Russian leaders, the Bush administration had paved the way through its surprising invasion of Iraq in 2003. As Iraq descended into near-civil war in the summer of 2014, the Russian point of view carried some weight.

However, the above picture of an eroded relationship is not the whole story, for signs of a convergence of perspectives characterized the post-Cold War world as well. Both powers had been targets and victims of attacks by Islamists committed to violence in order to punish them. Russia fought two wars with terrorists from its Muslim republics in the Caucasus, and additional attacks took place after those wars against a school in Beslan, a theater in Moscow, and the Moscow metro system. Terrorists from Osama bin Laden's al Qaeda movement caused thousands of deaths in the 9/11 attacks, and American security forces were preoccupied with preventing additional planned attacks in the years thereafter. However, the initial convergence of views after 2001 gave way to eventual doubts. Russian leaders envisioned the American invasion of Iraq and lengthy war in Afghanistan as overreactions, while the Americans had earlier not been particularly understanding of why the Russian military had reacted so strongly in the two Chechen wars or, later, in Georgia.

There was also an initial merging of concerns over the consequences of the outbreak of the Arab Spring revolutions, as key allies of both states were undergoing major transformations. Both sets of leaders agreed on the risk of the alarming changes that were taking place but had very different points of view about the identity of the culprits. This lack of convergence was particularly evident in the discussions about how to deal with the Syrian civil war. Perhaps the renewed interest of both in increased involvement in Asia had the potential to generate at least some common understandings. While the economic needs of the two states in the area differed, the issues were not by their nature primarily military ones. It is possible to imagine a future in which both Russia and America would occasionally jostle up against one another in Asia but not be constantly engaged in a military standoff. Economic convergence in an increasingly multi-polar world might balance the erosion that seemed so evident in the chaotic political and military relationships between the two nations in other settings.

Percolating through this concluding analysis of erosion and convergence will be and assessment of the impact of the theoretical approaches that formed the centerpiece of discussion in Chapter 1. To what extent do the five models of power and five theories both inform and explain the motivating forces behind erosion and convergence?

1

Theoretical approaches: models of power, systems theory, critical junctures, legacies, realism, and realism revised

In light of the eruption of American–Russian hostility during the Ukrainian–Crimean Crisis of 2014 and after, it might seem an unusual step to launch the analysis with the presentation of a multiplicity of analytical approaches. However, that is precisely what the situation requires. All parties to the conflict comprehend how searing and all-encompassing was the Cold War struggle between East and West. Although in that conflict there were interludes of understanding if not mutual respect between the two superpowers, for the most part it was a riveting and never-ending avalanche of worry for most participants in the international community. The collapse of communism was the phenomenon that brought it to an end, rather than the collective wisdom of the two nations' leaders over four decades in time. All the while, observer nations sat quietly on the sidelines and had little control over the comings and goings of the two superpowers. Why would it not have been possible to break up the political permafrost in the middle of the Cold War? Why did analysts not develop theoretical models that could have pointed the way to a new direction with more positive outcomes, instead of simply trying to explain the source and nature of the enmity? It is with this concern in mind that the center of attention in the opening chapter of this book is consideration of theoretical perspectives that can outline a path from Crimea to stability.

Cold War models of American–Soviet conflicts

The Balance of Power Model
First and foremost in interpreting the current relationship between Russia and America is the Balance of Power Model (Kissinger 1969, 5–6). Rooted in the

Austrian response to the overreaching power of Napoleonic France in the early years of the nineteenth century, this model can serve as both explanation and antidote to the current power drives of Russia and the United States.

A genuine balance entails a co-equal distribution of power between two nations or sets of nations. In the nineteenth-century case cited above, the Austrian foreign minister Metternich stitched together changing coalitions of nations with the objective of preventing any one country from dominating the continent as France had under Napoleon. There were no permanent enemies or friends in this changing coalition, for the objective was to prevent an imbalance of power. In many ways, the balance held for three decades, until a series of revolutions in 1848 awakened new aspirations among subject peoples against the monarchs who held sway in the key European empires.

Such a balance of co-equal forces did not emerge in later situations of major conflict. Following the German victory in the Franco-Prussian War in 1870, a new power emerged that would surpass Napoleon in the havoc that it caused on the European continent. Although the European nations collectively stumbled into war in 1914, the key problem was checking the Central Powers and eventually defeating them. Only with the introduction of American forces in 1917 did the tide of battle begin to undo the imbalance of power and pave the way for the defeat of Germany and its allies. It would be difficult to describe the interwar period as one of stasis, for key powers such as the United States withdrew into renewed isolationism, while new nations such as Poland struggled to maintain their fledgling democracies. An effective League of Nations might have been a deterrent to an aroused Germany, but it proved toothless without the involvement of America. The onward march of Nazi Germany in Europe and a militarized Japan in Asia required years of strategy making and military mobilization in order to restore some sense of equilibrium by the end of 1945.

Had the participants in the Yalta Alliance of February 1945, the Soviet Union, United Kingdom, and the United States, held together in any meaningful way, the restoration of a balance of power might have held for the immediate future. America hosted the founding of the United Nations (UN) in San Francisco, joined it with little hesitation, and agreed to host it permanently in New York City. Following the return or reemergence of their leaders who had been in hiding, the new states of Central Europe reestablished their youthful democratic frameworks. However, the break-up of the victorious World War II coalition led to the outbreak of the Cold War and the destruction of all key wartime hopes for a renewed balance of power that might have emulated the one established in Europe after the exile of Napoleon.

However, in the twenty-first century some analysts have shown renewed interest in adopting features of the traditional balance-of-power system. Andrei Tsygankov (Tsygankov 2014, 526) notes that Russia seeks equal treatment by the American leadership, a status that the latter has not accorded since the end of the Cold War. Prospects may exist for a "limited partnership" in which the two balance one another on key issues of global importance. It may also be the case that the emphasis on a "reset" of relationships at the beginning of the Obama administration incorporated a view of the balance of power that might underpin mutual actions on selected crisis areas. With continued emphasis on the importance of the state, Russian leaders also pursue western acceptance of "a Russian sphere of influence in former Soviet space" (Kotkin 2016). Their actions in Georgia and Ukraine reinforce that perception.

There are additional perspectives that would add new labels to the traditional balance-of-power concept in the current period. Perhaps a "Concert-balance" would be a more accurate description of a situation in which the "global primacism" of American policy in the first two decades of the post-Cold War period yields to a kind of concert of great powers who check one another through a realist focus on national interests (Naughton 2013, 675–677). Others describe the emergence of a new "multifaceted power balancing structure" whose fault lines coincide with the clash of civilizations concept initially presented by Samuel P. Huntington. In fact, economic and cultural variables may play a stronger role than military ones in this emerging balance of power (Ovie-D'Leone 2010, 72–86). Huntington (Huntington 1997, 19) himself anticipated the need for balancing in his analysis of emerging conflict among the world's powerful civilizations such as Judeo-Christian, Russian Orthodox, and Muslim. Thus, cultural splits may have the power to supplant political and military divisions. At the same time, others contend that the concept of balance of power has "declining relevance" in the current century, in the sense that the fears of people and leaders are no longer as state based as they once were (Mansbach 2005, 142).

The Bipolar Model

In the early Cold War a second model emerged that bore some resemblance to balance of power but had an edge and global sweep that were distinctive. For at least two decades, and perhaps longer, many observers used the term "bipolarity" to characterize the structure of relations that had emerged within the global community. It was common to describe the Soviet Union as leading one pole of power and the U.S. another, and the assumption was that other nations linked themselves with either Moscow or Washington (Brown 1988, 91–92). The timing of all of this had a larger-than-expected impact, for so many new states had emerged in Asia and Africa during post-World War II decolonization. Each of the new states felt considerable pressure to join one team or the other, and the two superpowers embarked upon a race to recruit them through economic assistance that often included military equipment. There was a tendency to conclude that it was imperative that each state in the global community should be part of one camp or the other.

A number of policy clashes and decisions reinforced this new concept of bipolarity (Ulam 1968, 409). World War II had ended in Asia with use of atomic weapons, a very new capability that both the U.S. and Soviet Union were pursuing during the latter stages of World War II. In fact, it was not until the late 1960s that a situation of parity developed, with both nations having approximately equal nuclear capabilities. By 1955 both camps had their own defensive and deterring military alliances. The West struck first in this regard with the setting-up of NATO in 1949. However, the admission of West Germany to that alliance was followed very quickly by creation in the East of the Warsaw Treaty Organization. While NATO rationalized its existence in the early days on the basis of a feared Soviet or Warsaw Pact on the other side of the imagined Iron Curtain, the Soviet Union's leaders brought up the old fear of western or capitalist encirclement, a concern buttressed in part by the number of American bases in Europe and Turkey that were close to their border.

The vulnerable situation of the city of West Berlin also lent itself to bipolar images, especially when the Soviet leaders limited access to it from West Germany. Similarly, Cuba became a vortex of the dynamics of bipolarity on numerous equations. The standoff between the Soviet Union and United States during the Cuban Missile Crisis of 1962 was startling and acted as a kind of glue that solidified the two camps, at least in the heat of the crisis. Conflicts between the two powerful nations over Iran, Guatemala, and the Korean Peninsula bore all the hallmarks of ambitious, well-armed nations seeking power and influence in any corner of the globe that they could. Bipolarity was the lens through which much of the world perceived these early Cold War struggles.

Within certain regions, bipolarity may still play a role in helping to define the root of conflict. For example, Eurasia is one region in which such tendencies are apparent to certain observers. With the Russian military build-up there, as well as in Syria, perhaps "European security by 2014 again became bipolar" (Trenin 2016). It is likely, too, that a continuing Russian focus in the near future will be the "vast neighborhood in Eurasia" (Trenin 2016). The Russian military strengthening of the enclave of Kaliningrad was also part of an effort to defend against both the United States and NATO. In fact, the Russian National Security Strategy for 2016 reflected the concept that American policy towards Russia was rooted in a new containment doctrine (Trenin 2016, 26–28). In that geographic area, then, bipolarity may again be a reasonable way of defining the situation between America and Russia.

The Unipolar Model

A third model is that of unipolarity, a conceptual apparatus that posits one power as having the preponderance of power and the corresponding ability to impose its will on key policy issues and conflicts. Such a model carries considerable weight when one considers the aforementioned eras of Napoleon and Hitler, for their authoritarian leadership enabled their nations to go unchallenged for a number of years. During the early Cold War, within the framework of bipolarity, there were instances and some evidence of unipolar power balances in several key issues. The Soviet Union was first to put a person in space, and held the edge in that scientific and policy arena that had important implications for the military balance of power. Similarly, the Americans had the advantage in nuclear capabilities for the first two decades of the Cold War, and that advantage may have been one reason why Khrushchev backed down in the Cuban Missile Crisis and withdrew the emplaced weapons from that critical island nation. Near to the end of the Cold War in the 1980s, it later became clear that the economic weaknesses of the Soviet Union were overwhelming, and this had much to do with Gorbachev's pullback of troops from so many locations, as well as his domestic reforms. In a sense, the U.S. had a unipolar advantage without knowing it. With the American emphasis on "New World Order" after 1991, there was a hope of preserving that near-unipolar structure of power (Hutchings 1997, 145–149).

If one looks beyond a pure focus on the variable of military preponderance, then there may be episodes of unipolarity in selected situations. For instance, ideological unipolarity may exist outside of exclusively power-politics situations (Haas 2014, Abstract). In that regard, the Russian effort to counter the West with aggressive actions in the Ukraine and Syria may have been rooted in an assumption that the United States had been exploiting a vacuum of power in an ideological effort to preserve its dominance within a unipolar framework (Lukyanov 2016, 31). While that theory may not have been the hallmark definition of the era, it may have explained certain policy assumptions and may have partly justified some policy decisions.

The Multipolar Model

Fourth, multi-polarity was a highly attractive model in the last two decades of the Cold War, and it was one which practitioners such as National Security Advisor Henry Kissinger shared. In some respects, that model was a reaction to the visible erosion of bipolarity in the 1960s and 1970s. Multi-polarity was a consequence of the lessened control of both the Soviet Union and the United States over their allies and the independent emergence of new regional powers that acted in a quite independent fashion (Brown 1988, 92–93).

For example, Moscow in the early 1950s had considerable control over nations in the communist camp, and challenges to its leadership were unthinkable. The Chinese leaders publicly declared the Soviet Union to be the sun around which all the others rotated. In the 1960s and 1970s this pattern was clearly no longer the case. The so-called Sino-Soviet split emerged in the early 1960s. It was partly based on the more ideologically committed Maoist leadership's having concluded that the post-Stalin era was replete with a pragmatism that compromised the original messianic messages that had accompanied the rise of the communist regimes in the twentieth century. Further, Tito in Yugoslavia had begun to carve out an independent path even in the 1950s. This was perhaps not so surprising, given that the Yugoslav leader and his forces had liberated their territory without Soviet assistance and had made an effort to be a regional player even in the late 1940s. Further, the Poles and Hungarians challenged Soviet primacy in 1956, while the Czechs repeated a similar process of revolt in their Prague Spring of 1968. While the Soviet-led bloc did not exactly unravel, the unquestioned dominance of Moscow could no longer be taken for granted.

Allies in the West were bold enough to challenge American leadership in quite different ways during the second half of the Cold War. While there had been incredible solidarity behind American policy during the Cuban Missile Crisis of 1962, very soon the French challenged both the United States and NATO. They requested that all alliance bases in France be dismantled, and in other ways they decoupled themselves from NATO without totally withdrawing. America's long involvement in and prosecution of the War in Southeast Asia led to many questions about both the motivation and goals of that struggle. It was much more difficult for presidents Johnson and Nixon to locate supportive and participative allies in that struggle than it had ever been in the Korean War in the early 1950s. All of this evidence of the weakening position of the United States' leadership of its allies was compounded by that country's international behavior following their departure from Southeast Asia in March 1973. In a faint echo of post-World War I isolationism, American leaders were very reluctant to take any bold stands on foreign-policy challenges for nearly a decade.

Multi-polarity was also in evidence as new regional powers burst onto the scene. Some were nation-states that had strengthened their global power position, while others were new alliances. In the first category, both China and Japan in the Asian theater achieved significant levels of regional strength in the 1970s and 1980s. China adopted some principles of the free market after the death of Mao Tse-tung, the Great Helmsman, in 1976, and this led to trading partnerships with various Western nations and the beginning of an end to Chinese isolation. Japan also rapidly moved forward economically. For a small island nation, the impact of its advances in technology and the automotive industry was nothing short of phenomenal.

There were also regional organizations that exercised special influence. For example, three leaders from developing nations had formed the Non-Aligned Bloc in the early 1960s in order to give nations a third choice that would be outside the bipolar structure of power. The leaders of India, Egypt, and Yugoslavia were the ones who had the foresight to set this course in motion, and at its high-water mark over one hundred nations had declared membership in the Non-Aligned Bloc. Also, the European Economic

Community, later the European Union, came to the fore and gave the individual nations of Western Europe more clout than they would have had on an individual basis.

Both of these pieces of evidence reinforce a model of multi-polarity that was a kind of symbol of the latter decades of Cold War. Declining superpower authority was combined almost seamlessly with the emergence of new and strengthened poles of power. After the Cold War ended, there would be no fear of a vacuum of power, for other rival power centers had already emerged to pick up the slack and supplement post-Cold War American and Russian influence.

There is evidence that the pursuit of multi-polarity guided Russian policy in much of the post-Cold War period, but especially after Vladimir Putin came to power (Silvius 2016, 1). Russia's above-noted perception that American policy represented a unipolar thrust probably led it to counter with a thrust toward multi-polarity. In that vein the Crimean take-over in 2014 may have reflected Russia's effort to discover "a credible role in the new, multipolar environment" (Lukyanov 2016, 35). In an increasingly diffuse set of power relationships, it may be in Russia's interests to pursue a "multipolar and polycentric system" (Pabst 2009, 170–175). Again, Eurasia offers terrain in which the Russian pursuit of its own center of power in the renewed multi-polar age may be understandable. One author (Pabst 2009, 166–168) enumerates five micro-power centers in that region that attract Russian interests. They include Turkey, Georgia, Azerbaijan, and Armenia in the west; Iran and Afghanistan in the south; the five Central Asian republics close by; China and Mongolia in the east, and the strategically vital Caspian corridor sandwiched in the middle. In addition, the busy travels of President Putin throughout that area and his effort to stitch together a variety of new alliances offer the potential to create a power center of considerable importance.

Chaos/Complexity Model

A fifth model is that of Chaos/Complexity Theory, and this is a kind of reaction against the previous four rather concrete depictions of the global structure of power. Instead of endeavoring to develop a model with clear definitional parameters, it is also possible to declare or conclude that there is no discernible pattern or structure of power at all (Northam 2013, 13–16). Such a picture would lend itself to the period of transition from the World War II alliance with the Soviet Union to conditions of hostility, the early days of the Cuban Missile Crisis, the long period of confusion over the War in Southeast Asia, and the period of American withdrawal after its exit from Southeast Asia. It may even be the case that the end of the Cold War also was conducive to the conclusion that there was no apparent pattern or power structure, and this may be part of the reason why there was so much bloodshed and unexpected war making in the Balkans, Afghanistan, and Iraq!

A number of writers have applied Chaos-Complexity Theory to the post-Cold War world in a number of settings. Sociologists have called attention to the importance of "nonlinear dynamics" in explaining "human social systems." The lack of predictability in many situations that social workers seek to unravel suggests that the human condition is often one of complexity and near chaos (Warren, Franklin, and Streeter 1998, 1). Often the line between social and political systems is a fine one, and so the existence of a global vacuum of power may lead to at least consideration of this model.

Clearly, each of these five models is useful in characterizing the dynamics and key events of the lengthy Cold War. No one of them served to depict all of the conflicts in 1946–91, and none was an accurate description for the entire period. However, often the models served to underpin key debates among rival political forces about potential policies for dealing with the per-ceived threats. For example, as new poles of power emerged in the 1960s and 1970s, some observers concluded that the Cold War superpowers held a weak-ening grasp over the underlying power structure of world politics. However, others developed the opposite interpretation, that the United States and Soviet Union were as dominant as ever and that decision making should hinge on that reality. In analyzing the post-Cold War relationship between Russia and America, it will be the case that this mix of five models will play an occasional role in explaining the direction that policies took.

Post-Cold War theories and Russian–American struggles

It is important to utilize theory in order to capture the underlying significance of Russian–American struggles after 1991. There are five theories that can assist in this analytical endeavor. Traditional Systems Theory is important, for it can help to delineate the ways in which the Russian–American dynamic has become an independent force outside the plans and decisions of the two countries and their leaders. A more recent theoretical tool is the focus on Legacies, for some post-Cold War developments were not totally new after 1991 but were rooted in both internal and external developments of the two nation-states. It is also necessary to study the breakpoints at which new policy departures occurred on both sides, and an informal theory of Critical Junctures can aid in that discussion. Further, Realist Theory is the heart of the matter in penetrating the basic motivations of both Russian and American leaders at different points after the Cold War ended. The last theory to receive attention will be Revised Realist Theory, an approach that takes into account the manner in which globalization forces have restricted the maneuvering room of all states. In light of occasional commentaries about the emergence of a new Cold War in the twentieth-first century, attention to such theories can cast light on the import of developments that appear on the surface to have no parallel or root in previous political machinations.

Systems Theory

Given the tension that has characterized the Russian–American relationship since the year 2000, it might seem unusual to speak about a relationship between the two that Systems Theory might depict. However, both nations and sets of leaders have been caught in a symbiotic relationship in which it is nearly impossible for one to ignore what the other has done, planned, or announced. From that perspective, they have developed a system of political behavior between them that may be rooted in Cold War interconnections that have taken on a life of their own, especially after Putin's rise to power in 2000. Their evolving behavioral system certainly possesses an environment that generates inputs that consist of demands on and supports for the system. There is also a "black box" in which decision making that leads to future policies takes place. There are mutual outputs that consist of signed agreements, informal arrangements, and sharply conflicting points of view and political stands. Unexpected and anticipated outcomes spin off from those decisional points, and a feedback loop pulls all of the components into a continuous process that influences future dynamics within the system (Almond and Powell, Jr. 1978, 3–24).

The environment in which the post-Cold War political system is contained consists of both a reduction of old tensions and the introduction of new centers of controversy. The various types of continuous polarization that were the hallmark of the Cold War have yielded to feints and starts that are typically of much briefer duration. In the early 1990s there was a substantial power disparity between the U.S. and Russia, to the disadvantage of the new Russian state. American preoccupation with the wars in Afghanistan and Iraq in the new century combined with the increasing prices that Russian oil could command, and the result was a rough evening-out of the power balance, although U.S. military capabilities remained at an overwhelming advantage. Globalization streams were also part of the global environment, for they bore on their surface new threats that were totally unrelated to decisions made in Moscow and Washington. Both nations took firm action to deal with terrorist attacks on their territory, but the mutual pivot towards Asia in the more recent years of the period under review was an indicator that cross-border trade pressures induced a kind of convergence between them.

There was also a duality of inputs that affected their decision making in individual and mutual ways. Rotation in office following democratic elections was now one common thread that affected both of their decisional processes. In the American case these pressures resulted at the presidential level in eight years of Democratic Party control under President Clinton, followed by eight years of Republican governance under George W. Bush, followed by eight more years of Democratic leadership under Barack Obama. Thus, there was a need for Russian leaders to adjust periodically to new counterparts at. These inputs to the process did not rock the boat very much, for a new policy towards Russia was not a campaign plank for any of the three elected American presidents in the period. On the Russian side, there was serious competition to President Yeltsin in the 1996 election in the form of communist candidate Gennady Zyuganov. The election of the latter would probably have led to increased hostility to the West in general; but the re-elected Yeltsin was not very healthy in his last term. As a result, inputs to the American–Russian relationship or system were unchanged. The 1996 election was probably the only competitive one in the Russian post-Cold War experience, for the rise of Vladimir Putin and the interlude of Medvedev were products of the manipulation of the dominant party, United Russia.

In terms of the impact on their mutual system, the dual but very different election systems produced credible leaders with electoral mandates that were unquestioned. This had not been true during the Cold War. Ironically, the one election that resulted in a dubious mandate was the tightly contested and controversial election of Bush in America in 2000. Unlike the three Russian presidents, Bush did not possess a mandate rooted in a popular majority in his first term in office.

The decision-making process within this system cannot be separated from policy-making processes generic to each nation. During the debate over the Missile Shield proposal in 2008–9, it was clear that key secretaries and cabinet ministers on each side served as, at least, spokesmen for the announced decisions that flowed from the presidential offices. President Bush sent both his secretary of state and secretary of defense to both the Czech Republic and Poland in order to sign the key documents in the agreement. Similarly, Russian counter-reactions such as a call for upgrading nuclear capabilities in Kaliningrad came from spokespersons such as their minister of defense and minister of foreign affairs. The case of the Missile Shield was a classic example of the decisional process within the American–Russian system. In the end, the United States cancelled the project, and Russian pressure correspondingly abated. The earlier-identified input of presidential elections was probably critical here, for the newly elected President Obama made the decision to cancel the Missile Shield in the fall of his first year in office.

Such a finding leads naturally to the assessment of policies as outputs of this burgeoning mutual system. There were in fact formal agreements that the two sides actually signed, such as the Strategic Arms Reduction Treaty (START), signed by presidents Obama and Medvedev in Prague in 2010. This agreement had been delayed for a long time, due to tensions within the system, but the two signatures did enact closure on a long debate. A very different process of outputs within the system occurred several years later, during the Crimean Crisis of 2014–15. With no conversations between Russia and America at all, President Putin worked with the Russian leadership on the Peninsula to hold a referendum that resulted in the annexation of Crimea to the Russian Federation. It was apparent that the key discussions occurred among the Russian president, the departing Ukrainian President Viktor Yanukovych, and the separatists in both Crimean and eastern Russian-dominated eastern Ukrainian regions. American and Western decisions, in turn, were ones in which Moscow did not share. They consisted of gradually escalating economic sanctions imposed on targeted prominent personalities and institutions in Russia. In sum, the differences between the output of the START agreement and the Crimean annexation were astounding.

Outcomes spin off decisions and often play out in very different ways than the actors anticipated in an earlier day. For example, while the START agreement offered hope to those who anticipated a reduced global threat of nuclear weapons, disappointment ensued, as it proved so difficult to get North Korea and Iran on board with any kind of similar agreements that would further stabilize the nuclear game. It may also be that the abandonment of the American Missile Shield proposal, although unrelatedly in tune with Russian demands, opened the door to those greater fears. Had the Shield been built, there might have been a greater sense of security in the West. Ironically, the Shield would also have protected vast areas in the western part of Russia, but the leaders in Moscow insisted on painting it as a project that was directed against them.

Similarly, there were all sorts of unexpected outcomes that stemmed from Russia's take-over of the Crimea. When the Crimean referendum was held, few in the West expected that military forces from Russia proper would play such a big role in the battles. Few envisioned the powerful effort by Russian militias in eastern Ukraine to set up independent geographic entities such as the Donetsk and Luhansk Republics. On the part of the West, the redistribution of troops from southern Europe to the Baltic nations and Poland probably did not figure in the original Russian calculus. Development by NATO of a new rapid-response force that could move quickly to trouble spots that Russia might stir up was another unanticipated development. Outcomes of these sorts certainly led to a perception that the Russian–American system was falling apart.

Finally, this leads the analysis to the vital feedback loop that is a critical part of Systems Theory. How are decisions and outcomes circulated back into the environment, thereby affecting inputs that become part of the next decisional process? One clear illustration would be the residue of Cold War decisions on decision making by both parties in the post-1991 period. References to the crisis over Ukraine as a renewed Cold War entails a cycling of decades of hostility back into the system. American mistrust of the 2012 Russian elections constitutes another example, for the degree of central control of those elections echoed the extreme of executive control of communist-era transitions in 1929, 1953, 1964, 1982, 1984, and 1985.

More concrete and micro situations make the impact of the feedback loop visible as well. For example, Russia's military entry into Georgia in 2008 and Ukraine in 2014 both impacted the Russian–American system. For instance, the U.S. took the lead in both situations to exclude Russia from the summer meetings of the Group of Eight (G8). Russian leaders had worked hard in earlier years to gain admittance to this elite set of developed nations that had been meeting since the early 1970s. Protests in Russia at the time of the 2012 presidential elections also circulated back into the system by making America somewhat more stand-offish, and wary of new Russian initiatives. For example, President Obama and other Western leaders turned down the invitation from President Putin to attend the Winter Olympics in Sochi in early 2014. A very different illustration centers on the decision of President Bush to invade Afghanistan after 9/11. This actually pulled the Russian–American system together more tightly, as President Putin said very little when the administration in Washington negotiated for base rights in both Kyrgyzstan and Uzbekistan. In these ways, a feedback loop is especially useful in outlining the exact way in which decisions by one set of leaders re-enter the mutual system of the two powers for better or worse at a future date.

It is also important to underline how fluid and in flux the defined system is at any point in time. In examining the American bureaucracy, Richard Stillman (Stillman 2004, 27) adopts "an open systems perspective" to guide his analysis of the behavior of public organizations. Such an approach underlines the critical importance of the feedback loop to the adaptive nature of a system of environmental and input changes. Bureaucratic or entire state systems clearly have the power to shape environments, but are in turn transformed by them. The energy in the process also matters, for analysts need to pay attention to and apply an "open dynamical system theory" (Fuchs and Collier 2007, 23). Clearly, there will be times when systems stagnate and times when they explode with change. This has definitely been true for the Russian–American relationship or system.

Legacy Theory

Milenko Petrovic (Petrovic 2014, 1–196) highlights the importance of legacies from the communist era for the experiences of post-communist governments. Importantly, he suggests that the Balkan nations did not register sharp challenges to their authoritarian regimes during the communist period. Therefore, they retained the same patterns and sometimes even the identical leaders after 1989. In contrast, the nations of East Central Europe did have at least one time when they challenged Soviet primacy in the bloc and therefore were more prepared to move in new directions after the 1989 revolutions. From the perspective of the EU, there was more interest in working right away with the second set of nations, further north. However, its approach to the Balkan nations more often took the form of efforts to help them to define their statehood. Legacy Theory more widely throughout the region took the form of physical, economic, societal, and political inheritances (Volgyes 1995, 2–19).

What might this type of Legacy Theory portend for a study of American–Russian relations after 1991? In conformance with the key components presented above with regards to Systems Theory, it may be a good idea to focus on each individual nation as well as on their joint relationship. Within each nation, an emphasis on leadership and the policy-making process can bear fruit. With regards to their informal mutual system of interactions, the policies themselves may bear scrutiny.

In the United States there were a number of presidents who focused in their foreign policies on the so-called Soviet threat. For example, President Truman articulated several themes that became foundational in the Cold War as guides for dealing with the Soviet Union. They included the Truman Doctrine, the Marshall Plan, and the overall comprehensive Containment Doctrine. Under the heading of the Truman Doctrine, financial aid to Greece and Turkey enabled the defeat of communism in those post-war settings. Marshall Plan assistance helped to rebuild Western Europe in order to make it more resistant to communist overthrow. Containment, the doctrine authored by George Kennan, offered a rationale for combatting the communist thrust in any corner of the globe.

In the 1960s President Kennedy offered a stirring inaugural speech in which he called upon his compatriots to pick up the burden and pay the price needed to defend freedom against the powerful regime in the East that had come to threaten freedom. His speech in West Berlin right after the construction of the Berlin Wall was also a stirring one that was able to build upon a new physical structure that hemmed in those who sought to escape to the West in search of an alternative system and life. Equally forceful was the imagery included in the policy-making process of President Reagan in the 1980s. Like his forbear President Kennedy, he went to West Berlin, where he challenged Soviet First Secretary Gorbachev finally to tear down the wall. His proactive efforts to take the struggle to the Soviet-backed regimes in Nicaragua and Angola were part and parcel of the same drive. Thus, at least three Cold War American presidents combined leadership style with policy themes in a concerted effort to stand up to the Soviet Union.

It is possible to see certain U.S. policy stands in the post-Cold War world in the mirror of these Cold War legacies. The quick condemnation of Russian actions in tiny Georgia in late 2008 bore the hallmarks of a reliance on old pre-1991 themes. There was no evidence of an American search early on for evidence that Georgian President Saakashvili might have initiated the conflict with a foray into the two controversial enclaves that included citizens who preferred to be part of Russia. There were also Cold War-type quick assumptions after the eruption of the Ukrainian crisis in 2014. The American leaders revealed a kind of wishful thinking that portrayed the Russian president as having escalated the Russian troop presence, first in Crimea and then in eastern Ukraine. Further, there was a quick rush to judgment about the complicity of the Russian militias in the shooting down of Malaysia Airlines flight MH17 in July of that critical year. Although American fears may have later been borne out when the evidence came in, the initial perceptions and condemnations in both situations were, in part, Cold War legacies.

Russian Cold War leaders and policies were equally strident and focused on the American threat. They even relied on pre-communist legacies such as the fear of capitalist encirclement that hailed back to the time of Napoleon. Khrushchev made strident threats, even with a shoe in his hand, that the West would live entirely under capitalism in the future. His emplacement of nuclear missiles in Cuba in the early 1960s was consistent with that rhetoric. His successor Brezhnev went on a very tough-minded mission to remake Soviet society in conformance with communist doctrine. His use of the legal system to lengthen sentences for dissidents and to send them to Siberia, and even to make exile the only option for others, reflected a tough-minded effort to purge the social order of those who may have flirted with American-style freedoms. There was a deep contradiction in such efforts, but he also was the leader who embarked upon the policy of détente with the West in an effort to defuse tensions.

Such leadership and policy initiatives were echoed strongly in some of the policy initiatives of President Putin in the twenty-first century. He was sharply critical of American-led efforts to bring some form of democracy to Iraq, of American critiques of the Georgia invasion, and overwhelmingly of Ukraine and the Western support in 2014–15. In some ways, his handling of the Crimean take-over resembled and resonated with Khrushchev's efforts to use Cuba as a wedge to reduce American influence in its own hemisphere. Both leaders, one in the Cold War and one in the next century, made ploys to gain enormous influence in fragile nations that were of great importance to the West.

What about post-Cold War American–Russian echoes of Soviet–American relations during the Cold War? Was there any sense in which a parallelism existed between those connections in such different time periods and conditions? In the 1970s and 1980s the two giants engaged in an awkward dance that went under the heading of détente. Governmental changes in the United States complicated the process, as the Republican President Nixon left office under the pressure of impeachment. President Ford, who succeeded Nixon by virtue of his office as Vice President, lacked an electoral mandate and was unable to win a term of office in the next presidential election. Ford was succeeded by the Democrat President Carter, who lacked foreign policy experience. On the Soviet side, the leader was the same Leonid Brezhnev, but towards the end of the process he was ailing in health. In spite of the weaknesses of leadership, the dynamics of their mutual system held sway, and progress continued unabated on arms control, the goal at the heart of the détente process. Strategic Arms Limitation Talks (SALT) agreements were signed and the START process on long-range weapons was engaged as well. Progress continued during the era of presidents Reagan and Gorbachev, as the INF agreement was signed and actually implemented within a three-year time frame. Clearly, the mutual system that included the two Cold War superpowers breathed with life, in spite of the leadership and policy differences that characterized the two national units.

There was a certain carry-over of systemic features in the relationship between Russian and American leaders over the Syrian crisis after the beginning of the Arab Spring in 2011. In the early part of the war President Obama's policy centered on the removal of Syrian President Assad from power, while Russian perspectives were focused more on the matter of reducing the threat of terrorism in the civil war that engulfed the nation. However, the discovery of the probable introduction of chemical weapons into the theater of conflict in fall 2014 brought the two together, for the American president agreed with the proposal of Vladimir Putin to have international inspection forces of the UN remove those lethal weapons. Similarly, as the threat of ISIS (Islamic State in Iraq and Syria) became such a powerful factor in the civil war, the American and Russian positions again moved into systematic convergence. American leaders such as Secretary of State John Kerry did not talk so directly about the need to remove Assad from power, and conversations moved in the direction of stabilizing an unbelievably complicated and multi-party conflict. In some ways, this set of interactions over a number of years was parallel to the détente-era negotiations over the limitation of armaments, especially those in the nuclear category. As such, the two case studies interact in ways that reinforce and lend credence to Legacy Theory.

Recent approaches to Legacy Theory have underlined the importance of the deep historical past, economic conditions, and efforts to get away from explanations that focus only on socio-political cleavages. In the Russian case, the sometimes "strident nationalist ideology" of President Putin is embedded in a past in which a blend of Tsarism and Russian Orthodoxy held sway and established a pattern of authoritarian leadership over centuries, and from which it was nearly impossible for post-communist leaders to extricate themselves (Orvis and Drogus 2015, 285). Economic legacies stood alongside political ones in impacting the post-1991 atmosphere and debate in Russia. The severe economic liabilities that acted as difficult inheritances within Russia included an obsolete economy, poverty among a large proportion of the population, corruption, a healthcare crisis, and a gap in responsive institutions (Aron 2002, 431–434). Finally, in contrast to many ethnic-based explanations of the hold of the past on current leadership, Sartes suggests that a kind of "ethnic-colonial communism" acted as a pressure on post-communist leadership in both Estonia and Latvia (Sartes 2016, 130). Clearly, the resulting "regime legacy" affected the Russian landscape as well.

Theory of Critical Junctures

Critical junctures have been central in the analysis of Russian political changes and policies, and the same is true for U.S. patterns. As Gel'man (Gel'man 2015, 3–5) asserts, critical junctures often coincide with regime trajectories that set off moves in new political directions. Attention to this theory that centers on transformations at critical time frames can supplement the previously outlined foci on Systems Theory and Legacy Theory.

In the American case, there have been decided regime changes in the period under review. For instance, the shift from Republican presidents Nixon and Ford to Democratic President Carter in 1977 had a big impact on budding détente and the success of the SALT negotiations in terms of a setback. America soon became engulfed in the Iranian hostage crisis, and Brezhnev decided to invade Afghanistan in order to prevent the growth of another Islamist regime that would approximate what the Ayatollah Khomeini had injected into the Iranian landscape. Similarly, the election of Ronald Reagan in 1980 generated a more purposeful stance in regard to Soviet adventures in Afghanistan, Central America, and even the continent of Africa. In his first term there was virtually no progress on arms control and détente seemed to be at an end. Another critical juncture was the election of Barack Obama in 2008, as he decided to "reset" relations with Russia after the strained relations under President Bush over Iraq and the war in Georgia. His speech at a Moscow university committed to economics education at the highest level was important, but its spirit was difficult to fulfill. Under the vagaries of the Arab Spring and the Ukrainian crisis, "reset" developed negative connotations. However, the idea of a new start with a different American administration was an important reinforcement for the Theory of Critical Junctures.

In the Soviet/Russian case, the significance of transformations at critical junctures bears even more meaning. Attention to the profound changes induced by the rise to power of Gorbachev in 1985, Yeltsin in 1991 and Putin in 2000 make this conclusion impeccably clear and persuasive.

Prior to Gorbachev's accession in 1985, the Russian leadership position had been in the hands of three different individuals in the previous three years. In spite of that instability, and in spite of their informal control of the levers of power, foreign policy towards the West and United States had remained relatively consistent. The Brezhnev strategy of maintaining a huge army along the Chinese border in light of the tensions of the 1960s remained intact, as did the location of medium-range nuclear missiles on the western border facing Europe. There was no effort to end the continuing occupation of Afghanistan as Soviet leaders wanted to bring a friendly regime into power there. All of those policies alienated the West and affected U.S. foreign-policy considerations.

Within the space of three years, Mikhail Gorbachev profoundly changed all three of those postures. He withdrew the forces from the border with China, and thus Soviet policy paralleled, if not dovetailed with, the softer and more trade-oriented approach that America had taken after the more pragmatic Deng Hsiao-ping came to power in 1976, following the death of Mao Tse-tung. The new Soviet leader also signed the INF agreement with the U.S., a step that reduced the nuclear threat in Europe as well as in the Soviet Union. Finally, he took the Soviet troops out of Afghanistan in 1988, a step that ended the need for the United States to fund a disparate group of freedom fighters that at one time even included Osama bin Laden. All of these moves improved at least the atmosphere of Soviet–American relations, and Gorbachev's invocation of the concept that "our common European home" was one feature of Soviet cultural orientations that injected a note of reality into that atmosphere.

In 1991 the transformation of the Soviet system into a Russian system with fourteen additional border nations added another dimension to Russian policy with the United States. Russia was indeed a stripped-down state territorially, but it was still a powerful geopolitical force in Eurasia. However, the Yeltsin leadership did not live up to the promise of his courageous stand against those who had sought to depose Gorbachev in August 1991. His attitudes wavered, for he sent Russian troops into Chechnya in 1994, and a two-year war that alienated the West resulted. Similarly, he unwaveringly supported the Serbian position during the highly controversial Bosnian War of the mid-1990s. And yet he did not seem overly troubled by NATO plans to expand eastward. At one point, he suggested that Russia might one day join the Western alliance, and on another day he was willing to sign the consultative agreement labeled the NATO–Russia Pact. Thus, Russian policies were not as consistent as Soviet policies had been under Gorbachev, but they bore no resemblance to the hostile stances that had characterized much of the Cold War.

Putin's sudden and unexpected rise to power in 2000 added yet another twist to Russian–American relations. He was determined to restore stability and strength to Russian foreign policy, a commitment that would lead inevitably to clashes with American foreign-policy leaders. He also had a dream to restore traditional Russian greatness, and thus the value of the Slavic-Orthodox culture and world moved again into prominence in Russian thinking and foreign-policy strategy. His seemingly innocuous search for a new Russian state anthem was a harbinger of things to come, for it spoke of a commitment for Russia to reach out expansively as she had in the late eighteenth century under Catherine the Great. Eventually, this would have policy implications that would greatly unsettle relations with the United States. Importantly, Putin's sweeping vision of the Russia future would add nuances to their relationship that were very different from those of the early Brezhnev, of Gorbachev, or of Yeltsin.

Donnelly and Hogan (Donnelly and Hogan 2012, 324) suggest that three components characterize a critical juncture, and they include a "crisis, ideational change, and radical policy change." If any one of these tests is absent, then it would not be accurate to utilize such a dramatic phrase as critical juncture. Often an "external shock" has such an impact that it does not really matter who the political leaders are, as any set would need to respond (Donnelly and Hogan 2012, 325). The crisis itself creates "windows of opportunity" that bring in new ideas and policies (Donnelly and Hogan 2012, 344). Many times, international events and dynamics constitute the "shock" that leads to new policies. Perhaps the "reset" between Russia and America in 2009 was such a force. Results included the American cancellation of the Missile Shield proposal and also the new START agreement signed the following year (Carter and Scott 2014, 205–210). There are other situations in which it is a series of domestic events that act as the creative force that leads to a critical juncture. For example, independence for Kosovo in 2008 may have been such a case. Smaller-scale domestic events in 2000, 2003, 2005, and 2007 culminated in independence resulting as the "default option" at the end of the process in 2008. The key "tipping point" in the decade was the 2005 assassination of the Serbian reform leader Zoran Dindič in 2005. With serious compromise no longer on the horizon, the announcement of independence came shortly thereafter (Cocozzelli 2009, 201–206). All three of these perspectives contribute to a more complete picture of the general contours of a critical juncture.

Theory of Realism

It has been a full century since idealism drove these two powers in their relations with each other in a consistent way. Each in their own way, Vladimir Lenin and Woodrow Wilson embraced sweeping values about human beings and about their foreign policies during and after World War I. For Lenin, the power of proletarian internationalism animated the earliest moves of the new Soviet state in the global arena. Similarly, Wilson's belief in the power of both democratic ideals and international organizations impelled his endorsement of military intervention in World War I as well as the League of Nations after the war ended. However, the pursuit of realistic policy was the motive force that generated both conflicts and periods of mutual understanding between the two superpowers in the ensuing century.

An assessment of the innate realism in their policies must center on a number of key components. What have been their principal hard-power capabilities over time, as these have risen and fallen in different epochs for both nations? To what extent have they often used soft-power tools as supplements to the military hardware that constitutes the essence of hard power? Further, how have asymmetric situations thrown off the rational calculations of realist leaders on both sides? Realism also incorporates theoretical approaches that can play out differently in nations that are pursuing contrasting regional and global strategies. Attention to both offensive and defensive strategies, as well as the tactics that implement those driving sets of goals, round out the picture of a realistic depiction of possibilities on the foreign-policy stage (Kay 2015, 24–45).

Hard power has been a major source of strength for both America and Russia during the Cold War and after. During the latter half of the Cold War, the United States fought a nine-year War in Southeast Asia, while the Soviet Union was embroiled in Afghanistan for exactly the same length of time. During the same period, both superpowers exerted additional leverage, due to their acquisition of nuclear weapons, a capability in which they were roughly equal after 1969. Clearly, the end of the Cold War was a circumstance that gave the advantage to the United States in hard power for a considerable period time. With great sacrifice of money and lives, America was able to fight a two-pronged war in Afghanistan and Iraq for over a decade. Russia's military recovery took time after 1991, but it was able to fight wars with success in Georgia in 2008 and in the Ukraine in 2014. Both were much shorter than the American wars, but each resulted in Russia's new hold on exclaves from each nation that had Russian-leaning populations. There was also a tendency on both sides to react in terms of Cold War rivalries whenever an issue relating to new military capabilities emerged. For example, the United States signed the Missile Shield project with both the Czech Republic and Poland in 2008, and this would have established over time a protection against surprising missile strikes from challenging nations such as Iran. Russia responded with announced plans to upgrade its military capabilities in the exclave of Kaliningrad, in order to counter the alleged U.S. pressure.

The use of soft power has played out differently on both sides, but it has fitted the realistic goal of enhancing global credibility and clout. For example, the U.S. sponsored the Dayton Peace Conference in 1995, and this had the result of bringing an end to the Bosnian War that had led to so much sacrifice. In a parallel way, Russia informally mediated a quick halt to the Syrian War's chemical weapons crisis in 2013. In both cases, the sponsoring power gained global credibility that multiplied its hard capabilities and expanded the basis of the advancement of national security goals. In a number of cases, individual diplomats have had a substantial impact on the evolution of Russian–American relations. With her roots in Central Europe, Secretary of State Madeline Albright in the late 1990s became a respected voice on matters pertaining to that region as well as to the Balkans further south. In a similar way, the Russian Minister for Foreign Affairs Sergei Lavrov managed to present balanced messages and points of view through the tumultuous years that surrounded the Crimean crisis of 2014 and after.

Both powers have also dealt with asymmetric situations that have sharply challenged their ability to exercise the kind of control that they would like over certain countries or situations. Soviet frustration in Afghanistan and

Poland in the late Cold War period was very similar to U.S. partial paralysis in Southeast Asia in the 1970s and Central America in the 1980s. In the post-Cold War period, the Americans found surprising challenges in Somalia in 1993, while the Russians were unable to cope with the gravitation of small former Eastern Bloc nations to the EU and NATO in the 1990s. The realistic protection of national interests was compromised, but this was not a mortal blow, due to the multi-faceted nature of the national security policies of both powers.

Realism in policy has benefited from doctrinal formulations as well. For the United States, the Containment Doctrine served as a convenient rationale for a variety of defensive policies aimed at restricting and reducing the use of power by the Soviet Union. For Soviet leaders at the time, the driving goal and doctrine seemed to be the breaking-up of the capitalist encirclement that had been their fear since the allied intervention during World War I. Following the collapse of the Soviet Union in 1991, it was more difficult to identify on either side a realistic doctrine of similar cogence and clarity. However, expansion of the universe of democracies, as troubled as resulting policy has been, has been a rough guide to American actions from the Persian Gulf War of 1990–91 through the long war in Afghanistan. For Russians under Putin, restoration of Russian, Slavic, and Orthodox greatness has much to do with its interest in and pressure on exclaves and other regional powers. For leaders in both nations, the pursuit of realistic policies has contained both offensive and defensive tactics. American leaders have initiated wars, such as in Iraq in 2003, with a shaky foundation, as did Putin's Russia in the Crimea in 2014. At the same time, the U.S. engaged in a seemingly defensive war in Afghanistan in 2001, while Russia came up with a plan for renewed military capabilities in response to the Bush Missile Shield proposal. All told, doctrine has included on both sides an overarching sense of purpose, offensive moves, and defensive reactions to new tactics embraced by the other.

Hans Morgenthau was a founder of the modern Realist Theory that had such a strong emphasis on pragmatism and the protection of national interests. Perhaps, as a reaction to the emphasis of American foreign policy on nurturing and building democracies in the post-Cold War period, there has been renewed interest both in what Morgenthau meant and in how that applies, following the disappointment of the Afghan and Iraqi wars. Some analysts have pointed out that Morgenthau's realism was in fact a "normative theory highly concerned with ethics and morality" (Book Review 2011, 49). Further, Angela Stent calls for clarity in the post-Obama presidency on exactly what U.S. national interests are. Such an emphasis would be understandable to Russian leaders and would reduce their ability to "unravel the post-Cold War order" (Stent 2016, 106–113). Other analysts have called for a revival of Morgenthau's realism after several decades of American over-emphasis on extending the universe of democracies that themselves rely heavily on soft power and legal norms. It would be to the advantage of the United States to emphasize the right of a state to self-defense in order to begin a series of steps that might result in more "balance and order" (Jones and Smith 2015, 937–952). There would be an ensuing expectation that any such renewed American focus on realism would be greeted in kind by the leadership in Moscow.

Revised Realist Theory

However, there is a state-centeredness to Realist Theory that does not correspond perfectly to the swirl of twenty-first-century dynamics. Correspondingly, protection of solely national interests does not necessarily guarantee the preservation of national security in the broadest sense. Nations are not sharply divided from one another as they were in the mid-twentieth century, while national leaders often perceive themselves as powerless to shape events in ways that they might have in the past. In order to come to terms with the whirlpool of currents that affect both countries and leaders, it is imperative to examine a theory that preserves some of the elements of Realist Theory but modifies them in significant ways as well (Kay 2015, 42–60).

For many leaders, an emphasis on regional and global security competes for equal space with furtherance of national security goals. For example, two nations labeled simplistically as "rogues" in the 1990s have received attention from small clusters of nations that include both Russia and America. Discussions with and about the North Korean dilemma typically include six nations that either are its neighbors or played an instrumental role in the region in decades past. Similarly, negotiations with Iran bring together the U.S., Russia, the EU, and individual European nations that share a concern about Iran's future possession of nuclear weapons. Thus, a narrow focus by either America or Russia on the threat from North Korea or Iran would be less effective than consultations that included a broader set of players.

In order to display the key features of Revised Realist Theory, it is helpful to focus mainly on the cross-national forces that often are classified as part of the globalization dynamic that so often transcends the parameters of the state and even makes national goals seem outdated. Some of those forces include globally based terrorism, immigrant flows across national borders, and economic imperialism exercised by powerful corporations. Perhaps, these globalization pressures disclose the extent to which long-standing civilizations that predate the existence of the nation-state may have become the predominant entities that "clash."

As stated earlier, the attacks of global terrorists have at times provided a common ground of understanding for both Moscow and Washington. For Russia, the attacks have emanated from one of their own republics, but Chechnya in 1991 declared itself to be an Islamic republic. Thus, its various attacks on public centers of activity almost seem to have originated on a planet very different from the one in which most Muscovites live. Correspondingly, the al Qaeda attacks on the east coast of the United States in 2001 were unexpected and raised the question of the ability of U.S. security forces to protect the homeland, a question that had not emerged since the surprise attack on Pearl Harbor in 1941. In the early twenty-first century al Qaeda appeared to operate almost without control across the borders of Afghanistan, Syria, Yemen, Nigeria, Somalia, and Mali. Even more challenging to the national units of both West and East was the explosion of ISIS onto the world stage in 2014 and after. That barbaric group targeted soft spots in the public sphere that were relatively unprotected, and countries such as Australia, Tunisia, France, the United States, Iraq, and Syria suffered greatly in terms both of personal and family tragedies and of a profound sense of vulnerability. The powerful nation-state that Realist Theory celebrates was victim rather than initiator and actor.

The movement of populations across state borders in an uncontrolled way has come to constitute the fifth plank of public discussion in many of the world's more economically developed nations. Again, the vastness of Russia explains why its challenges stem from areas in the south that used to be republics in the Soviet Union but are not independent but struggling nations. People from those largely Muslim nations meet with hostility when they arrive, looking for work, in cities such as Moscow and St. Petersburg. In America, the inflow of people from Hispanic societies across its southern border has caused considerable discussion and tension over several decades, and it became one of the key issues in the early stages of the 2016 presidential campaign. In 2015 this phenomenon had a principal impact on Europe as stories abounded of a tripling of the number of people seeking admission to European nations. The human tragedy was compounded when a number of faulty vessels experienced disaster at sea, and the resulting pressure on EU nations to control the process became nearly overwhelming. Instead of coping with the needs of citizens of North African countries to seek a better livelihood across the Mediterranean, European leaders had to cope with the civil wars in Syria, Afghanistan, Pakistan, and Iraq that drove people to seek a better life in Western Europe. Crises of a severe magnitude occurred at the point of crossing through the tunnel from France into the United Kingdom and in Balkan nations that had become a way-station into the wealthier countries of West Europe. In fact, the nationalist government of Hungary erected a wall in an effort to halt the flow of immigrants. However, the enormous flow of refugees into Germany in September 2015 revealed the powerlessness of the nation-state that is at the heart of Realist Theory.

Economic forces of a global nature also undermined the authority of the state, as well as the Realist Theory that depended on its intactness. A number of American-based companies such as Apple penetrated large foreign markets, such as that of China, until nationalist reactions and barriers resulted. Russia's Lukoil spread its reach into European markets such as Belgium and earned significant profits from gas-thirsty European drivers. Further, the growth of regional economic organizations became a factor that at least provided cues to national leaders and, in some cases, direction. For example, Russia stitched together a new Eurasian Economic Community in 2014, and its efforts were focused on Russian-directed coordination among the membership. In a broader fashion, the EU negotiated with the newly elected Greek government in 2015 and offered both a carrot and a stick. On the one hand, loaned Greece considerable amounts of money in order to lift Greek prospects of recovery. On the other hand, it demanded that the Greeks enact and follow a series of austerity measures in order to prevent the worst in future years. Cross-border economic pressures thus fitted into an evolving pattern of interdependencies that again compromised state-based realism.

In the 1990s Samuel Huntington (Huntington 1997, 19) offered his thesis about the clash of the world's traditional civilizations as a substitute for the state-based conflict that was so characteristic of the Cold War and its antecedents. In many ways, two of the key indicators of globalization reinforce this picture and point to the long-lasting credibility of the Huntington thesis. For instance, the terrorist challenge that ate into the intactness of the state was frequently based on the clash between Islamic civilization and the Judeo-Christian world. Islamic offshoots such as the Taliban and ISIS, while enacting twenty-first-century tactics, reinforced that picture with their reliance on practices from earlier ages, such as restrictions on the role of women, the inoculation of the young with the dreams that accompanied jihad, the destruction of artifacts such as those in Palmyra, Syria that predated the seventh century and the life of Mohammed, and barbaric cruelty meted out to innocent Westerners who fell into their hands. The announced plan of ISIS to create a Caliphate based on traditional territorial lines that included portions of Syria and Iraq revealed an effort to replace modern national borders with older, civilization-based ones. In addition, the Ukrainian conflict of 2014–15 included the minor theme of a clash between Russian Orthodox civilization and that of the West. In addition, the movement of immigrants entailed a flow of many Muslims into Europe, while the influx into the United States greatly increased the presence of persons from Latin American civilizations and their families in the geographic U.S. Each of these examples revealed the extent to which underlying civilizational differences had become better explanations of regional conflict than national distinctions. The phenomenon of globalization thus reinforced the wisdom of Revised Realist Theory.

Fully understanding the implications of globalization and Revised Realist Theory entails a responsibility to broaden the range of analysis into additional academic disciplines. For example, Robinson (Robinson 1998, 1) calls for devotion to a "new interdisciplinary transnational studies." In his view, it is important to depict the state as a "specific social relation" rather than as a stationary object in the global arena (Robinson 1998, 565). From that perspective, it may make sense to some begin discussions with an emphasis on NATO or the G-20 rather than on the United States or Russia.

Periodization of Russian and American patterns

Having outlined a number of key models as well as theories of importance, it is important to conclude with a brief outline of key periods of Russian and American foreign policy themes, for the models and theories underpin them.

For Russia it is possible to identify four key periods in the period after 1985. First, in 1985–91 Gorbachev articulated his concept of a New Foreign Policy, and this entailed a serious cut-back in military commitments that had been so costly. Realist Theory helps to explain this effort to protect basic national economic interests, and it also fits the Multipolar Model that posited increasing challenges from medium-strength nations to the superpowers. Second, the Yeltsin administration from 1991–2000 was characterized by a continuing effort to engage with and even placate the former enemy in the West. A unipolar model with U.S. dominance is helpful in this analysis, while the Critical Juncture Model may be helpful in suggesting the overwhelming importance of the events that occurred in the East in 1991. A third period includes the first Putin presidency from 2000–2008, and the general foreign policy themes about the resurgence of the great Russia of the past that reverberated throughout the general effort to move beyond the passivity of the Yeltsin years. The Theory of Legacies is surely pertinent, as is the model of restoration of a balance of power. Finally, the Putin–Medvedev leadership after 2008 applied the previously stated effort to restore Russian greatness to Georgia in 2008 and to the Ukraine in 2014.

There are also four distinct periods of American foreign policy after 1985. With the advent of the second Reagan presidential term in 1985 through 1993, America emerged much stronger and more active than the Soviet Union/ Russia. A hint of the Unipolar Model was evident in President George H.W. Bush's articulation of the New World Order, at least in the thinking of U.S. administrators, while Systems Theory with its emphasis on conversion of new inputs to the policy process may be a worthwhile explanatory device. Second, the Clinton administration from 1993 to 2001 attempted to cope with new challenges in the Balkans and elsewhere, in spite of the president's commitment to a domestic policy focus. Probably a Multilateral Model is instructive, while Realist Theory explains the efforts of the U.S. to maintain its position in a world in which the clash of civilizations was becoming more apparent. The 2001–9 time frame of the George W. Bush administration was, of course, a shocking one with 9/11 and wars in both Afghanistan and Iraq. Perhaps, the Chaos Model is instructive, with its expectations of a lack of firm patterns, while the Critical Juncture Theory explains some of the uncertainty of how to cope with a new foe of uncommon threat capabilities. The Obama years from 2009 to 2016 were again transitional, for the president talked of resetting relations with Russia and ending both wars. He was much more successful with the latter set of goals than with the former. With Russia's growing strength in its own region, it is tempting to conclude that a kind of bipolarity was beginning again to emerge, but one much different from Cold War patterns. Revised Realist Theory may be helpful in identifying some of the policy themes, for the lack of impact by the U.S. on the crises provoked by the Arab Spring, by the ISIS onslaught, and by unpredictable Russian policy surely demonstrated the power of globalization and the futility of a strong nation-state to channel it or even have much impact on it.

2

The Cold War root of post-Cold War tension: duality of détente in the 1970s and neo-Cold War in the 1980s

Introduction

In the post-Cold War decades, Russian–American tension has alternated with more tranquil periods of open discussion.

There were two clearly defined periods of mutual understanding between America and Russia in the late Cold War. The first was the era of détente, admittedly hard to define in terms of years but probably at its high-water mark in 1972–79. The second accompanied the rise to power of Mikhail Gorbachev and his reformist period from 1985 to 1991. In each period the two powers and their leaders seriously sought mutual agreements that would better their own relationship as well as reduce global conflict. At the same time, there were definitely times of great tension between the two. Clearly, their general objectives about what they sought to accomplish in foreign policy diverged considerably from one another's. Further, Soviet ambitions both in Afghanistan and in key countries in the developing world perturbed Americans who had grown too comfortable with the relaxed atmosphere of détente. In addition, leadership changes on the American side made a difference. President Carter had an awakening at the end of 1979 to what he considered to be the true assumptions of Soviet policy as revealed in its invasion of Afghanistan. Thus, he took firm steps to counter Soviet power after that. Incoming President Reagan developed a new doctrine of pro-active tactics that would counter ambitious Soviet moves after he took over the presidency in 1981. Thus, waves of change swept over the Soviet–American relationship in the last two decades of the official Cold War.

In explaining late Soviet Cold War policy towards Afghanistan, Bialer (Bialer 1986, 313, 330) argues that the overall policies of the superpower alternated between "offensive, expansionist periods" and "defensive coordinating ones." He envisioned the 1979 invasion of Afghanistan as encapsulating both of these power drives. On the one hand, the occupation was defensive, for it prevented the creation of another unstable border nation in addition to Iran, and one that also bore the potential for an Islamic resurgence that could infect the USSR's Central Asian republics. On the other hand, control of Afghanistan could serve to establish a Soviet springboard in the region for further expansionist moves to the south. In a somewhat parallel way, American leaders were torn by policy indecision after the extraction of U.S. forces from Southeast Asia in 1973. A driving and persistent motivation for U.S. leaders was the need for accommodation to public pressure that would not countenance another war that would cost so many American casualties. At the same time, there were strong internal pressures to restore a tradition of bipartisanship in foreign policy, "executive branch coherence," leadership with regard to European allies, and development of a new Cold War agenda that would lead to greater stability (Hutchings 1997, 10–11). This double motivation on both sides contributed heavily to the duality that characterized the last twenty years of the Cold War.

Ambiguity in terms of both strategy and policy afflicted the two nations and highlighted the duality of the period. In the late 1980s the Soviet leadership took steps such as denuclearization that would give it a "breathing spell" from policy overreach. However, it did not give up its ambitions in the Third World or for a new outreach to Asia. By the same token, American strategic objectives continued to underline the importance of containing the Warsaw Treaty Organization but also reflected the importance of taking new steps to avoid nuclear war (Nye 1988, 404–405). These parallel dualities are important, as they came near the end of the Cold War. This was a time when many observers expected future moderation in the rhetoric and effects of the Cold War. However, neither power was thinking about giving up its entrenched position of leadership in regional or even world politics. Thus, a spillover of the mixed set of strategic motivations would undoubtedly penetrate into any period of renewed détente, or one in which the Cold War was surprisingly over.

Periods of mutual understanding and reliance on soft power

Détente, 1972–79

The Nixon–Kissinger thrust to foreign policy did not eliminate containment of the Soviet Union as the overall strategy, but it did express that negotiation rather than confrontation would guide tactics in the future. During the War in Southeast Asia, Soviet leaders had strengthened their nuclear capabilities to the point that they equaled overall those of the United States (Paterson *et al.* 2005, 371, 375). Given the nuclear parity between the two superpowers, it made sense for the incoming American administration to seek some sort of accommodation that would freeze capabilities at the co-equal level. Another component of this search for balance by Nixon and Kissinger was the proposition that multi-polarity had replaced bipolarity in the general global structure of power. In Kissinger's view, American leaders must negotiate in a setting that gave credence to the reality that Japan, China, and Western Europe had grown in the power scenario. Thus, it became imperative that there be a constant focus on a pentagon of power that included them as well as the United States and the Soviet Union (McCormick 2010, 105).

With those realities in mind, the American leadership duo reached out to Secretary Brezhnev with proposals to freeze and eventually reduce the size of the nuclear capability on each side. They met in a summit in 1972 and signed the "Basic Principles of Relations" agreement that reflected the hope of moving beyond the frightening reality of mutual assured destruction (MAD). They signed the Strategic Arms Limitation Treaty I (SALT I) that put in place serious limitations on certain categories of nuclear weapons. The agreement permitted the USSR to have a quantitative advantage in nuclear weapons that would be balanced by the qualitative edge in the nuclear arsenal of the U.S. (Jentleson 2007, 140–142). Further, the agreement froze the existing numbers on both sides of intercontinental ballistic missiles (ICBMs) and limited each to development of two ABM sites. Secretary Brezhnev met with the new President Ford in 1974 at Vladivostok in far eastern Siberia. They agreed to freeze the number of delivery vehicles on each side at 2,400, and they further decided that only 1,320 of each set could contain Multiply Independent Reentry Vehicles (MIRVs) (Paterson *et al.* 2005, 375). This was a significant concession by the Americans, for they had always held a considerable advantage in the relatively new MIRV technology.

Even though it was a multilateral meeting of thirty-five nations, the United States and Soviet Union were very much central players in the Helsinki Accord of 1975. This was a unique agreement, for it included signatories on both sides of the Iron Curtain for the first time. Key categories of agreement included advances in human rights protection, economic cooperation, and cultural interaction (McCormick 2010, 108). The centrality of the U.S.–Soviet relationship in this agreement was revealed through later disagreements about whether the Soviet leadership had gained economic advantages through it but failed to follow through on its human rights provisions. Finally, the two leading nations signed the SALT II agreement in the summer of 1979, a year that turned out to be the last one in a period of understanding and even concord. That agreement maintained the Vladivostok number of nuclear delivery vehicles at 2,400 but lowered the number that could have multiple warheads from 1,320 to 1,200. In addition, limits were imposed on the number of warheads that each delivery vehicle could carry (Paterson *et al.* 2005, 427). At the time, this agreement appeared to be a simple stepping-stone from previous ones dating back to 1972. However, it had a more storied history than the others, for the Soviet invasion of Afghanistan later in 1979 caused President Carter to withdraw the treaty from Senate consideration. And yet, both sides eventually agreed to comply with its limits, even in light of the failure to fully ratify it.

In this defined period that was the high-water mark of détente the two superpowers used the soft power of diplomacy and actually signed agreements in lieu of the harsh rhetoric that had accompanied earlier episodes such as the building of the Berlin Wall, the Cuban Missile Crisis, the War in Southeast Asia, and Soviet crack-downs on reform movements in Hungary (1956) and Czechoslovakia (1968). Even though the period of accommodation came to an end, it is likely that its importance lies also in the fact that post-1991 leaders could look back on these negotiations as a precedent for future linkages.

The late Cold War Gorbachev era, 1985–91

Although the theme of duality in the late Cold War era is the key reality and organizing concept of this segment of the analysis, it is apparent that the Gorbachev factor on the Soviet side was the unexpected stimulus that led to a thaw in relations in the last six years prior to the collapse of the Soviet Union. With Ronald Reagan still in the White House, there was not really much of a push from that side of the Atlantic to melt the iciness of neo-Cold War. However, as time passed, both sides worked to sign mutual agreements that appeared to pick up the pieces of the unfinished work of the earlier period of détente.

In Gorbachev's own words, his effort to break out of the isolation of the period included pursuit of "the growing tendency towards interdependence of the states of the world community." Conversion to Marxism-Leninism was no longer the key Soviet concern in foreign affairs, for the need to incorporate the experiences of all peoples was the higher priority. Thus, the mutual focus on global issues held in common as well as the use of "dialogue" as a key tool of diplomacy would come to command center stage (Gorbachev 1987, 137–159).

The emerging foreign policy on the Soviet side reflected in part one feature of Gorbachev's domestic reforms. *Perestroika* entailed an emphasis on restricting the economy in the direction of market forces that might increase its efficiency. In order to have more financial resources to fire up the economy, it was necessary to reduce spending on military and defense projects (Sakwa 1990, 333). Further, definitions of security would increasingly be anchored in political matters rather than exclusively military ones (Light 1989, 178). The practical side of this approach entailed meetings with Western European leaders, restating goals in terms of interdependence, acceptance of the Western multi-polar approach, and more frequent references by Gorbachev to "our common European home" (Light 1989, 188–189; Sakwa 1990, 327).

Gorbachev's speech to the UN in December 1988 was a centerpiece of the new strategic approach, as it incorporated surprising new tactics that shifted resources in new ways. In that speech he indicated that there would be a 10% cut in the army and reduction of its ranks by 500,000 (Sakwa 1990, 334). A follow-up to this speech was permission for the Polish Roundtable in April of the next year, a meeting at which the leaders made the critical decision to hold largely free parliamentary elections (Hutchings 1997, 9). Soviet reactions to those plans differed markedly from work with the Polish military to crack down on Solidarity and its reforms less than a decade earlier. Thereby, Gorbachev signaled to other Warsaw Pact members that reforms were a possibility in their states as well (Hook 2014, 58).

Troop reductions in other locations fleshed out the 1988 UN speech in important ways as well. Some of these initiatives included the pull-out of all Soviet troops from Afghanistan, an end to efforts to jam Voice of America, the reduction of support for the Sandinistas in Nicaragua, and pressure on Cuba to take its troops out of Afghanistan (Paterson *et al.* 2005, 442). Significantly, there were sharp reductions of Soviet military personnel in Eastern European countries as well. Khrushchev had ordered an invasion of Hungary to halt its reform movement in 1956, and occupation troops had remained to keep control after that critical event. In 1968, Soviet leaders had organized a Warsaw Pact invasion of Czechoslovakia in order to end its Prague Spring. In conjunction with his overall "new thinking" in foreign policy, Gorbachev pulled 15,000 of 60,000 troops out of Hungary, and he also pulled out two of the five Soviet divisions in Czechoslovakia, while announcing plans to take all 72,000 out by 1991. The largest Cold War military presence of Soviet forces was that in the German Democratic Republic, and the Soviet leader indicated that he would take out a symbolic three divisions of the nineteen that had a presence in that front-line state. There had also been a major Soviet military presence in Mongolia and Central Asia, in light of the need to check Chinese ambitions. The plan entailed a reduction of 200,000 troops in that Eurasian presence. By 1990, Gorbachev had also begun to pull out military capabilities from Cam Rhan Bay in Vietnam (Sakwa 1990, 343–345).

Accompanying this considerable drawdown of military forces in regions that had been critical to the achievement of Soviet goals during the intense period of the Cold War was a renewed willingness to negotiate with the West in the area of arms control. Even before Gorbachev acceded to the top position in the Soviet leadership, the previous Chernenko regime had put out feelers about its willingness to restore the arms-control process. Preparations began in September 1984, a year that bore some significance. President Reagan was only weeks away from the presidential election and had taken considerable criticism from his opponent, Walter Mondale, for the lack of progress on arms control in his first term in office. It is also possible that Reagan's earlier proposal in 1983, for a Strategic Defense Initiative (SDI), may have captured the attention of the Soviet political elite (Hyland 1988, 451).

The Reykjavik Summit in October 1986 bought both Reagan and Gorbachev to the negotiating table in an effort to restore the spirit of 1970s-style détente. Both agreed to reduce nuclear weapons by 50% over the next five years and to maintain only 100 warheads on their respective Intermediate Nuclear Force (INF) weapons (McCormick 2010, 138). They also agreed to preserve the ABM Treaty and President Reagan confirmed that the U.S. would not deploy the SDI in the near future. They also decided then to eliminate the short-range and intermediate-range missiles that the Soviet Union had emplaced in Eastern Europe and America in selected Western European states (Hyland 1988, 452). All of this bore fruit in December 1987 when the two leaders actually signed the INF Treaty in Washington, D.C. In order for this treaty to work, there needed to be complete openness about the removal and destruction of the weapons from their theaters in Eastern and Western Europe. This was made possible as a result of the Stockholm Conference of 1986, a meeting at which both sides agreed to on-site inspections (Tucker 1987, 155). As a result, both sides actually fulfilled the requirements of the INF Treaty before its three-year deadline.

In a number of ways, the reforms and changes of the late 1980s had some similarities with the processes utilized in the 1970s. Arms-control agreements were central to both periods, and progress occurred in the areas of SALT, START, and INF. However, there were marked differences as well. There was much more openness about the aims and procedures of both the United States and the Soviet Union in the second period. The Soviet leadership situation was a unique characteristic of the second period as well. Finally, there were barely noticed signs that the Cold War was winding down in the second period, indicators that were not present at all in the 1970s.

Periods of hostility and reliance on hard power

Underlying tension during détente in the 1970s

Although agreements of considerable meaning took place in the 1970s, that decade was in many ways similar in tone to the early decades of Cold War. In the wake of the Berlin and Cuban crises of the 1960s, the West continued to be "mobilized as if for war" (Hutchings 1997, 2). As a result of American provocations such as the expansionism in Southeast Asia and continued presence in military bases along the extended Soviet border, the same could be said for Moscow. One example of this continued ill will was American apprehension about the way in which human rights protections suffered under Brezhnev's leadership. The treatment of dissidents such as Aleksandr Solzhenitsyn and Andrei Sakharov was a central issue, but so also was the matter of Jewish immigration. While Nixon and Kissinger trod lightly on the issues of human rights, in the hopes that détente would continue, the American Congress was of a different mindset. In 1973 Congress passed the Jackson-Vanik Amendment that linked the granting of Most Favored Nation treatment for the Soviet Union to its willingness to grant more immigration visas for persons of the Jewish faith (Jentleson 2007, 143). Thus, an undercurrent of hostility made the overarching framework of détente somewhat shaky.

Divisive Latin-American issues involved more than the lingering Cuban sore spot, but Chile was under the elected communist leadership of Salvador Allende from 1970 to 1973. Although the link between Chile and the Soviet Union was not nearly as tight as that between the USSR and Cuba, still the crisis bore all the hallmarks of being a microcosm of the Cold War. The Central Intelligence Agency (CIA) covertly poured considerable financial resources into opposition hands in order to overthrow the communist leader (Jentleson 2007, 147). In fact, for a decade (1963–73), the CIA utilized "black propaganda" in an effort to keep Allende out of power and then to dislodge him from his elected post. Involvement by the United States in the politics of Chile was very extensive and included efforts to play communists off against both socialists and labor union organizations. They supported opposition media outlets such as *El Mercurio* and on behalf of moderate and conservative political parties they injected $8,000,000 into the election process, ("U.S. Covert Action in Chile (1963–1973)," 2005, 464–465). In many ways, the persistence in such projects made the arms-control agreements in the same decade even more remarkable.

Tension continued over additional battlegrounds in the Middle East and Africa. For example, the Middle East War of 1973 ended in a ceasefire, but President Nixon put all U.S. forces on nuclear alert. Clearly, the audience he had in mind was not the set of players that included Israel and its neighbors but Brezhnev and the Soviet Union. Similarly, the Ford administration of the mid-1970s took Soviet involvement in the Angolan Civil War seriously. When it became clear that Moscow was supporting the Popular Movement for the Liberation of Angola, President Ford took the remarkable step of banning the term "détente" from official American vocabulary (Paterson *et al.* 2005, 380–385). However, such posturing did not undermine his commitment to the furtherance of arms agreements with the same global rival.

Provocations by the Soviet Union

By the late Cold War it is probably the case that traditional Russian self-perceptions and world views had replaced the early twentieth-century drive to expand the number of fellow workers' states in the world. Russian leaders brought to the negotiating table with the United States a sense that they had an "exceptional status" as the "third Rome" in global relations. Some provocations were nationalist in nature, but others bore the stigma of the nineteenth-century Slavophile mission with its sense of a "universal mission" for Russia and its huge successor state (Bialer 1986, 260–266). Western European nations, based on distinct "social communities," looked with a lack of understanding at the huge "territorial empire" to the east. Since its experience as a multi-ethnic state with "overlapping identities for citizens" was so different from the polities of Western Europe, understandings between the two were hampered (Remington 2004, 17–18).

In that light, perhaps some of the Soviet provocations fit into a more comprehensible framework. Soviet support for like-minded third-world allies was not confined to Angola but also included Ethiopia and North Vietnam in the early 1970s (Jentleson 2007, 146). However, the invasion of Afghanistan at the end of 1979 was perhaps the key event that undid the détente spirit of the 1970s. The Brezhnev regime sent 80,000 troops into that border nation, with very uncertain goals from the perspective of the West (Hook 2014, 58). The war itself became a quagmire from which Moscow could extract itself only after nearly a decade of futility. This was combined with the coming to power of the Sandinistas in Nicaragua earlier in the same year and the stifling of the Polish reform movement two years later, and so it is not surprising that the American leadership perceived the Soviet Union again to be on the move as it had been in the first decades after 1945.

Following the temporary collapse of détente in 1979, it could be argued that additional Soviet offensive moves preserved the atmosphere of hostility between the two superpowers. In fall of 1983 the Soviet military shot down a South Korean airliner, flight KAL 007, that had gone off course and seemingly flown over Soviet air space. Moscow argued that the plane was on a spying mission for the U.S., while the West provided evidence that it was actually in international air space at the time when the Soviet air force shot it down (Paterson *et al.* 2005, 438). One year later, the Soviet Union boycotted the Los Angeles Olympics in retaliation for a number of alleged provocations by the West (McCormick 2010, 131). While all of these apparently hostile and offensive moves by the Soviet foreign policy planners occurred prior to Gorbachev's emergence in the top leadership position, it is also clear that ensuing American reactions were not just defensive but also provocative in their own way.

American provocations

President Carter entered the presidency with an idealistic component to his foreign policy that he saw as having been lacking in the previous two Republican administrations. In addition, he hoped to repair damaged relations with allies that had persisted even after the end of the War in Southeast Asia. One consequence of this new thrust in foreign policy was a downgrading of the importance of the Soviet Union in his calculus, an emphasis that would harm Soviet–American relations in the long run (McCormick 2010, 112). In addition, he met with Solzhenitsyn, the dissident Russian writer of considerable stature (Jentleson 2007, 143). This was a move that former President Ford had turned down, and one that alienated the Brezhnev regime.

However, the Soviet invasion of Afghanistan in the third year of the Carter administration was the event that pushed the two nations much further apart on a whole host of issues. There had been considerable differences of opinion within the top levels of the Carter administration on key foreign-policy questions. Secretary of State Cyrus Vance consistently looked for diplomatic solutions, while National Security Advisor Zbigniew Brzezinski advocated more hardline approaches on a number of questions. The latter's views certainly came to the fore after the events connected with Afghanistan. President Carter pulled the SALT II Treaty back from Senate consideration, halted high-tech sales to the Soviet Union, limited Soviet fishing rights in U.S. waters, imposed a grain embargo on a state that had difficulties producing enough for its own population, due to its proportionally small amount of cultivable land, and boycotted the 1980 Moscow Olympics (McCormick 2010, 125).

It is important to note that these steps bore an offensive as well as a defensive stamp. Limiting fishing rights and adding a grain embargo hurt citizens and consumers in the USSR in the short run. An Olympics boycott led to retaliation by the Soviet Union against the Los Angeles games four years later, due to the coincidence that the competitions were scheduled successively in the two states. Foremost, though the Moscow boycott hurt American athletes who had been preparing for the games for four long years. Their dreams of winning medals evaporated, and the action violated the long-standing value that the Olympics should be free of politics. Furthermore, the SALT process had proceeded through careful negotiations through three presidencies and was of overwhelming importance for creating a sense of global security. The SALT process was a profoundly different national security issue than the invasion of Afghanistan. There is no doubt that the invasion itself was a bold gambit in an effort to gain strategic advantage for the Soviet Union. In the eyes of the Soviet leaders, it was less provocative and more justified than the involvement of American military forces for so long in Vietnam. Thus, the complete cycle of reactive moves by the United States was probably overdone and itself a provocation.

The U.S. reactions, however, did involve a number of "in kind" steps that matched the nature of the Soviet military move, for there were genuine concerns that the Soviet leaders might move further into the region in an effort to finally acquire access to warm-water ports. For example, the Carter administration made new arms sales to Pakistan, which shared a concern about the instability in its neighbor to the east. The U.S. Navy set up military facilities in Oman, Kenya, Somalia, and Egypt to help contain any further Soviet aggression. For its part, the U.S. Air Force dispatched two carriers to the region, while the administration required young males to register for the draft, as they had prior to the War in Southeast Asia (Paterson *et al.* 2005, 429). This last requirement was meant to signal that the nation was on standby, although the call to active duty never took place. Hauntingly, thirty-five years later, the type of tactics considered and used by the Obama administration after the Russian annexation of the Crimea in spring 2014 bore a resemblance to this range of measures that seemed defensive to the United States and offensive to the Soviet Union.

The election of Ronald Reagan in 1980 was a step that continued the stepped-up Carter national security policy of the previous year but took it much further. Whereas President Carter had initiated a number of individual actions that would impact various corners of life in the Soviet Union, his successor advocated a fully fledged upgrade in military capabilities, both conventional and nuclear. This approach may have been responsive to currents that swirled in American political life as well. Not only did President Carter go down to defeat in the elections, but so also did senators Culver of Iowa, Bayh of Indiana, McGovern of South Dakota, and Church of Idaho. All had been critical of American intervention in locations such as Southeast Asia, and so their collective defeat may in part have reflected a public desire to get out of the post- Southeast Asian quagmire and step forward into a position of world leadership once more. In the background were the conclusions of the 1976 Committee on the Present Danger, a neo-conservative group that perceived the Carter administration as generally too weak on foreign policy (Paterson *et al.* 2005, 431). In sum, President Reagan envisioned his foreign policy mandate as one that should focus on the use of military power to halt Soviet expansionism in its tracks and thereby generate on the American side a "revival of the national will" (McCormick 2010, 127).

In the conventional arena, the new administration announced its intention to double spending on defense in the near future (Hook 2014, 58). Specifically, America would spend $1.6 trillion on defense between 1981 and 1986. There would be a strong effort locate more military capabilities overseas in order to be ready to counteract new rounds of Soviet adventurism. Increasing naval strength to the level of a 600-ship navy was also part of the calculus (Papp *et al.* 2005, 176).

However, it was in the area of nuclear capabilities that the moves of the administration were most eye catching. Thinking that a new window of vulnerability had developed, as the Kennedy campaign had worried in the 1960 election, Reagan proposed the building of the B-1 bomber, a project that President Carter had cancelled. Nuclear submarine strength was upgraded through the construction of a second generation of the Trident submarine, with bases in Bangor, Washington and Kings Bay, Georgia. Those submarines would carry significantly more warheads than did the Trident I category. The MX Missile would be located in the West of the nation and would provide advanced land-based capabilities. All three "legs" of the nuclear arsenal would thereby receive an inoculation of new energy and capability. The SDI or "Star Wars" would protect the United States from any attacks by other nuclear powers. The Soviet Union clearly envisioned that defensive system as provocative, for it would provide protection for an America whose leaders may have already decided on a first strike by its own weapons. Advisors made a difference in the Reagan administration, as they had under President Carter, for Ambassador to the UN Jeanne Kirkpatrick helped the administration to justify all of this through her distinction between totalitarian enemies who needed to be checked and authoritarian friends who could work with the U.S. in the global conflict (Jentleson 2007, 155–159).

In conjunction with the advances in the American capabilities noted above, the American president also presented his own "Reagan Doctrine" that called for a more proactive American policy that would essentially take the fight to the Soviet Union and its allies. Efforts to roll back perceived Soviet gains in locations such as Angola and Nicaragua would enhance America's role in the world and restore it to what it had been in the pre-Southeast Asian era. The plans and actions may have had more impact than the administration realized. In fact, the enemy was weaker economically than American economists knew, and age plus ill health resulted in a situation in which the Soviet Union experienced a succession of four top leaders between November 1982 and March 1985 (Papp *et al.* 2005, 179). The American provocations may have put the Soviet Union on the defensive, but they also paved the way for its collapse. In any event, they undercut the gains of détente in mutual understanding and set up a contradiction in policy that penetrated well beyond the end of the Cold War.

Conclusion

Which of the five analytical models holds the most sway in interpreting the late Cold War relationship between the United States and the Soviet Union? The Balance of Power model reveals a number of important realities about the period under review. During these two decades there was rough parity in nuclear capabilities between the two superpowers. There had been an imbalance between the two in the early Cold War era, and the USSR was at a distinct disadvantage at that time. Balance also characterized the competition in third-world settings such as in Nicaragua, Angola, and the Middle East. Both Washington and Moscow either pursued objectives in those countries and their neighbors, or checked the ambitions of the other. At the same time, there was over time a kind of staggered nature within the power equation. Soviet leaders took advantage of American passivity in the post-Southeast Asia time frame and took initiatives in Afghanistan and elsewhere. If the United States did not respond immediately, its leaders eventually did through a number of the national security initiatives of the Reagan administration. Overall, balance at the regional and global levels held sway.

Another model that was a realistic part of the equation was that of Multi-Polarity. If most nations in the world had leaned towards one or another of the big powers in the early Cold War, that was no longer true with the advent of détente. Western European nations in particular pushed the two nuclear giants to moderate their hostility and cut back both on their nuclear arsenals and on the nuclear weapons emplaced on both sides of the Iron Curtain. Japan and China became powerful and independent forces in East Asia, the former through its economic strength and the latter due to its population, economic growth potential, and rivalry with the Soviet Union. Powerful nationalism infected developing nations such as Vietnam, Nicaragua, and Iran. Such nations did not prefer alliances with either the United States or the Soviet Union, and their domestic struggles were perplexing and stymieing for the larger entities. These power patterns were notably different from the bipolar positioning during the early Cold War.

Which of the important theories played a role in explaining the duality of power between the two during the late Cold War? Realism is important in explaining how state centered and focused on national self-interests each power became in the 1970s and 1980s. Protection and expansion of the power of the Soviet Union in the traditional Russian pattern had replaced the ideological drives of Marxism-Leninism to create fellow worker states wherever possible. Maintenance of control over Eastern Europe, largely through the Warsaw Treaty Organization, had the objective of protecting the vulnerable western border of the Soviet Union. Perhaps the invasion of Afghanistan performed the same service in a southwest that may have seen the revival of Islam in Iran as an inspiration. It also served American national interests to preserve the balance in the nuclear weapons area, especially after the advantage was lost to Moscow during the 1960s. What was the purpose of the Reagan revival of American power and stature, if not to protect national interests after a decade of irresolution in foreign affairs? Interestingly, the power of globalization pressures that flooded across national boundaries in the twenty-first century was far more limited at the end of the Cold War, and thereby Realist thinkers and planners could more carefully plot how to advance the interests of their own nations. To say that multi-polarity had replaced bipolarity is not the same as saying that the new sources of global power and the nations that embodied them could really paralyze the actions of the two strong players on the world stage.

Potentially, Legacy Theory had an important beginning in this two-decade-long conclusion to the Cold War. So many events and decisions in the 1970s and 1980s reverberated after the end of the Cold War. The Reagan legacy served as a reminder to later presidents of what values America stood for and could spread on the world stage. Arms-control agreements that had come to fruition in very difficult times offered hope for even sharper reductions after East–West hostilities had eased somewhat. However, the Soviet disaster in Afghanistan over nearly a decade was a legacy and reminder that might have influenced American planners more than it did as they sought to nation-build in that country after the invasion of 2001. Obviously, legacies of the communist patterns of state control and planning profoundly influenced the evolution of the Russian state after 1991. Perhaps the strong-man nature of Soviet-style rule and leadership explains the Russian receptivity to the single-minded rule and authoritarianism of Vladimir Putin.

In conclusion, Balance of Power, Multi-Polarity, Realism, and Legacy Theory all help to illuminate the shadows of superpower objectives, strategies, and tactics in the late Cold War. Elusive as those explanations are in trying to explain what the Soviet Union and the United States aimed to accomplish in that time frame, they look to be very firm in contrast to their uneasy hold and unpersuasive power after 9/11 sent the world nearly spinning out of control.

3

The imbalance of power in 1991: collapse of the Soviet Union and allied victory in the Persian Gulf War

Introduction

Two symbolic sets of events occurred in 1991 that underlined the sharp foreign-policy changes in the destinies of both Cold War superpowers. At the beginning of the year President George H.W. Bush led a coalition of thirty nations in a successful effort to dislodge Iraq from Kuwait in the Persian Gulf War. At the end of the year, President Gorbachev tendered his resignation amidst the collapse of the federation known as the Soviet Union. On the surface, it appeared as if the apparent late Cold War equity in power between the two nations had yielded to a sharp imbalance that worked considerably to the disadvantage of the new Russia while providing some in the United States with the conviction that America had somehow "won" the Cold War. Both sets of perceptions and conclusions turned out to be gross oversimplifications, for Russia gained considerable strength over the next two decades while the United States struggled at times to maintain its central position in the global power equation.

Analysis of this new relationship will take two paths. First, it is important to examine carefully the way in which the external challenges that the two states faced bore some similarities, or at least parallels. On the one hand, prior to the break-up Soviet leaders had been dealing for two full years with the strategic challenges that emanated from Warsaw Pact allies in Eastern and Southeastern Europe. By overthrowing their own communist-led regimes, each of those nations changed the regional power balance in which Moscow had been the dominant partner and even the director. Gorbachev's response had been an accepting one, as he acknowledged the changed relationship with them and their new freedom of orbit. On the other hand, American leadership dealt with strategic challenges from key nations in the Middle East such as Iraq. However, its response differed from that of its counterpart in the Soviet Union, for America resisted the changed status quo after the Iraqi invasion of Kuwait and essentially brought a halt to it. Thus, the United States and the Soviet Union reacted in very different ways to changes presented by medium-power nations in regions of great importance to them.

Second, both American and Russian leaders needed to cope with severe doctrinal challenges to thinking and assumptions that had been in place for some time. The Soviet Union's central place in the universe yielded to the new and shrunken Russia, a state that had lost fourteen regional units that previously had been republics in the vast entity that Moscow governed. What would be the identity of the new unit that continued to be deeply and broadly multi-ethnic? For the United States, the pressing need was to evolve a new self-definition that was tied neither to the defense of interests against Soviet power nor to its post-Southeast Asian sense of passivity about its possibilities in world politics. In both cases, new definitions and doctrines would emerge. In the Russian case, there would be a renewed emphasis on the greatness of the past, its rulers, and its achievements. For the United States, the concept of New World Order emerged much more quickly and seemed to imply that victory in the Persian Gulf War would be a model for a future in which the United States would fill any vacuums of power in virtually any region of the world. While the focus on doctrine was common to the leaders of both states, the results were very different. For America, military and political power would be the key ingredients, while for Russia, emphasis on history and culture would be substitutes for more tangible components of power but, hopefully, foundations for the reconstruction of a principal political role in regional and world politics.

Meeting strategic challenges from new regional powers

Russia and the Eastern European revolutions
The Eastern European revolutions occurred in rapid fashion in 1989, a full two years before the collapse of the Soviet Union. In Poland, continuing pressure from Solidarity led to the scheduling of relatively open elections in the summer. Non-communist candidates ran in an open way and, for the most part, defeated their communist opponents. Within a few months Hungary opened its border with Yugoslavia and many people from throughout the bloc flowed in so that they could use the Yugoslav "tunnel" into the West. The climactic moment was surely the opening of the Berlin Wall on November 9. East German border guards had received the order to withhold fire as people climbed onto the wall and went into West Berlin. Soon people were flooding into West Germany and beyond in order to see what life was like in those countries. At the end of November, huge crowds demonstrated in Wenceslaus

Square in Prague, and after a number of days the communist leaders gave up their positions of power. Changes came to the Baltic States later, but the Romanians chased their leader, Nicolae Ceausescu, from power and executed him and his spouse on Christmas Day (McCormick 2010, 161). It was as if a string of firecrackers had gone off in a region that had been under tough communist control since the end of World War II.

How did the Soviet leaders justify their inaction or grant of permission to their former client states? Some argued that the economic weaknesses of the Soviet Union made control over a broad swath of territory to the west no longer possible. In Gorbachev's own words, the Soviet Union had decided to get more fully involved in Europe and its global structures. He acknowledged that this was a profound "change of the political arrangement known as the Yalta agreement." More important, Moscow had decided informally to give the Eastern European nations back to their own peoples (Gorbachev 2008). Whatever the rationale, the consequences were enormous for both Central Europe and the Soviet Union.

The United States and the Persian Gulf War

Whereas the Soviet Union had sponsored the communist take-overs of the Eastern European nations partially in an effort to establish a firm buffer against Western nations and their potential aggressiveness, the United States decided to take firm action in the Persian Gulf in order to protect others of its oil-rich allies such as Saudi Arabia from potential moves by Iraq. Iraqi control of an oil empire that included Kuwait and Saudi Arabia would have been a sharp challenge to the national interests of the United States and its allies. In fact, there were those who depicted the Iraqi invasion of Kuwait as parallel to Hitler's invasion of Poland in 1939 (Papp *et al.* 2005, 197). With the stakes so high, an American-led response was inevitable. In contrast to the situation of the Soviet Union, which confronted less of a threat from the Eastern European states, the United States perceived the threat in the Middle East as one that was growing in importance in terms of the economic, political, and strategic stakes that were involved.

President Bush addressed the American Congress just prior to the war itself and made a strong case consistent with the reasoning cited above. He argued that there was a need to stand up for the rule of law, freedom, justice, and, especially, respect for the rights of the weak. Further, not only did the Iraqi invasion eliminate the national autonomy of Kuwait, but it also threatened many of its oil-producing neighbors (Bush 2005, 550–551). There was also a strong dimension of the old Cold War containment doctrine in this perception of the crisis, as the president feared that the fall of one domino would lead to the toppling of others as well. As such, this was also an echo of lessons learned in the 1930s. Hitler had convinced British Prime Minister Chamberlain at Munich that the take-over of the Sudetenland was a needed defensive move that was justified by restrictions on the German community in Czechoslovakia. However, the conquest of the entirety of Europe, with the exception of Great Britain, was the result. President Bush and a number of his advisors had lived through that period. Therefore, it was no surprise that their mindset in confronting Saddam Hussein's invasion was colored by their own previous history.

In prosecuting the upcoming war against Iraq, the American president mobilized the American Army, Navy, and Air Force in preparation for a gigantic struggle against Iraq's "crack troops" and its undefeatable Republican Guard. He then proceeded to stitch together a coalition of thirty nations that shared his perceptions about the nature of the crisis in the Persian Gulf (Papp *et al.* 2005, 197). Interestingly, the American leadership was successful in generating support from Gorbachev in the Soviet Union, the nations of Western Europe, and many key players in the Middle East (Jentleson 1997, 55). With the threat including "naked aggression," economic factors, and possibly nuclear weapons, the president's persuasive powers with these other nations were considerably enhanced (Jentleson 1997, 51).

In light of all these factors that pointed towards the need for military mobilization, it is surprising that presidential persuasiveness was even necessary. However, the shadow of Southeast Asia loomed large in the minds of the decision-makers, just as the Munich analogy did. Would the war, like its Southeast Asian predecessor, be an unending one in which the enemy was battling on its home front and able to evoke the powerful nationalism of its people? Thus, key presidential advisors argued for reliance on multilateralism and hoped that the use of force would be the ultimate last resort. The continuation of economic sanctions on Iraq was clearly the choice of many others, and that concern helps to explain why the Senate resolution that supported the use of force in Kuwait passed by only a 52–47 majority. Senator Sam Nunn had chaired the Armed Services Committee and he voted for the continuation of sanctions rather than the outright use of force in Kuwait (Lieber 1997, 4–15).

The American mobilization of military force was an impressive display of what was possible after more than a decade of hand wringing about what might have been done differently in Southeast Asia. In August 1990 the United States sent 150,000 troops to Saudi Arabia in preparation for the allied counterattack. Americans were stunned to see so many military vehicles moving south on interstate highways 95 and 75 at a time when many of them were thinking only about enjoying their needed vacations. In addition, the Arab League sent forces, as did many Western European allies. The Security Council of the UN passed ten resolutions that pressed economic sanctions upon Iraq. The final resolution called for the use of "all means necessary" against the aggressor, but all observers understood that this was a euphemism for advocating the use of force against Iraq. On January 15, 1991, the allies set a deadline for Iraqi withdrawal from Kuwait and began their air attack when their target did not observe it. A second ultimatum from the allies called for an end to the Iraqi aggression by February 22 of the same year. The Iraqis' failure to meet that deadline led to the 100-hour war that resulted in victory for the allies (McCormick 2010, 170–171). General Schwarzkopf dispatched his forces to the west in a surprising end-run around the Iraqi Republican Guard that was mobilized in the Persian Gulf. The Iraqi withdrawal from Kuwait occurred very quickly and the allied objectives were fulfilled. In this way the United States took firm action to back up a jeopardized and needed ally in the Persian Gulf. Perhaps its leaders fulfilled national interests with this involvement in parallel fashion to Soviet leaders who were liberating allies to pursue their own destiny. Regional and global security was served by both sets of decisions from the leaders in Washington and Moscow.

Developing new doctrine to settle the contours of the post-Cold War world

The doctrine of Russia as a successor state to the Soviet Union

Pressure from the existing republics in the Soviet Union for greater autonomy or even independence commenced at the same time that the Eastern European client states were actually breaking away. In 1989 a human chain four hundred miles in length stretched throughout the Baltic republics of Estonia, Latvia, and Lithuania. Specifically, the participants were protesting against the Nazi–Soviet Pact that had linked the three republics to the Soviet Union. In fact, their life as republics within the Soviet state was several decades shorter than that of the other twelve republics and many of their citizens had memories of pre-Soviet times and still held a bitter resentment about the incorporation of their home countries into the communist-dominated empire to the imme-diate east. It is thus not surprising that the Baltic republics were the first to effectively break their bonds with Moscow, as early as summer 1990 (Paterson *et al.* 2005, 469). At the same time, changes were also percolating in the huge Russian Republic, for Boris Yeltsin won the presidency there in an open election process in June 1991 (Huskey 1999, 25). His willingness to stand for election in the face of several contenders stood in sharp contrast to Gorbachev, whose assumption of the Soviet presidency was anchored in the elite appointment process that had been characteristic of the Soviet pattern since 1917.

Of course, the domestic reforms of Gorbachev preceded the Eastern European revolutions and paved the way for demands within the Soviet Union for even more wide-ranging transformations. In his own mind, Gorbachev's *perestroika* reforms, changes that opened up the Soviet economy gradually to free-market forces, were also linked to foreign-policy needs. The involvement in Afghanistan for nearly a decade had been so costly that domestic adjustments were a necessity (Gorbachev 2008). However, it was probably the case that the changes accompanying *glasnost* were the ones that provoked symbolic demonstrations such as the human chain across the Baltic republics. That category of reforms centered on protection for freedom of expression, although Gorbachev probably never dreamed that it would lead to such a crescendo of demands for more deep-rooted changes. Democratization was another category of reforms, but one that the leader imagined would take place totally within the container of the Communist Party and its institutions. Clearly, it provided a taste of a new day that only whetted appetites for more (McCormick 2010, 162). Finally, new thinking in foreign policy was part and parcel of the Gorbachev package of reforms, and its crystallization was clearly evident in the Eastern European revolutions of 1989. In the end, Gorbachev had no choice in embarking upon this four-pronged reform package, for clearly "the old system was broken" (Snow 2004, 114).

There were efforts to develop doctrine that would correspond to these enormous political changes, even prior to the break-up of the federation in December 1989. A popular characterization of the events was that Soviet leaders were adopting the "Frank Sinatra Doctrine" encapsulated in his famous song "My Way." The nations of the Warsaw Treaty Organization as well as Soviet peoples and groups were liberated to follow their own styles and preferences. Soviet reformer Georgi Arbatov called upon both superpowers to follow a foreign-policy doctrine of democratization that would allow other nations associated with them to breathe more freely. If Soviet leaders were able to "reverse the militarization of life," then ideal circumstances would exist for the pursuit of substantive and meaningful domestic reforms ("Soviet Reformer Arbatov Explains the 'New Thinking' in the Soviet Union" 2005, 506). However, the reforms did not bear only positive consequences, for their results made the people's lives more difficult in many ways and would eventually include increased inequality, poverty, corruption, and criminality. Some concluded that it had been a mistake to concentrate on so many political reforms before relaxing the centrally controlled economic system to the same extent (Remington 2004, 3–6).

A combination of institutional changes within the Soviet Union and activities within the various republics led to the undoing of Gorbachev and the implosion of the Soviet Union. In March 1990, the Soviet leaders created a new appointive office called the presidency in order to anchor the authority of that leader outside the framework and traditional institutions that were either part of the Communist Party apparatus or within its control. The republics then started a parallel process of setting up their own regional presidencies. A key decision was that of the Russian Republic, for its leaders decided to make the position elective and Boris Yeltsin was successful in winning office after standing before the general electorate in June 1991. A few months earlier, in April, Gorbachev had signed a new Treaty of Union with nine of the fifteen republics in what turned out to be a last-gasp effort to keep the federative entity alive. This was clearly an exercise in decentralization that offered expanded autonomy as a substitute for the republics' independence (Remington 2004, 46–49).

In the late summer of 1991, while Gorbachev was on vacation in the Crimea, the conservative opposition to that Union Treaty removed him from power. The conspirators included people from the Communist Party, military, and legislature. Reformers headed by Yeltsin restored Gorbachev to power and brought the president back to Moscow. However, by December the temporary solutions were unraveling and the official final blow came at a meeting in Minsk on December 8. The presidents of the Russian, Belorussian, and Ukrainian republics met in private and agreed on the dissolution of the Soviet Union. Their republics were large and very central to the administration of the state, and their decision marked the end of the federation. On December 12 the Russian Supreme Soviet withdrew from the 1922 Treaty of Union that had created the state, and the new day was at hand (White 2011, 25). Gorbachev himself resigned the presidency of the Soviet Union on December 25, for he no longer had a territorial entity over which to preside. The efforts to create a doctrine for the Soviet Union in its last years then yielded to a need to create a rationale for Russia at home, in its region, and indeed in the world as a whole.

Central to the dilemma of reshaping late Soviet institutions and simultaneously maintaining workable relations with all the republics was the issue of the presidency. There was a sharp contrast between Gorbachev's assumption of an appointed executive office in 1990 and Yeltsin's ability to obtain 60% of the votes for the office of president in the Russian Republic in 1991. Yeltsin thereby was clothed in a "mantle of popular legitimacy" that Gorbachev could not claim (Huskey 1999, 25). The Soviet presidency was severely harmed by the August coup that removed Gorbachev from power (Huskey 1999, 24). Later, in 1993, Yeltsin used his presidential powers to attack the legislature when it resisted his plans. Of course there was a huge outcry and questions were raised about the powers and limits of this new office. The answer to this dilemma of the ambiguity surrounding the presidential office during its first three years led to the writing of a new constitution for Russia that was ratified by a referendum on December 12, 1993 (Huskey 1999, 34–35).

The office of president was very clearly defined in the new constitution, which gave it considerable authority. The president appointed the prime minister, served as commander-in-chief of the armed forces, and could dissolve the Duma if the need arose. In fact, the constitution itself included the statement that the elected leader "exercises control over almost every policy." The president also possessed the power to settle differences between the Russian Federation and its various republics. Further, he could suspend the actions of republic executives if they conflicted with federal laws or international obligations. Finally, the president could invoke martial law and announce a state of emergency (*Constitution* 1994, 7–51). The strengthening of the presidential office did not substitute for an ideology or doctrine for the new Russian state. However, it did provide a powerful foundation for a strong-minded president to outline a compelling doctrine based on Russian history and culture.

American doctrine after the Cold War

President George H.W. Bush had two remarkable opportunities to develop new doctrine as a replacement for the Containment Doctrine that had played such a continuing role during most of the Cold War. In early 1990 his State of the Union message followed the last of the Eastern European revolutions by just one month. In that speech he celebrated the new reality that America stood "at the center of a widening circle of freedom." With the Soviet system struggling with so many internal tensions, he was bold enough to proclaim that only the United States could provide the needed leadership in the future (Bush 2005, 509). In September of the same year he spoke to both chambers of the Congress during the drama that surrounded the preparations for the Persian Gulf War. At that time he went further in terms of doctrine and spoke about the emergence of a new world order that had specific characteristics. It would celebrate western values that the American constitution embodied, to include protection for the rights of the weak (Bush 2005, 550). That value was certainly compromised by Iraq's take-over and occupation of Kuwait, but the same could also apply to the treatment of minority groups within Iraq and other nearby nations.

One observer described the situation at the time as a "unipolar moment" that pushed the United States to the center of the stage. The first term of that phrase coincided with Bush's emphasis on the unique circumstances that had led to such a special role for the United States, but the second implied a temporary situation that would have some sort of end point. All other potentially strong players had adopted a smaller role in world affairs for reasons unique to them. Germany was in the process of getting a new start as a unified nation. The Soviet Union had broken up, and the European Union itself had just adopted a new, staged strategy that pointed towards tighter internal integration. China's potential was enormous, but it had just gone through the conflict over Tiananmen Square and was not yet politically strong in its own region and beyond. This fluid situation that affected key players reinforced a dominant role for America by all measures: "military, economic, technological, diplomatic, cultural, even linguistic" (Krauthammer 2007 556). Such a doctrine was heavily dependent on American power rather than on a set of ideas, but it did serve for a time as a substitute for the Kennan's Containment Doctrine that President Reagan had been able to revive as late in the Cold War as the 1980s (Gaddis 2007, 251–253).

President Bush himself was not a grand visionary in the sense that either Franklin Roosevelt or Ronald Reagan had been. His strength lay in smart tactics rather than grand strategy. He generally pursued policies that were "pragmatic and prudent," and the true test of them was their results rather than ideological content. He had chosen advisors such as Secretary of State James Baker whose earlier experience was also in tactics rather than strategy. Baker had done an excellent job as an election campaign manager, though that was quite a different role than that of the architect of new foreign policy doctrine. He and National Security Advisor Brent Scowcroft focused on an "incremental strategy," and so the general result was a different kind of doctrinal approach (McCormick 2010, 155–156). There is no reason why pragmatism might be incompatible with grand strategy, but this may have been responsible for its shorter life span.

There were also other players on the scene, and that reality undercut any leading role outlined for the United States. For many leaders such as President Havel of Czechoslovakia, the OSCE was an ideal organization for mediating future conflicts (Snow 2004, 118). The OSCE was a product of the 1975 Helsinki Conference and included nations from both sides of the old Iron Curtain. If the EU were successful in further integrating is members based on the 1989 Single European Act, then that organization's Common Foreign and Security Policy might become a central actor as well. Also, any effort by the American leader to stimulate new agreements with Russia might come to naught, since Russia was spending so much time getting internally organized after the momentous events of December 1991 (Lieber 1997, 11). American power over global doctrine also faced the challenge that it was difficult to rally the nations of Europe in light of the inability of all concerned to figure out the exact nature of threats to that continent. Finally, President Bush's domestic position was weakened after the end of the Cold War and the Persian Gulf War victory. The public was ready for a re-focus on domestic policy matters, and the election year and campaign were just around the corner (Lieber 1997, 175).

During 1992, the last year of the Bush administration, a number of test cases raised real challenges for implementation of the New World Order. In Haiti, local forces overthrew the elected leader, Jean-Bertrand Aristide, and America might have taken a tough and leading stand. However, economic measures were the only tactic utilized, and the preferred option was to use the Organization of American States to implement a trade embargo. Many refugees from Haiti sought asylum in the United States, but they were sent home. In Somalia, a long drought had led to much suffering among the population, but ethnic rivalries and struggles between tribal warlords complicated international efforts to assist. President Bush sent 28,000 U.S. troops to Somalia in December 1992, but they did not arrive to carry out an American doctrine (McCormick 2010, 175). Rather, they arrived under UN auspices and under the Clinton administration they actually submitted to UN command (Jentleson 1997, 62). In spite of such situations of shared leadership, the in the election campaign of 1992 the president depicted the United States as "the ultimate guarantor of world order and stability," while Bill Clinton opted for a broader, multi-lateral approach that may have been more congruent with the reality in settings such as Haiti and Somalia (Schneider 1997, 29).

It is also the case that Yugoslavia broke up into separate nation-states in 1991–92, and the Bush administration did not jump in with arguments about how that fit into New World Order. Instead, the opening of the Bosnian civil war in 1992 led to American support for UN sanctions and eventually a NATO-run "no-fly zone" (McCormick 2010, 173–174). In a variety of foreign policy settings in his previous diplomatic career, George Bush had shared the common perception of successive administrations that Yugoslavia during the Cold War was a kind of mediator between East and West. After all, its communist leader Josip Tito had been one of the key founders of the Non-Aligned Movement in the early 1960s. Since Yugoslavia had been so independent of Moscow's controls for a full four decades, American leaders such as President Bush initially preferred to see it remain intact after the end of the Cold War. However, the reality was very different, and the West held back while many suffered during Yugoslavia's civil wars. Another contributing factor was the American perception that several West European nations such as France and Germany had long-standing ties with ethnic groups such as Serbs and Croats, respectively. Why did they not step into the breach and take action to prevent the suffering? In any event, New World Order did not mean American leadership to prevent the blood-letting in Croatia and Bosnia in the last year of the Bush administration.

It is also the case that the Bush post-Cold War effort at doctrinal formulation was very much state based. In other words, one powerful state outlined the elements of a vision that would guide other states to adopt values and principles that would lead to a better future after the end of the Cold War (Hutchings 1997, 148). However, the states that emerged from the old Yugoslavia were themselves afflicted with sharp internal ethnic tensions. Bosnia's population consisted of Muslims, Serbs, and Croatians. Croatia had a relatively large Serb population. State-based solutions did not speak to this multi-ethnic reality. The declaration that Bosnia had become a state did not correspond with the underlying tensions and open conflict among its three major ethnic groups. Building a state from so many different pieces would take time and external support as well as internal convictions. A state-based concept such as New World Order did not jive with the reality that the forces of globalization sharply challenged state domestic controls in ways that made it impossible for domestic progress to occur in a planned way. Serbian attitudes and actions were such a globalization force. From nearby Yugoslavia, the Serb leader Slobodan Milošević called for the protection of Serb minorities in nearby states such as Bosnia and Croatia. The invasion of both Croatia and Bosnia by Yugoslav Serbian military forces skewed state-based planning and created perplexity in the minds of those in the West who thought that the new day had come with the fall of communist leadership in so many places.

Perhaps, the image of the United States in the early 1990s as a "benign Goliath" is a starting point for clarifying the doctrinal dilemmas of New World Order (Mandelbaum 2007, 568). It was a Goliath in terms of its military power and the vacuum created by the fall of the Soviet Union and the preoccupations of European nations. However, it was a benign giant, due to its blindness to the profound changes that were taking place in the post-communist world and in the Middle East. In an age of globalization, state and non-state actors could react to and limit U.S. initiatives through a balancing of interests, balking at U.S. initiatives, obstructing U.S. actions, and blackmailing local forces in conflicted nations. At the same time, they might also occasionally jump onto the U.S. bandwagon or bond with U.S. officials when it was to their advantage (Walt 2007, 571–571). Such images help to explain the challenges that accompanied clear and decisive doctrinal formulations in the immediate aftermath of the Cold War.

Russian–American diplomacy

In the midst of all the confusion that accompanied the end of the Cold War and the complicated venture in the oil-rich world, the two states made progress on the nuclear arms-control agenda that had its roots in the early 1970s. In 1989, Bush had stated that his goal was to integrate the rapidly changing Soviet Union into the "community of nations" (McCormick 2010, 157). One important piece of unfinished business was the START diplomacy that sought to limit the long-range nuclear capabilities of both sides. Therefore, in June 1990, both leaders met at the Washington Summit to plan the future in this regard. START would build on the halting progress made to date on the SALT regime that dealt with defensive, short-range offensive, and medium-range offensive categories of missiles. Limitations on conventional, non-nuclear weapons, were also very much part of the discussion. One result was the signing of the Conventional Forces Europe (CFE) treaty at the end of 1990. This signified that both sides had withdrawn and destroyed the conventional military weapons that they had promised to eliminate in the agreement of 1987. In July 1991, Bush and Gorbachev met once again and agreed to conclude the START details and process (McCormick 2010, 165–166). This became known as the START I Treaty and resulted in agreement of each side to reduce the number of warheads on long-range missiles from 10,000 to 6,500 (Papp *et al.* 2005, 198). After the changes of late 1991, Boris Yeltsin picked up the baton from Gorbachev and met with President Bush in Washington, D.C. in June 1992. They laid the groundwork for START II that would reduce the numbers of warheads and weapons even further. By the time President Bush left office in January 1993, work on that treaty was completed (McCormick 2010, 172).

It should also be noted that the United States and Soviet Union were both part of the process that led to German unification after the fall of the Berlin Wall in November 1989. The quick move of Chancellor Kohl in West Germany to unify with East Germany was somewhat of a surprise, for many observers had predicted that West Germany and a non-communist East Germany would persist for some time. Once Kohl put his support behind the objective of unification, "Two Plus Four" talks were set up to bring about that objective. The two Germanys were involved as well as the USSR, U.S., France, and the United Kingdom (Papp *et al.* 2005, 198). In previous years, Soviet leaders might have opposed German unification, due to their World War II experience of the unexpected Nazi invasion. However, they did not feel a threat from German revanchism in the early 1990s and proceeded to play an integral part in the process.

Progress on nuclear arms agreements, conventional arms treaties, and German unification demonstrated that the Soviet Union/Russia could work on integrated as well as parallel paths with the United States. These foundations of commonality helped to reduce stresses and uncertainties created by visions such as New World Order on the American side and Soviet implosion on the other.

Conclusion: models, theories, and the end of the Cold War

The Balance of Power Model is useful in assessing the changed situation of the Soviet Union and United States in the late 1980s and early 1990s. During the last two decades of the Cold War, each had sufficient power to check or contain the other, even though hidden problems in the Soviet economy in the 1980s probably made the situation unequal. Challenges to the leadership of Moscow from Eastern Europe bore no counterpart in the West. Nations such as France had certainly challenged American leadership and that of NATO, but the U.S. alliance was nowhere near collapse. Imbalance between East and West was thus the result. Similarly, the collapse of the Soviet Union itself had mixed results in terms of the balance of power. While the United States had the strength to put together a broad coalition to dislodge the Iraqi military from Kuwait, Gorbachev was dealing with challenges from the Baltics, the Ukraine, Yeltsin in Russia, and other Soviet republics. From that perspective, Soviet power did not match that of the U.S. However, Russia as a republic and, later, nation was huge and had considerable potential by itself to eventually challenge the United States and match it in certain dimensions of power and capability such as the nuclear area. The potential for a balance of power between them existed.

Elements of the Chaos/Complexity Model also help to cast meaning on the Russian–American relationship at this time. The situation was certainly complex and unexpected for both sides. Most observers had not anticipated the possibility either that Eastern European nations would be free to go their own way or that the Soviet Union would break apart so quickly. At the same time, the United States had been reluctant to play a forceful role in world politics after the pull-out from Southeast Asia in 1973. While its military operation in the Middle East was under new rules of engagement that it had not used in Southeast Asia, still the willingness to intervene was somewhat of a surprise. The use of the Weinberger or Colin Powell criteria did make a difference. For example, the Gulf War coalition used overwhelming power to make a difference, instead of the measured increases in troop numbers as in Southeast Asia. Similarly, there was an end game in the Gulf War that there had not been in Southeast Asia. Victory meant pushing Saddam Hussein out of Kuwait but did not involve removing him from power in Baghdad.

There were additional components of Complexity Theory that were germane to the overall situation between the two powers. The system that linked them was now a much more open one, in contrast to the rather fixed relationship between them during the Cold War. Leaders on both sides had to be quite adaptable to new conditions and to develop new behavioral codes and practices. Spontaneity in terms of policy was a requirement for leaders in both Washington and Moscow, and they basically created a new order between them, and one that continued to evolve. It may even be possible to conclude that some of the changes in that period could correctly receive the label of chaos events (Northam 2013, 64).

One theory that informs the challenges in the period is that of Critical Junctures. It is almost a given that the end of the Cold War was such a transition in the relationship between the United States and the Soviet Union/ Russia. Instead of shaking a fist at the Berlin Wall and Soviet leadership as President Reagan had done, in a variety of ways Americans extended an open hand to Russia. For example, academic specialists such as Jeffrey Sachs of Harvard University went to Russia on an invitational basis in order to work with their counterparts in setting up free elections and opening the door to multi-party political contest. When the two nations met at the bargaining table it was no longer the case that one leader came out of the cocoon of a very closed and authoritarian political system while the other had probably achieved power after a long and harrowing dialogue with voters in the primary/caucus system as well as the general election. Of course, it was also a critical juncture in terms of the respective foreign-policy clout of the two. Over two dozen allies followed American leadership in the Gulf War, while about the same number pulled away from the control of Moscow. This was indeed a crossroads in their relationship.

Finally, Realism Revised was also a pertinent theory at the time, with its emphasis on the decline in authority of the state itself, as well as its leaders. Globalization pressures are a hallmark of this theory, as they challenge even strong states to either modify their behavior or develop new strategies for protecting the status of their own unit. In the East, it was as if a powerful dam had broken all of a sudden and washed away many of the traces of the valley below. What was now the meaning of the state in Hungary or Kazakhstan? How would President Yeltsin preside over a rational decision-making model and devise realistic policies to buttress the new Russian state? In the West, it was as if the roof had blown off and leaders looked up at a clear blue sky. The Cold War had ended, but what did that mean? Would democracy now become the preferred system of all freed national units, or would new global pressures flow across state boundaries and confound the rational planning of political leaders? Answers to these questions arrived very quickly, and some of them will be evident through analysis of the relationship between Russia and America in the 1990s as the Balkan wars took the stage.

4

Making different choices in the Balkan wars of the 1990s: Bosnia in 1992–95 and Kosovo in 1999

Introduction

Yeltsin and Clinton. Different choices. One key crisis that involved both Russia and America shortly after the end of the Cold War was the violent ethnic conflict that accompanied the break-up of Yugoslavia in the early 1990s. Russia had historically been deeply involved in the Balkans from the time of Catherine the Great. The common Slavic bond between Russians and Serbs as well as between Russians and Bulgarians was a strong one, and a protective attitude had been displayed by the larger Slavic brother towards the smaller one. Further, what was the identity of the Balkans? Were they mainly connected to the East, on the basis of the Slavic tie and past historical events? Or had they been mainly part of European history, in light of the individual links between key Western European nations and certain Balkan peoples? For example, the Romanian language is Latin-based, and thus the tie to European nations that shared that tradition was an important one. As already indicated, leadership in Washington and Moscow was an important factor, and in both cases there was a kind of avoidance of purposeful action during the Bosnian and Kosovan conflicts. The Yeltsin administration was critical of the Western drive to do something about the Serbian aggression but did not intervene. The Clinton administration was reluctant to get directly involved until the tragedy had become a very major one, in the Bosnian case, but was much quicker in the case of Kosovo. It may be that domestic preoccupations had much to do with this somewhat detached approach of the two leaders.

It is important to outline how the Bosnian War evolved and eventually pulled in the West through NATO's Operation Deliberate Force, and how the conflict in Kosovo resulted in the use of the Western military alliance to halt the suffering through its Operation Allied Force. While the first intervention was directed at protecting the national sovereignty of the new Bosnian state, the rationale for the involvement in Kosovo was a humanitarian one. In both cases, NATO maintained a military presence, at the invitation of the UN, after the end of hostilities in order to preserve the results. It is also the case that that involvement focused on rebuilding and protecting key institutions that the wars had damaged or destroyed. In addition, there was a link to the issue of NATO expansion, for the new PfP members contributed to those important post-war efforts. In that way, the Balkan crises brought another divisive issue between the United States and Russia to the table.

The impact of Russian history

Catherine the Great (1762–96) had considerably expanded the Russian Empire, beginning with her involvement in the first partition of Poland in 1772. In return for Russia's engagement in that critical action, the empire obtained the eastern sections of Bielorussia, Polotsk, Vitebsk, and Mogeilev (Walsh, 1958, 155). Even more significant were the gains that came with annexation of the Crimean Peninsula in 1783. Such a bold move certainly broke the harmony that had come with the 1774 peace with the Ottomans that was signed at Kuchuk-Kainardji. That armistice brought to an end the Russo-Turkish War of 1768–74 (LeDonne 1997, 241–242). In the Black Sea region, Russia conquered the port of Kherson, a former Greek city. It also conquered Azov, Taganrog, Nikolaev, Odessa, and Sevastopol (Billington 1966, 225). This made its presence in the Crimean Peninsula a formidable one. Given Russia's stated intentions to take Constantinople, it was no surprise that the Turks declared war against Russia in 1787. The Russian General Alexander Suvorov (1730–1800) annihilated the Turkish fortress at Ismail, and the Turks were eventually willing to sign the Treaty of Jassy in 1791. Russia ended up with Crimea in its possession, as well as the Black Sea coast from the River Bug to the Caucasus (Walsh 1958, 156).

The Russian gaze turned next Northern Europe, and Catherine directed the coordinated move to divide up Poland twice more. In 1793 and 1795, Russia obtained much of the Polish frontier region, but left the core of the former and future nation intact (LeDonne 1997, 241). The 1793 partition was particularly important for Russia, as it acquired both Lithuania and the Western Ukraine (Walsh 1958, 156). Catherine's aims were quite far reaching in Asia as well, for she sent out three exploratory missions into Siberia and the Far East. As a result, Russia later asserted claims to the Kuriles, the Aleutians, and Alaska (Walsh 1958, 157).

It is no surprise that Russia would want to commemorate all of this expansionist activity with its first state anthem, "Let the thunder of victory sound!" This anthem rejoices in the defeat of enemies and seems to celebrate the "groans" of the fallen Turkish fortress at Ismail. While the hymn was actually inspired by the victory of the Russians over the Ottoman army in 1790, its main themes were absolutism, the imperial concept of boundless territorial expansion, and the dominance of Christianity over Islam and Judaism. Catherine, the "gentle mother of us all," the "Brilliant Empress," surely gets plenty of credit. However, all of this is tied together in the anthem with a focus on how "Russia's glory sparkles brighter" and on how Russia now stretches "over mountain peaks and seas" (Giles, 2016). Surely, this commemoration constituted both historical facts and a realm of memory that would carry over to future generations. The anthem included too many topical references related to Catherine's time on the throne. It was all too natural for subsequent Russian tsars to dislike the idea of the state's being identified solely with Catherine the Great and her victories.

The Balkans were on the doorstep of this region of eighteenth-century conquests and two of the Balkan states, Bulgaria and Romania, straddled both Southeastern Europe and the Black Sea region. Russian expansionist gains in Slavic geographic areas such as the Ukraine led to a natural interest in the areas further west. Containment of the Turkish Empire could be achieved with greater Russian influence in geographic entities that encircled the Ottomans, who had penetrated into Bulgaria, Albania, Serbia, and Bosnia. Therefore, the outreach to members of the Slavic family in the Balkans was deeply rooted in Russian history.

What are the Balkans?

From the perspective of Russian history, then, the Balkans are a natural region in which Russia had imperial interests. Until World War I, there was a constant need for Russia to defend its interests by checking the Ottoman Empire as much as possible. After the collapse of that empire during the war, the new Yugoslav federation bore a strong Slavic imprint in its regions such as Serbia, Croatia, Slovenia, Montenegro, and Macedonia. The nurturing of that state was important in principle and echoed through the fascist period, Cold War, and beyond. Thus, Russian interest in the plight of the Serbs, in particular, in the 1990s was a natural one.

At the same time, the Balkans had become a part of Western history too, for it was the allies from Europe and the United States that had mobilized to help liberate those areas from control by the large empires. In fact, both Slovenia and Croatia had been members of the Austro-Hungarian Empire and thus had a much more European experience than had their Serbian counterparts, who were liberated from the Ottoman Empire. It is also true that the leader of the new Czechoslovakia, Thomas Masaryk, shared his experiences in federation building with the founding figures of Yugoslavia and thereby helped to put an imprint on the new state. During World War II it was the West and Russia both that took on responsibility for the liberation of the region from the Nazis, although Tito played a major role from within as a leader of the anti-fascist resistance. At the commencement of the Cold War, it seemed that Yugoslavia under Tito's rule would be comfortable as a part of the Moscow-led East. However, within a few years of this orientation, Tito led his state in a neutralist, albeit communist-ruled, direction. In the early 1960s he assisted in formation of the Non-Aligned Movement, and the state acted as a kind of meeting place between East and West rather than as a formal member of alliances in either region.

Unique role of presidents Yeltsin and Clinton in the 1990s

Yeltsin had come to power as the courageous president of the Russian Republic who had challenged Soviet controls and helped to tear that federation into fifteen independent states. His agenda as president of the new Russian Federation was to hold it together under pressures from within that considerably threatened it. In 1993, when he was meeting considerable opposition to his proposals for a referendum on constitutional change, he took the unexpected and perhaps outrageous step of dispatching the military to the White House or parliament. As noted above, one result of Yeltsin's action was a new constitution, written in the same year, that considerably enhanced presidential powers. In addition, there had been a swirl of controversy about the pace of the move to a free-market system in the economic realm. Yeltsin's advocacy of the 500-day plan of conversion to capitalism had met with much resistance even while Russia was still a republic in the Soviet Union. As economic change proceeded, there were major problems with the large scale of corruption and the unbelievable wealth acquired by certain entrepreneurs such as Khodarkovsky. An additional internal pressure was the violence that emanated from the Islamic separatist Republic of Chechnya. The two-year war of 1994–96 coincided with all the pressure and global concern about Bosnia, but Yeltsin was preoccupied with countering the challenges from this unit of Russia that had actually declared its independence as an Islamic republic in 1991. These internal stresses and pressures prevented Russia from doing much more than protest in a defensive way against evolving Western concerns about the Serbian moves in the states that had emerged from the old Yugoslavia.

President Clinton had developed an approach that guided his choices in the Balkans during his two terms in office. Although he had come into office mainly to inject new ideas into economic planning, crises such as those in Bosnia and Rwanda led to a change of emphasis during his first term. The 1993 disaster in Somalia also affected his thinking and pushed him toward work on a foreign policy doctrine that would bear the hallmarks of practicality. By 1995 he was warning against a new isolationism and committed to the exercise of "our military muscle through NATO." He also acknowledged that it had been difficult to develop a new doctrine, as there had been no "overarching framework" since the end of the Cold War ("President William J. Clinton Applauds America's Globalism and Warns Against a New Isolationism" 2005, 510–511). He eventually developed a concept of selective engagement that called for the enunciation of clear criteria before the dispatch of military forces to distant locations. Instead of using military force to restructure the global order, the focus would be on containment and control of conflicts. Presidential Decision Directive (PDD)-25 in May 1994 established a doctrine that set out criteria for multilateral peacekeeping operations after the Somalia embarrassment. PDD-56 in May 1997 set out the criteria for humanitarian intervention after the Dayton Accords that ended the Bosnian War (McCormick 2010, 186–192). In this way, powerful events pulled Clinton away from an exclusively domestic focus in a way that differed from the situation of Boris Yeltsin.

Clinton and Yeltsin met on many occasions during this troublesome period. In April 1993, they met in Vancouver at a time of extreme Russian vulnerability, and the American president offered $1.6 billion in financial support to assist in the economic changes that were occurring in Russia. In January 1994, both leaders met in Russia and agreed that they would no longer target each other's nation with their nuclear weapons. Further, Yeltsin agreed to protect the rights of Russian speakers in the three Baltic nations. The Moscow Summit of May 1995 commemorated the fiftieth anniversary of the victory over the Nazis in World War II (White 2011, 272–274). Thus, the two leaders worked to establish a common agenda on significant foreign-policy questions, in spite of the underlying disagreement over the Balkans.

Civil war in Bosnia

The rise to power of Slobodan Milošević in the Serbian Republic of Yugoslavia in 1987 had a profound impact on the Balkans for the next decade. After the collapse of that large and complex federation in 1991, the Serbs in the truncated state that bore the same name became either protective or aggressive on behalf of the Serbs who were now locked as minorities in the new nations that emerged. For example, the geographic area of Croatia had lost 400,000 Serbs to the Nazis in World War II, and consequently the Serbian population felt a great sense of vulnerability to the leaders of the new Croatian state (Papp *et al.* 2005, 463). The result was pressure that drove their Serbian descendants towards the protective Milošević in the early 1990s. Of course, this trend was just as pronounced for Bosnian Serbs during their longer war against both the Croatians and the Muslims. The residue of history thus had much to do with the outcomes of the war in the Balkans.

After the break-up of Yugoslavia in 1991, there was a delay by the United States and Europe in granting diplomatic recognition to the successor states.

Perhaps, the Serbs of Yugoslavia concluded that the West had no real stake in the future of the new state and would not get much involved if the situation became a complicated one. Once the civil war broke out in 1992, peacekeeping forces from the UN played the largest outsider role in controlling its worst effects for the first few years. The UN utilized two organizations to bring a halt to the suffering. One was called UNPROFOR and attempted to uphold ceasefire lines, with mixed success. When UNPROFOR sent out humanitarian relief lines of trucks, these often encountered blockades set up by Bosnian Serbs. Many Muslims and Croats fled their homes and villages under Serb pressure, and thus there was a need to assist them in relocating to new places of residence. UN High Commission for Refugees was the organization responsible to assist in that needed project (Hutchings 1997, 315–317).

The UN met with many frustrations in its Bosnian missions. For instance, in 1993, Bosnian Serbs took several hundred UN peacekeepers hostage, and three UN officials were killed by a landmine (Jentleson 2007, 441). Notably, the UN peacekeepers located in the town of Srebrenica were unable to prevent the Serbian military under General Ratko Mladić from massacring thousands of Bosnian men and boys in 1995. In July 2014, the World Court held the Dutch UN peacekeepers accountable for three hundred of those deaths (Süddeutsche Zeitung 2014a). This kind of futility on the part of the key international organization increased the pressure on the United States and the Clinton administration to inject force in a more effective way in order to protect Bosnian Muslims and Croatians. Ironically, the Clinton campaign of 1992 had emphasized the need both to consider the use of air strikes and to lift the arms embargo on Muslims. However, his administration did not follow through immediately on those plans, and the consequences were grave (Jentleson 2007, 441). By 1995, the pressure was consequential, and the above-noted massacre led to firm Western action.

NATO had not fought an actual war before, for its mission in the Cold War had been mainly a defensive one against possible Soviet aggression against key West European states. However, the alliance did engage in air strikes against key Serbian positions within Bosnia, and these led to the end of the civil war. NATO was a broader organization in 1995 than it had been in the Cold War, for it had brought in many former communist nations as observers through its PfP program that commenced in 1994. Thereby, the pool of assistance from these potential NATO members was much broader than would have been the case prior to the Bosnian War. The NATO mission was called Operation Deliberate Force, and the London Summit conference of July prefigured its role by permitting NATO to take aggressive action under three sets of circumstances. The conference gave the green light to retaliation following Serb military strikes on targets of significance in the struggle (Hendrickson 2006, 70–84). As a result, the Serbs agreed to meet with all enemies and concerned parties at the Dayton Conference in fall 1995.

What impact did this Western military involvement against the Serbs have on Russian–American relations? One clear piece of evidence about the Russian influence on the process of the war was the eventual switch from a UN peacekeeping operation to a NATO set of aggressive moves. Russia could have vetoed any resolution that came to the UN Security Council, and thus firmer action by that organization would have been impossible. The shift in emphasis from the UN to NATO was thus a logical step by the West in response both to conditions on the ground and to Russian strategies (Hendrickson 2006, 51). Of course, the NATO bombing campaign pricked Russian sensitivities and led Russia to make critical comments. Some concluded that Russia might have done more to bring those responsible for the Serbian excesses and the atrocity at Srebrenica to justice, but Russia's general attitude of resistance to Western policy in the region made that impossible (Peterson 2013, 106–107). Thus, it is possible to conclude that the Bosnian intervention by the West was a setback in Russian–American relations that had considerably warmed up after 1991, and even after the earlier rise to power of Gorbachev.

The Kosovo conflict

Kosovo was a republic in Yugoslavia that was 90% Muslim and became the object of escalating Serbian attacks in 1998. The Muslims had been pushing for more autonomy since 1997, and they had also developed their own military force called the Kosovo Liberation Army. Western pressure on Milošević escalated much more quickly than it had during the Bosnian War, probably in order to prevent the casualties that had occurred during battle in the early 1990s (Papp *et al.* 2005, 465–466). President Clinton and British Prime Minister Tony Blair were equally convinced of the need to take firm action (Berger 2005, 5). The resulting NATO attacks under the name Operation Allied Force (OAF) lasted seventy-eight days and resulted in pushing the Serbian troops north and out of the Kosovo region. Approximately 800,000 Muslims fled the violence, crossing the borders and into Macedonia and Albania (Paterson *et al.* 2005, 481). It is possible that casualties might have been lower if ground troops had been used. However, the alliance was divided on that question in light of the fact that the West was protecting a republic within a federation, rather than one country against invasion from another (Jentleson 2007, 442).

The Kosovo War embittered Russian–American relations in a number of concrete ways. In 1997, Russia had agreed to the NATO–Russia Founding Act that was aimed at keeping the lines of communication open between them. However, Russia temporarily exited from that framework after the Kosovo operation. The UN had initially endeavored to assist in easing the crisis and ending it as soon as possible. In summer 1998, the UN Security Council had passed Resolution 1199 that looked ahead to firm action if needed. However, both Russia and China added reservations that another authorization would be needed if force were actually to be used. The result was the same as it had been in the Bosnian crisis, as the pressure then switched to NATO to take firm action (Hendrickson 2006, 91–94). Russia was also quite critical of the eventual NATO bombing campaign, describing it as violation of the territorial integrity of Yugoslavia (Peterson 2013, 107). Another complicating factor in Russian–American relations was the fact that the three former communist countries of the Czech Republic, Poland, and Hungary had just joined NATO indirectly and were part of the operation. Overall, the alliance operation was a substantial one, with 50,000 NATO troops taking part, of which 5,000 were American. In addition, there were a full 6,000 bombing missions (Peterson 2014, 111–112).

Russian actions in the crisis included a mix of international and domestic considerations. They did not want to see a precedent set that could act as an invitation to other nations to be aggressive towards nearby states if they wanted to make a border change. In terms of internal considerations, Russians had just completed the first Chechen War that some might have perceived as parallel to the Serb actions against Kosovars. Both entailed wars by a national government's military against one of its own republics. Russia had also suffered from a financial collapse in 1998, and this accentuated its desire to obtain great power status again in some way. In light of later Russian goals and tactics in the next century, it is noteworthy that Vladimir Putin became Secretary of the Security Council in the same month as the Kosovo operation. Finally, Russia was willing to give sanctuary to members of Milošević's own family, and that step surely unnerved the West (Peterson 2011a, 70).

There were later repercussions of OAF on future Russian–American relations. On the one hand, Russia firmly opposed the declaration of independence by Kosovo in 2008, and was particularly bothered by the decision to keep 1,600 Western troops there afterwards. The Russian leadership also worried that Western involvement in the divided states of Georgia or Moldova might occur if ethnic tensions resulted in violence in those two places (Peterson 2011a, 74). On the other hand, Russia did contribute to the Kosovo peacekeeping operation by sending its 15th Separate Motorized Rifle Brigade to be of assistance (Peterson 2013, 108). In a totally different issue, the Kosovo tensions in 1999 may have convinced Russia that another such conflict between East and West was not a good idea after tensions began to develop over Iran in 2006 (Baev 2008, 91).

Organizational issues and Russian–American relations

The Russian factor was clearly behind the duality of UN and NATO engagement in the Balkans at this time. Many partners in both may have preferred the use of the UN in both Bosnia and Kosovo. However, UN peacekeeping operations proved unable to stop Milošević and the Yugoslav Serbs from their offensive actions, and the potential Russian veto in the UN continually put the pressure for action onto NATO and the U.S. In 1994, a dual key solution was adopted in which both organizations would have an equal say in actions to be taken (Hendrickson 2006, 49). However, the military alliance had the capabilities to protect those who were targeted by the Serb attacks, and so it ended up playing the most significant role. It is also the case that NATO Secretary-General Manfred Wörner pushed for alliance action as early as May 1993. He advocated a policy that included the use of restricted military options on behalf of limited objectives in resolving the crisis. He also envisioned a new strategic approach for NATO after the end of the Cold War, and that would entail a call for new security roles that the players in the Cold War had never imagined. In 1993 and 1994 Wörner was unable to persuade either President Clinton or Secretary of State Warren Christopher to adopt such an approach, and the result was the unfolding of a continuing tragedy. His untimely death in August 1994 removed a strong voice on NATO action from the discussion table (Hendrickson 2006, 52).

In spite of the delay of firm alliance military intervention until the fall of 1995, there were earlier limited contributions that the alliance was able to perform. These included a heavy focus on Bosnia in formal discussions within the North Atlantic Council (NAC), the expansion of exclusion zones in Bosnia in spring 1994, and the expansion of no-fly zones in the same period. NATO forces downed four Serbian Galeb aircraft that were in violation of the no-fly zones and also hit small command posts in April and November, 1994. At the same time, the dual key agreement often led to situations in which UN personnel overruled ground commanders who wanted to perform additional strikes (Hendrickson 2006, 57–62).

The alliance leadership looked particularly at Kosovo as a real test of its credibility. The alliance hit all three categories of targets, and that meant strikes on areas near Belgrade where civilian casualties could have resulted. There were strikes on oil refineries and talk about how the Serb attacks on Kosovo were a "moral outrage to Europe." Clearly, In Kosovo the alliance took over the military mission from the UN more quickly than it had in Bosnia. It had learned that waiting could have serious consequences (Hendrickson 2006, 110–114). These organizational steps were useful in ending the crisis quickly, but did put Moscow in a more defensive position.

Consequently, it is no surprise that NATO played a principal role in the supervision of both Bosnia and Kosovo after the end of conflict. After the Dayton Conference there were 60,000 alliance personnel stationed in Bosnia under Operation IFOR, and they worked with a UN High Commander. Similarly, the alliance left 50,000 troops under Operation KFOR in Kosovo directly after the conflict ended. Western leaders were committed to the creation of a more substantial security structure in the Balkans. Partly, this was a lesson from the Persian Gulf War, for UN forces had departed so quickly after that conflict and trouble continued to rage in the Middle East. Additionally, there was a strong effort to include the Balkan nations in NATO's PfP program, even if several of them would not be prepared for full membership for quite some time (Peterson 2014, 109–119). The aims of the two operations were similar on paper but different in some respects. In Bosnia, Operation IFOR was aimed at enabling Muslims, Serbs, and Croatians to work together in new ways and make the political system a viable one. In contrast, in Kosovo Operation KFOR had the objective of protecting that republic from any future incursions by the Yugoslav Serbs. Another difference resulted from the decision to turn over the peacekeeping operation in Bosnia to the EU in December 2004. The renamed Operation SFOR included activities by all ten new NATO partners by the end of 2005 (Peterson 2011a, 66).

Mr. Walter Andrusyszyn, former National Security Officer for the government of the United States, served at the American Embassy in Sarajevo during the Dayton peace talks and for the first months of the subsequent IFOR deployment. His recollections include the following conclusions about Russian–Serbian links prior to the talks:

> Russian–Serbian ties had historically been close, dating back to the pan-Slavic Movement. The reality is that the Russians provided no real support to the Milošević government. A few weapons here and there; a few statements of support, so nothing truly substantive. The Russians were not a significant player in the confounding conflict (confounding for the West). The Russians had their own problems in Chechnya and there was growing public animosity towards Muslims in general and the Bosnians were seen as part of that world-wide trend. That said, the Russians did not obstruct the Dayton process and they really were not a factor in the process until Kosovo at the end of the nineties, and even more so after Yeltsin's resignation in December 1999. (Andrusyszyn 2015)

Conclusion: theory and practice in the Balkans

Struggles within and over the Balkans impinged on American–Russian relations in several significant ways. They evoked images from a Russian past that had included both outreach into the region and special ties with members of the Slavic family such as the Serbs. In addition, they revived an American sense of responsibility that had become submerged after Southeast Asia but was revived in the years after the Persian Gulf War. New leaderships on both sides made purposeful efforts to come to terms with the collapse of the European and Eurasian communist systems in ways that would benefit their nations as well as the region. Also, the wars in Bosnia and Kosovo stoked the fires of conflict between Russia's hope to regain its shrunken global status and America's leadership of the NATO alliance in moving in new directions to establish frameworks of security. Finally, the presence of two global organizations that both shared in the mission of providing personnel and capabilities in crisis areas both raised hopes for solutions and set up organizational struggles between them.

What models of power can help to cast light on this very new and most difficult period for the leaderships in both Moscow and Washington? The Balance of Power Model is an appropriate one to consider, for both nations used that baseline as an instrument for establishing their goals and strategies. For the United States, the members of the Clinton administration eventually came to the conclusion that Western power was the sole capability available to check the bold military invasions by Milošević on behalf of fellow Serbs who were now minorities in other regions. In the case of Bosnia, the Serbs were now in second place, in terms of numbers, to the Muslim plurality, while in the case of Kosovo they were a minority of only 10% in a republic of the Yugoslav Federation itself. Russia's considerations focused on restoring a stronger position for the Russian Federation in the global balance of power. Much was lost with the twin collapses of communist rule and Soviet power in 1991, and Russia's situation in the 1990s did not correspond very well with the upward line of Russian progress since the time of Catherine the Great.

Multi-polarity had emerged with full force at the time of these events. President Yeltsin no longer had a commonwealth of nations with which to bargain and sometimes to coerce. He needed to establish some linkages to former Soviet republics through the CIS, and he made trips to Western capitals and forged new linkages with Western powers in order to shore up the Russian regional and global position. At the same time, President Clinton needed to cope with the dynamism of the EU and its members after the path that they had set through the Maastricht Accord in 1989. The president also needed to bargain with a variety of strong-minded leaders as he nudged NATO towards firm action in the two troubled Balkan locations. As Russia became a stronger player by the end of the decade, there was a need to treat seriously the moves and objectives of the purpose-driven new Russian president, Vladimir Putin.

Theories also can shed light on the dynamism of the Russian–American relationship in the 1990s. Since both powers were attempting to evolve a new pattern of multidimensional connections in several directions, the features of Systems Theory can help to illuminate what was happening throughout the decade. The environment of the Cold War system had dramatically changed, with the result that inputs to their decision-making processes underwent alteration as well. There were new public and electoral pressures in Russia that had never really been present in a history replete with rule by tsars and first secretaries of the CPSU. As such, their own inputs to regional crises like those in the Balkans were constrained by domestic considerations that had not played much of a role before. On the American side, a newly energized NATO provided countless ideas about what tactics were possible for the newly emergent America in hot spots that its leaders deemed vital to its national security. The resulting outputs or policies thus bore a very different stamp from Cold War decisions. Both Russia and America waited longer before issuing firm statements, and both needed to take account of pressures well beyond their own borders. All of these realities circulated through a feedback loop into future decision-making processes. The responsible actions that the U.S. took on behalf of Balkan security fed smoothly into its injections of military power into Afghanistan in 2001 and into Iraq in 2003. For Russia, resistance to American-led initiatives toward the Balkans at a time of alliance expansion to former communist nations prefigured its outright opposition to Western sensitivities at the time of the Georgia War in 2008 and the war in the Ukraine in 2014–15.

The period was also one of critical junctures, for both nations were emerging from the restraints and relative passivity of the earlier decades. Washington was throwing off in major ways the restraints that the war in Southeast Asia had put on its ability to commit troops abroad or to lead the Western military alliance with force. Russia was at a crossroads in terms of its own self-conception and ability to impact unfolding crises in its own region. As recently as 1981, Brezhnev had been able to order the Polish military to break the backbone of the Solidarity resistance movement. Only one decade later, Russia's hold over Poland was broken and Russia as engaged in a new march in its own region with new partners such as China and new hopes to restore the greatness of the Russian past.

Each of these models and theories can illuminate some of the shadowy areas of the Russian–American relationship in the 1990s. At critical junctures in their own political situations, there was a natural tendency for both sets of leaders to fall back on recreating a predictable balance of power. After all, their spheres of activity might be restricted by the need to bargain with each other and with regional partners. Creating a balance of power would avoid the greater danger of a power vacuum. By the same token, an emergent and changed balance of power could feed into frameworks that would set up more predictable regional systems that could replace those developed during the Cold War. Multi-polarity would be a clear hallmark of these new systems, and both sets of leaders understood the wisdom of leading but not dictating to new partners in that evolving multitude of state and non-state actors.

5

The admission of twelve former communist states and republics into NATO and the bitter Russian reaction, 1999–2009

Introduction

Soon after the end of the Cold War, America led the West to embrace the concept of expanding the membership numbers in NATO. There were other international organizations, such as the OSCE. However, NATO received the call from the West, and it had real implications for the relationship between the United States and Russia. Key decisions that will receive attention in this chapter include the setting up of the PfP program in 1994, the inclusion of three former communist nations in 1999, the admission of four more plus three former Soviet Republics in 2004, and the admission of two in 2009 and one more in 2015. It is important also to assess the significance and role of the NATO–Russia Founding Act of 1997, a step that was to keep connections alive between East and West on security issues. Finally, there have been echoes of these decisions in the diplomatic history between Russia and America since the 2004 expansion, and these issues will also receive attention.

The PfP in 1994

In 1991, the year that the Cold War ended, NATO created a North Atlantic Coordinating Council (NACC), and all Central European nations joined it. The Warsaw Treaty Organization was dissolving, and a connection with the long-standing Western alliance became a substitute and a guarantor of security in the event of newly emerging security threats. Importantly, all the former republics in the USSR, including Russia, became members of this organization as well. In fact, these nations also had the opportunity to participate in joint maneuvers alongside the traditional members of the alliance. Under this framework, Russia eventually sent 2,500 troops as part of the eventual peace-making mission in Bosnia (Papp *et al.* 2005, 207).

The issue of Poland's early membership in NATO became a kind of trip wire that activated Russian concerns and led to a change in Western tactics. President Yeltsin initially gave a green light to the move of Poland from NACC status to full NATO membership. However, he later backed off from that position and the alliance proceeded to develop a new plan that was called PfP. NATO approved that new program in January 1994, which included observer status as well as a welcome to take part in alliance exercises. Russia expressed immediate concerns that Cold War blocs might emerge from this new step, and President Yeltsin cast about for alternative solutions such as heightened use of the OSCE structures (White 2011, 282). By June of 1994, Russia had agreed to join the PfP under certain special circumstances. Since Russia had greater size and significance than other PfP partners, there were special arrangements for Russia. For example, there was a promise to develop an Individual Partnership Program, and there was also a concession that Russia and NATO would have a relationship outside the formal PfP structures. In addition to participation with a brigade in the IFOR program in Bosnia, Russia sent a general to Supreme Headquarters Allied Powers Europe for a few weeks in October 1995 (Williams 1997, 230).

At the time of these negotiations the Western alliance took account of the uncertainties that accompanied the Russian factor in NATO expansion. Would the Ukraine and the three Baltic republics be threatened at some time in the near future, given the role that they had played in the former Soviet Union? Concerns about the Russian reaction may have led NATO also to place restrictions on its connections with other PfP members. For instance, the alliance would limit its forward presence in those nations and would not station troops within their territorial boundaries. In this sense, Norway became a kind of model for alliance connections. During the Cold War, Norway had been a full member in NATO, but the promise had been given to it that troops would be stationed on its territory only in an emergency. Further, the West sought to partially compensate Russia for the dislocations of PfP by expanding cooperation with it on trade, World Trade Organization membership, science, and technology (Asmus *et al.* 1997, 99–109).

The PfP process itself entailed a number of challenging conditions. The continued progress of the former communist states on democratization was one important criterion, and so was civilian control over the military. Potential members needed to demonstrate a purposeful effort to reduce conflict among states, to set up market systems, to cope with their own ethnic conflicts in meaningful ways, and to develop the capability to promote the "common security" (Michta 2006, 17). Interestingly, several Scandinavian nations also became PfP members. However, unlike the Central European new democracies, they did not aspire to full membership in the future. For Sweden and

Finland, there was an aspiration to contribute to NATO peacekeeping missions but not to submit to Article 5 expectations of providing military support to a partner under attack. Nonalignment continued to be their abiding preference (Michta 2006, 47–49).

Even after the advent to power of Vladimir Putin, Russia continued to work within the framework of PfP status. In September 2000 it took part in a PfP military exercise in Kazakhstan. There was also a small connection with a ten-day long PfP training session near Odessa in southern Ukraine. This time Russia sent only observers rather than direct participants (Black 2004, 66). It is thus evident that the Russian–NATO relationship was a complex one. Expansion through PfP status touched on Russian nerves in a painful way, but Russia also had a chance to observe what the alliance was about by taking a limited part in its operations.

The NATO–Russian Founding Act of 1997

In order to formalize the relationship between Russia and NATO beyond admission to PfP status, the two entities signed the NATO–Russia Founding Act in 1997 (White 2011, 283). This Act created a Permanent Joint Council (PJC) to streamline activities between the two. Topics for discussion within the PJC included ways to combat terrorism, methods for achieving greater nuclear security, developing joint military doctrine, and cooperating on the establishment of peacekeeping forces (Papp *et al.* 2005, 207). Since the PJC included Russia, its leaders asked that the Council have the power to veto alliance decisions, but the American leadership declined to accept that request. Russia also did not take up a liaison presence in Brussels and perceived its role as that of an outsider. After all, in the PJC it seemed as if the math after 1999 added up to nineteen regular members plus the one outsider that was now part of the consultative process (Webber 2007, 274). The 1999 expansion to include three post-communist states itself threw Russia off stride as well, so that there was considerable distance between Russia's leaders and NATO at the end of the Yeltsin regime on the last day of the twentieth century.

However, the 9/11 crisis resulted in stimulating greater understanding between American and Russian leaders, with the result that the latter's links to the Western alliance improved somewhat. In May 2002, NATO issued its Rome Declaration that replaced the PJC with the NATO Russia Council (NRC), with an eye to smoothing out the linkages between the one state and the multi-member alliance. After this change, Russia would be one of twenty players in the new Council instead of just one sitting opposite nineteen others. Further, Russia was seated alphabetically, between Portugal and Spain, and that gave the new Council a more equitable cast. If Russia created huge contro-versy in terms of blocking motions, the other nineteen council members could simply retreat into their regular committees and make decisions without the presence of Russia (Mahnke 2004, 59–60). President Putin actually took part in the Rome deliberations on the creation of the Council and then dispatched a Russian general to serve as a Supreme Allied Commander Europe deputy in Brussels. As a result of this effort over several years to incorporate the unique position of Russia into the alliance, Russian soldiers ended up serving in Bosnia, Kosovo, and Afghanistan (Thompson 2004, 107). Simultaneously, a new permanent NATO mission opened in Moscow on May 2, 2002 (Black 2004, 175). Finally, in 2005 the NRC signed a NATO–Russia Status of Forces Agreement that led to the participation of Russia in the alliance's Operation Active Endeavor in the Mediterranean (Webber 2007, 275).

The admission of three new NATO partners in 1999

In 1999 the Czech Republic, Hungary, and Poland were admitted to full membership in NATO, and this was a direct consequence of decisions made by alliance planners at their Madrid Summit in July 1997. This decision was linked, in Russia's perspective, with the announcement by the EU six months later in Luxemburg that it too planned an expansion that included former Central and Eastern European states. Russia had hoped for a common and open security space in the area, but now felt somewhat hemmed into a corner (White 2011, 283–284).

A number of benefits for NATO followed on the heels of the expansion. All three new members gave at least moral support and over-flight rights during the alliance's Kosovo operation shortly after moving into full membership status. The Polish–German connection was solidified, as the two were now co-equal NATO partners. In fact, Poland would play a key role in administering a broad geographic area south of Baghdad in 2003, and NATO supported that action even though it was not the sponsor of the intervention itself (Michta 2006, 18, 37). Czech contributions included the provision of niche capabilities such as field hospitals to both Afghanistan and Iraq. In the latter case, the field hospital was in a stand-by position outside Iraq prior to the beginning of the war in 2003. The 601st Czech Special Forces unit played a role in hunting for terrorists in the craggy mountains of eastern Afghanistan, while other Czech units rotated in protection of the airport at Kabul for a period of time. Finally, Hungary offered a number of contributions to the alliance, such as provision of rights to use Base Papa in its territory, as well as involvement in the Strategic Airlift Capability in 2006. In addition, the proximity of Hungary to the old Yugoslavia provided Hungary with a potential role in case the Balkan agreements became unglued (Peterson 2011a, 26–30).

Intriguingly, Slovakia did not become an alliance partner at this time, even though it had been part of Czechoslovakia as recently as 1993. Partly, this exclusion was due to its provocative leadership in the person of Vladimir

Mečiar. However, the exclusion was also partly due to Slovakia's closeness to Russia on the mid-1990s. For example, it discussed with Moscow the possibility of a free trade zone between the two states in 1996. The practical results of the discussions included Slovakia's permission to Russia to deliver natural gas through its territory. This bilateral connection fitted into the Russian hope of becoming part of the evolving European security system from the Atlantic to the Urals. Russian pressure also encouraged Slovakia at this time to think of its security protector as the OSCE rather than the NATO alliance (Balmaceda 2000, 92–96). The result of Slovakia's responsiveness to Russian pressure was postponement of its membership in the Western alliance for several years.

The admission of seven new NATO partners in 2004

The states admitted to NATO in 2004 included Estonia, Latvia, Lithuania, Slovakia, Slovenia, Bulgaria, and Romania. The events connected with the 9/11 attacks had much to do with both the timing of this expansion and the choices of states to be included. The decision about their admission was taken at the NATO summit in Prague in November 2002. While the inclusion of three former Soviet Republics bore the potential to stimulate a sharp Russian negative reaction, in fact Russia's response was somewhat mild. The fallout of 9/11 made a difference, but so did both Russia's hopes for economic assistance and its greater participatory role through the NRC (Mahnke 2004, 63).

Each of the newly admitted members had the potential to make substantive contributions to the alliance mission. For example, Estonia sent twenty-one soldiers and one officer to be part of the KFOR peacekeeping operation in Kosovo. In addition, in 1998 it had set up a Baltic Defense College that could provide alliance-based training for new partners. Together with Latvia, Estonia provided "specialized ordnance and minesweeping units" for use in areas subjected to conflict. Lithuania offered the use of a medical unit in similar situations (Michta 2006, 90–91). All three Baltic states needed alliance assistance in creating their own military capacities from scratch, as they had not been able to do so while under Soviet sway (Michta 2006, 18). Slovakia provided assistance to the Polish units responsible for the management of Iraqi territory and towns after 2003, while Slovenia chose to focus on giving assistance in the NATO Response Force Bulgaria and Romania were late add-ons to the class of 2004, and the rationale was that they could be a deterrent against the chaos in Afghanistan and Iraq. More particularly, Bulgaria eventually provided assistance to nearby Ukraine. Embedded in the discussion was the matter of the new Russian enclave of Kaliningrad. Arrangements to ensure Russian access to this alliance-surrounded piece of Russian territory would be a future agenda item (Peterson 2011a, 34–42). However, its geopolitical situation guaranteed that Kaliningrad would be a divisive factor in future conflictual situations.

The admission decisions of 2009 and 2015

NATO's Bucharest Summit in April, 2008, was a momentous one indeed in terms of full alliance memberships. The leaders of the alliance considered the possibilities of moving five nations with PfP status into the category of full members. They included Croatia, Albania, Georgia, Ukraine, and Macedonia. In the end, NATO decided to admit the first two but not the last three. Croatia had been one of the more developed republics in the old Yugoslavia but had to sit on the sidelines and watch Slovenia gain full membership in 2004. Croatia's delay was parallel to the delay in admitting Slovakia between 1999 and 2004. The Tudman leadership in Croatia was authoritarian, and the consequence was that the political system was not a good fit for the alliance's criterion of democracy building. The delay in admission for Croatia was thus five years, exactly the same as it had been for Slovakia. Croatia had also been part of the Austrian-Hungarian Empire prior to World War I and was the last of its remnants finally to enter the Western military alliance. The argument on behalf of Albania was very different, for its political history had been highly unusual. During communist times, Albania was first an ally of Moscow, then of Beijing, and finally isolationist. Another factor in Albania's case was its predominant Muslim population, a fact that would enable its personnel to communicate, in different ways than traditional alliance partners, with some of the key groups in Bosnia and Afghanistan (Peterson 2011a, 46–49). Thus, for different reasons, both Croatia and Albania fitted the needs and criteria of NATO by the time of their official admission in 2009.

However, Georgia and the Ukraine were different cases and thus did not receive membership. However, the alliance made a promise to both that they would be admitted in the future (White 2011, 285). Both of these PfP members were somewhat removed from NATO's center of balance, and they might have drawn the alliance into engagements in areas far removed from the hub of the alliance's operations. After all, NATO had been formed in 1949 with an exclusive emphasis on defending Western Europe from Soviet inroads. Both Georgia and the Ukraine had also been republics in the old Soviet Union, as had been the Baltics. However, Russia's connections to the Ukraine and Georgia were more historically rooted than had been those to the Baltic States. The Ukraine had been the center of activities of Kievan Rus, the cornerstone of the Russian Empire, and its Crimean Peninsula was the birthplace of the Russian Orthodox faith. Georgia was not Slavic like Ukraine, but it was part of the Caucasus region that was part of Russian history, literature, and lore. The long-standing Soviet leader Stalin had come from Georgia and had first worked his way up the political ladder in that region.

In some ways, the unwillingness to admit the Georgia and the Ukraine led to a series of "what if" questions later on. Russia invaded Georgia in 2008 and the Ukraine in 2014, and their membership in the Western alliance would have raised provocative questions about the possible invocation of NATO's Article 5 in both situations.

The Macedonian petition for full membership of NATO was tabled, as the old issue of Greek concerns emerged once again. Macedonia had been part of the Greek Empire and was the birthplace of the Greek founding figure Philip of Macedon. Its formal name was a cumbersome one that served as a reminder of the Greek period in its history. However, Macedonia had been part of the Yugoslav Federation and was of the same category or status as other segments of that large and complicated geographic unit. Clearly, the alliance's priority on potential Balkan members was in part due to the bitter ethnic conflicts that had occurred in Bosnia and Kosovo.

The emphasis on the Balkans' importance figured largely in the invitation to Montenegro in 2015. It had been connected with Serbia in the Yugoslav period and stuck with it after the 1991 break-up. There were strong cultural and political similarities between the two linked regions, but in 2015 Montenegro was successful in gaining a promise of formal admission to the alliance in the following year. Russia expressed exasperation with NATO's willingness to admit yet one more eastern state and stated that it was prepared to take countermeasures, as yet to be defined (SME 2015a). Along with Slovenia and Croatia, Montenegro gave a Southern Slav imprint to an organization that was anchored in Western and Central European culture, values, and politics. Bosnia, Kosovo, Serbia, and Macedonia would need to fulfill their PfP responsibilities in the short range but wait for some time for the benefits and responsibilities of full membership.

The overall impact of NATO expansion on Russian–American relations

The result of inclusion into the alliance of so many new, formerly communist states between 1999 and 2015 had a mixed impact on the relationship between America and Russia. Of course, the residue of good and bad periods extended beyond the alliance leader, the United States, to the other members, as well as to the NATO administrative center in Brussels. Prior to the 1999 admissions, Asmus *et al.* (Asmus *et al.* 1997, 116) argued that there were three ways in which upcoming NATO expansion could generate Russian reactions. First, the "modalities of enlargement" would be a factor that would influence responses from Moscow. In other words, would the rationale for inclusion of a new member be what it could contribute to clearly defined missions? Further, what would the process and criteria of expansion approximate? Second, the time frame of enlargement would matter as well, for too rapid an inclusion of controversial nations would speed diplomatic and security responses by Russia. Third, how would the changing alliance reshape its posture towards Russia?

The nature of the expansion process in a rough way approximated these sensitivities. NATO included first those states that possessed the capabilities to contribute to missions such as those in Bosnia and Kosovo, and established strict criteria in terms of political, military, and economic measures for membership. The alliance also spaced out the expansion, with an interval of approximately five years being the norm between incorporations of new categories of states. The largest group came in 2004, but the reality was that 9/11 generated a need for additional partners such as Bulgaria and Romania as barriers against the trouble further east. The passage of the NATO–Russia Founding Act of 1997 assisted in allaying some Russian concerns about expansion, and the reforms of that program that occurred several years later upgraded the Russian role to a more respectable one. The 9/11 attacks also clearly played a role in at least temporarily easing the pangs of Russian readjustment to the new geopolitical reality (Webber 2007, 271).

There were others who worried about the impact of NATO expansion on domestic developments in Russia itself. In a fledgling way in the early 1990s, Russia had been moving along a path of democratic development. Would the specter of a new threat from the West obliterate that process? The country's leaders might react by settling back into a more familiar authoritarian pose, or radical nationalists might carve out more political influence and distort election results. Russia might even acquire more allies if states that pounded on NATO's door but were denied entry opted to move closer to their former leader in Moscow (Brown 1997, 128–129).

In the early twenty-first century, greater involvement in NATO activities by potential members did stir up Russian sensitivities and signaled future dilemmas. The 2000 Cossack-Steppe military exercise took place on Ukrainian soil. It was a training exercise for PfP and new alliance partners, and some of the activities took place in East Crimea. Later in the year, Operation Transcarpathia took place nearby, and both operations pricked Russia's nerves. During the next year, Operation Cooperative Partner took place in the Black Sea near Georgia. Russia approved Georgian participation, but the Russian Ministry of Defense was "bitter," as it was rather large. Participating were 4,000 servicemen, 34 warships, and 2 submarines (Black 2004, 239–256; Thompson 2004, 110). By 2005 the spotlight had shifted to the Baltics, as NATO made the decision to deploy aircraft in Northern Europe to defend the Baltics. Russian leaders asked what threat would lead the West to think that there was a need to defend the Baltics. Russia was able to rely on its confidence that the Baltic militaries were new and developing, while its forces in Kaliningrad were much more developed and sophisticated. A constant concern of Russia was that of encirclement, for military exercises in the Ukraine and Georgia hinted at a NATO concern about Central Asia. With American access to bases in Uzbekistan and Kyrgyzstan in light of the war in Afghanistan, would the West move further east with its security network, and would Russia in the end be surrounded (Michta 2006, 83–87)?

Following the Russo-Georgian War of August 2008, relations between NATO and Russia became very bitter, to the extent that Russia temporarily stopped participating in the NRC. Once again, NATO planned and executed military exercises in Georgia in 2009. It also upgraded the importance of the Black Sea region in its planning process. The enclaves of South Ossetia and Abkhazia in Georgia were also a center of contention, for Russia ended up occupying them and declaring them to be independent of their territorial homeland, Georgia. NATO issued warnings about the enhanced involvement by Russia, but to no avail (Peterson 2011a, 50–52). Ukrainian connections to NATO were also nettlesome, for Russia had such long historical links to that geographic unit, and especially to Crimea, the location of a Russian naval fleet at Sevastopol. While the U.S. provided economic assistance to liquidate the vestiges of the former Soviet nuclear arsenal located in that nation, the Ukraine was the first PfP nation to contribute in material terms to the NATO Response Force. However, in 2010 the election of ethnic Russian Viktor Yanukovych as president in 2010 pulled the Ukraine further towards the Russian fold (Peterson 2011a, 54–56). In conclusion, the reality of the American–Russian relationship in 2010 was some distance from the openness and understanding that had existed between them at the beginning of the decade, immediately after the 9/11 attacks in the United States.

Mr. Walter Andrusyszyn, former National Security Officer, has commented with force on the initial views of Russia in regard to NATO expansion:

> Yeltsin was in power at the time and even though some key Russian thinkers (Karaganov) opposed NATO enlargement, the internal debate was whether or not it was in Russia's interest for NATO to provide stability in the East. The Russians generally view the world in terms of camps, so if there is a vacuum (which some in the West thought was the best approach), the Russians thought that one day they would have to choose between taking in the Poles or the Bulgarians (let's say) as renewed allies. Many Russians did not believe they had the security apparatus or the economic ability to provide that kind of anchor.

> The Baltics were an emotional issue for the Russians. It had been part of Russia for centuries even if the Latvians and Estonians didn't like it, so there was no interest in giving up Latvia and Estonia in particular. Lithuania was always a bit different.

> Our approach was to reassure the Russians that we wouldn't do anything either bilaterally or in NATO to upset the Russians. It was a tribute to Bush's relationship with Putin that, in November 2004, when the Balts were formally admitted to NATO, a smiling Putin waited at the bottom of Air Force One for the symbolic

stop that Bush had insisted on before heading to Vilnius for his visit. At the time, neither Yeltsin nor Putin were vigorously opposed to Baltic membership in NATO. That has now changed, but it is done. (Andrusyszyn 2015, interview)

Expanded NATO and coping with crises

How well did the enlarged alliance perform in confronting crisis situations that fitted within the purview of its defined scope of responsibilities? Continued skirmishing with Russia demanded a certain amount of attention from NATO planners. However, the emergence of ISIS as a huge threat in the Middle East demanded even more thought and planning.

Visits to the new partners took place in an effort to allay concerns about Russian adventurism after the Ukrainian War of 2014–15. For example, the American Secretary of Defense Chuck Hagel made such a visit to Romania in summer 2014. He reassured his hosts that NATO reinvigoration was one cost to Russia of its annexation of the Crimea. Given the long-standing historical Romanian connection to Moldova, the American delegation also promised to assist that nation in the event of any Russian moves in its Trans-Dniester region. American defense links to Romania were increasing, as well, with the opening of an air base there to replace the transit hub in Kyrgyzstan as the primary means of getting flights into Afghanistan. In addition, the U.S. was planning to locate a missile defense installation in Romania later in the year, while military exercises and naval visits to the nation were increasing as well (*USA Today* 2014a). On the other hand, some nations were reluctant to get much more involved in NATO planning in the midst of the crisis over the Ukraine. Initially, Czech Prime Minister Bohuslav Sobotka was not interested in seeing an expanded NATO military presence in Europe (*iDnes* 2014a). Perhaps some nations wanted to keep their distance from the areas in which Russia had now demonstrated such an enhanced interest.

The Ukrainian crisis did place Russia and NATO at loggerheads over their individual desires to upgrade military capabilities in the region. The NATO exercise Saber Strike in the Baltics in 2014 included 4,700 soldiers from ten partner nations. There had also been separate maneuvers earlier in Poland and Estonia. Russia's reaction included military exercises in Kaliningrad that were, in its own words, comparable to the NATO activities in Poland and the Baltics. For instance, twenty-four warships were active along the coast of the Baltic Sea (*iDnes* 2014b). As the Western alliance prepared for its Wales Summit in early September 2014, President Obama and NATO Secretary General Anders Fogh Rasmussen agreed to increase defense assistance to partners located close to the Russian border (*USA Today* 2014b).

NATO plans to counter Russia accelerated in early 2015. In February, NATO command announced plans to establish six new command units within the territory of the Eastern allies and also to create a 5,000-person "spearhead" force that would possess rapid-reaction capabilities. This upgraded military presence was the first step in reversing a long post-Cold War reduction in NATO military capabilities in Europe. Further, the Saber Strike exercise in Poland and the Baltics was expanded from the 2013 exercise. This time it included 6,000 troops from fourteen allied nations, and the number of soldiers was actually triple the number from the exercise two years earlier, before the advent of the crisis in the Ukraine. In addition, the individual Baltic nations had been engaged in expanding their own military capabilities. Latvia possessed both demolition experts and ground spotters who could call in air strikes. Estonia had created a "defense league" that consisted of 30,000 civilians, while Lithuania planned to add 3,000 further conscripts to its military forces (*USA Today* 2015a).

Alliance partner Turkey moved into the center of the stage following heightened preoccupation with the ISIS threat. After a summer 2015 terrorist attack that took many civilian lives in Turkey, the new Secretary General, Jens Stoltenberg, expressed solidarity with Turkey and promised assistance in the near future. However, it was important for the alliance that Turkey should not use NATO assistance for attacks on the Kurds who were helping the allies in Syria against ISIS (*Dagensnyheter* 2015a, b; *SME* 2015b). However, in the fall of 2015 Turkey's downing of a Russian air force plane embittered relations between the Russia and Turkey and, indirectly, the NATO alliance. Turkey argued that the plane had violated its air space, but Russian leaders denied that was the case. President Putin used tough language in condemning Turkey's leaders, and called the incident a stab in the back and a move by Turkey down a blind alley (*USA Today* 2015b, *iDnes* 2015a). At the end of November, Russia placed sanctions on Turkey as a punishment. The sanctions would include the end of visa-free travel by Turks to Russia, the end of chartered Turkish flights into Russia, and the prevention of Russian tourist companies from selling vacation plans that included a stop in Turkey (*USA Today* 2015c).

All of these conflicts indicated that NATO–Russian relations would never be at a standstill. The alliance had too many partners that were close to Russia and subject to intimidation of one sort or another. Inevitably, major incidents would have an echo effect on Russian–NATO relations in a negative direction.

Conclusion: NATO expansion and its impact on Russia in theory and practice

In terms of the models used as the framework for this analysis, the Balance of Power and Multi-Polarity models have the most pertinence in understanding the impact of NATO expansion on the two strong global powers. At the same time, Legacy Theory is a useful lens through which the familiar Cold War themes are illuminated, or through which at times they even glared. Realism also is a central explanatory theoretical tool, as both America and Russia sought to impose a grid of their own cost-benefit analysis onto a fluctuating system of regional politics.

In many ways, Boris Yeltsin and Vladimir Putin sought to counter-balance what they perceived as U.S. gains through the admission of thirteen former communist states and entities into the long-standing Western military organization. To Moscow, the admission of so many new members into NATO unsettled the existing balance of power, and this helps to explain Yeltsin's early preference for reliance on the OSCE. The OSCE includes nations from both East and West, and so it had the potential to deal with initiatives from both sides in an even-handed way, with the result of preserving the equilibrium of power. From this perspective, a number of Russia's initiatives aimed at restoring what to it was a lost sense of balance. The Russian willingness to take part in the NATO–Russia Founding Act of 1997 and its modification in 2002 revealed those interests. The annexation of the Crimea and the subsequent military build-up in Kaliningrad were additional balancing steps.

Part of the dilemma for both Russia and America was the emergence of multiple new poles of power. The end of the Cold War resulted in a new theme that resonated throughout Europe. Certain Central European nations such as Poland, Hungary, and the Czech Republic were more prepared than the others to join first NATO and later the EU. Along with Slovakia, they actually constituted the Visegrad bloc that held meetings based on their commonality of history and current objectives. The Baltic States were not militarily strong but did make up a unit that shared geographic space as well as the experience of having been republics in the Soviet Union. The Balkan states were more troubled and less committed to a particular direction in future political development. Bringing all of these new blocs into the Western military alliance would strengthen collective defense but was not aimed at or able to produce commonality in any dimension. That was particularly the case in light of the rich but complex historical development of each of them in past centuries. From this angle, the Russian courting of Slovakia in the early 1990s and Serbia throughout that decade looks to be an effort to exploit multipolarity in order to help protect Russia's own national interests.

A strong dose of Legacy Theory reverberated throughout the entire post-Cold War period in terms of the Russian–American relationship. At times, it seemed as if each purposeful move by one side generated a parallel counter-move by the other. Russia sought to pull some former Soviet republics into a framework called the CIS as the West unified under the NATO or EU banner. Russian moves into the Crimea and eastern Ukraine in the Donbas region in 2014 led to strong action by NATO to move military capabilities from southern Europe into the seemingly more threatened northeast of the continent. If Russia could move with lightning speed after the Sochi Olympics to peel Crimea away from the Ukraine, then the Western alliance would create a new Spearhead Force that could move quickly to prevent any other such aggressive Russian action in Eurasia. After all, the Cold War had looked like this, with a move by the one leading to a countermove by the other.

Realism posits that states will do everything possible to hinge decision-making on calculations of what is in their own self-interest, and the result is a strong dose of state-centeredness. They will do all they can to control fluid forces and power centers in the world outside their borders, as well as to prevent them from flooding into their own decision-making process. What is pertinent in this perspective is the fact that both Moscow and Washington sought to contain the ocean of changes in the region after 1991, so that they would still fit into and reinforce their own national interests. There was some sense in this as well, for Russia faced continued challenges from terrorist forces within, while the United States dealt daily with the extreme Islamist threat that had led to the first attacks on its territory since the attack on Pearl Harbor in 1941. In the end, it was not just that Russia and America were straining so much to protect their own state-based interests in a realistic way. It is also the case that each understood the extent to which their own state had become a regional leader and encapsulated the needs and motives of an assortment of other nations.

In sum, the pursuit of Balance of Power by both Washington and Moscow meshed with their Realist approaches to each maximize their own power through their linkages to newly freed European states that were looking for positive direction. The Balance of Power would not be the same as it had been in the time before the break-up of the Soviet Union, but both powers sought to mold it into a shape that was as familiar as possible. Similarly, the Multi-Polar Model fitted in some ways with Legacy Theory. The late Cold War had been a time of the rise of new power centers such as Japan, China, and the European Union. None of those units was particularly focused on doing the bidding of either superpower. In parallel ways, Russia and America brought out earlier assumptions about how they had coped with those new power centers as they struggle to fit the former communist entities into new frameworks. NATO membership turned out to be a quick and easy answer for the United States and its traditional alliance partners. However, its expansion touched on numerous Russian nerves as that state perceived itself as operating in a near-vacuum of allies and political friends.

6

Russia and America confront terrorism, 1994–2004: a foundation of understanding

Introduction

If the experience of NATO expansion was in many ways a troubled time for Russian–American relations, their respective targeting by terrorists acted as a force pulling them to positions of mutual understanding. However, the undercurrent of tension connected to the widening of the Western alliance generated moments of high drama at other times. By the turn of the century, the challenge from the Republic of Chechnya had created a perception in the Russian leadership that the global terrorist network was beginning to choke the Russian Federation. In reaction to the 9/11 attacks in the United States President Bush chose to wage war against the geographic center of the al Qaeda network, with broad domestic and international support. In some ways, the two sets of world leaders reacted in parallel fashion. While the Russians perceived the first Chechen War as imperative to hold the Russian Federation together, the Americans understood the attacks on the Twin Towers and the Pentagon as the first serious violation of American territorial integrity since the 1941 attack on Pearl Harbor. Both sets of national leaders eventually concluded that the respective attacks were part of vast and threatening terrorist network. There was also a modicum of mutual understanding between Washington and Moscow during the white heat of the threat, from 2001 to 2003. Each reached out with support to the other in words and deeds. However, misapprehension by each about some of the conclusions drawn by the other side became evident at certain crisis points. The United States had joined with its allies in criticizing the brutality of the First Chechen War in the mid-1990s, while Russia now distanced itself in large part from the Bush decision to invade Iraq as part of the mission against the terrorist thrust. In the end, there was an ironic overlap in the experiences of the two nations in spring 2013. Native Chechens who had moved into Dagestan to escape the Russian military thrust into their own republic moved with their families into the eastern part of the United States. Two brothers chose to express their hostility to the American values and system by setting off explosives at the Boston Marathon, resulting in several deaths and the serious wounding many others.

Russia responds to challenges from Chechnya

The collapse of the Soviet Union in 1991 led to the existence of a number of weakened successor states, and some of them were republics in the Russian Federation. The Caucasus, in the southwest area of Russia, was particularly vulnerable, and some republics became a "hotbed of terrorism." Chechnya was the most troubled and visible of those geographic units, and the tensions within it spread to its neighbors as well. Those states also were porous ones through which drugs, organized crime, and arms flowed. While al Qaeda's attacks against the West were largely ideological in nature, those that emanated from Chechnya were principally based on ethnic and religious differences (J. White 2009, 338). It is also the case that the Soviet military forces departed from a number of new states and regions after the 1991 implosion of the USSR and left behind many weapons in Chechnya (Gakaev 2005, 26). Within a decade of the 1991 transition, Moscow would fight actually two wars in Chechnya for quite different reasons.

The First Chechen War took place between 1994 and 1996, and preoccupied the Yeltsin presidency in the years just prior to his re-election. In that first war the primary goal of Russia was to "restore constitutional order" (Sakwa 2005, 17). The Chechen leader, Dudayev, had declared an independent Islamic republic in 1991 and the federal government was committed to holding the territorial unit of Russia together so that it too would not implode as had the USSR. The war itself was characterized by a high number of casualties, large-scale attacks by the Russian military that took many civilian lives, and widespread international condemnation. In the end, there was a real uncertainty about the outcome of the presidential election, and thus the war came to an end just prior to the re-election of the president.

The Second Chechen War was quite different and occurred primarily between 1999 and 2001, although it technically did not end until 2009 (Van Herpen 2014, 196). One analyst (Sakwa 2005, 17) characterized it as a "counter terrorist operation." Chechen terrorist attacks on Moscow apartments had taken about 300 lives in 1999, and the Chechen leaders chose to intervene militarily in Dagestan in the same year. Vladimir Putin had just been appointed prime minister and he showed a firm hand in the few months that remained before his accession to the presidency. Like Yeltsin a few years earlier, he worried about the potential break-up or "Yugoslavization" of Russia. Perhaps

Chechen aggression would encourage terrorist groups in Dagestan and in other Russian Republics along the Volga River. Concern about the intactness of Russia was the older theme and the combat against terrorism the new one. In 2000 the plan switched from emplacing Russian leaders in Chechnya to placing reliance on local Chechen leaders who were loyal to Russia. As a symbol of this "Chechenization", Putin appointed Akhmed-hadji Kadyrov as the administrative head of the republic. Kadyrov worked closely with Moscow until his assassination in 2004 (Sakwa 2005, 17–19). The war itself forced 200,000 persons into exile in neighboring Ingushetia, and Russia hit the Chechens hard with air raids and heavy artillery. Election needs again played a role, when Putin stood before the voters for the first time in spring 2000 and needed to demonstrate to them that he was a man with a firm hand (Gakaev 2005, 35–36). The new Russian leadership offered the promise of stability and victory, after all the failures of the 1990s (Pain 2005, 70–71).

Further terrorist attacks occurred in Russia after the initial phase of the Second Chechen War ended in 2001. In 2002, commandos attacked the Dubrovka Theater in Moscow and held the audience captive for several days. "Black widows" or female suicide bombers whose husbands had died in battle were a notable feature of this attack. The Russian military eventually put an end to the siege, but the loss of life was high. In 2004, terrorists took over a school in Beslan on the first day of term, and again intervention by the Russian military led to a high number of casualties as the standoff ended. Shamil Basayev was identified as the leader of the terrorist forces, and the Russian military hunted him down and killed him in 2006. However, the overall Russian losses were very high (J. White 2009, 340–344).

America responds to the 9/11 attacks

The attacks on the Twin Towers in New York and the Pentagon in Washington evoked a powerful American response that was broad based and multidimensional. The initial emphasis centered on punishing Afghanistan for harboring al Qaeda and permitting Osama bin Laden to plan the attacks. A full-scale invasion of Afghanistan took place a few weeks after the 9/11 attacks and resulted in the quick initial defeat of the Taliban, which had ruled the nation since its military conquest in 1996. The Bush administration soon opened another front, with the invasion of Iraq in 2003, and the indirect connection of this action to the original attacks on the U.S. led to considerable criticism at home and abroad. Key variables that played a role in this U.S. response included the attitudes and support of allies, domestic public opinion, and the restructuring of domestic administrative capabilities for coping with the nature of the new terrorist challenge.

A number of analysts characterized the 9/11 attacks as reflecting a situation of asymmetric power. Neither the Taliban nor al Qaeda had the conventional military capabilities to challenge the American military. Thus, they resorted to "unconventional methods" and selected target areas "outside the realm of military conflict" (Kay 2015, 255; J. White 2002, 285–287). In order to prepare defenses against such attacks in the future, the Bush administration enacted a number of administrative changes, some of which require congressional approval. One reform included the erection of the Transportation Security Administration to provide the national government with a supervisory role in airports over the screening of passengers. In addition, the Bush administration set up the Homeland Security Office, which it soon upgraded to the status of a full cabinet department. After much deliberation by president and Congress, new legislation established a Directorate of Intelligence to manage the CIA and other intelligence apparatuses under one roof. Further, the USA PATRIOT Act provided law-enforcement personnel with additional powers to gather intelligence about future possible attacks. This latter act was the most controversial, for it sparked a continuing national debate about what compromises of civil liberties and privacy rights were necessary for the "war on terror" to succeed.

In terms of strengthening military and intelligence capabilities, American leaders activated the Counter-Terrorism Center of the CIA in the knowledge that the battle against terrorism would be a continuing one (Howard and Sawyer 2004, 22). On the battleground of Afghanistan there was a renewed interest in utilizing the military activities of Special Forces, who would operate in a difficult terrain, trying to root out and destroy enemy forces (Jenkins 2004, 138). A rethinking of overall military strategy also occurred, and the new approaches centered on the realizations that the U.S. was a special target due to its visibility in the Middle East, that the military needed to make greater use of unconventional tactics, that the American public should conceptualize war as a process that might not end quickly, and that current and future enemies would not probably always be nation-states (Hook 2014, 16).

Allies became an important component of the American strategy as well. NATO invoked Article 5 for the first time, as there had been an attack on the territory of one of its members, and Australia followed suit by putting into operation Article IV of the ANZUS Treaty. Initially, thirty-seven nations offered assistance (Downing 2004, 154). However, the Bush administration took full charge of the Global War on Terrorism and did not rely very much on the allies. NATO partners were more geared up for the defense of Europe rather than the pursuit of terrorists in desert locations. Their military structures were designed for Cold War struggles, and the Balkan Wars of the 1990s were unlike those to come in Afghanistan (Michta 2006, 108–109). However, offers came in from the United Kingdom for 4,200 troops, from France for 2,000 troops on naval vessels, from Germany for 3,900 soldiers, from Italy for 2,700, and from the Netherlands for 1,200. Substantively, the U.S. and the EU formed an agreement to intensify cooperation on matters such as targeting terrorist financing, imposing tougher border controls, and improving the exchange of information and intelligence (Rees 2004, 176–178).

Within the United States, President Bush received high approval ratings, general support from Congress for his policy initiatives, and the public's willingness to support military action. Much of this support continued even after planning for the Iraq War took place, but it did erode after the war began in 2003. Clearly, in the short run there was a "rally around the flag" effect that had notable consequences. Perhaps President Bush had been successful in convincing domestic constituencies that this was a different war than the Persian Gulf War or the war in Kosovo had been, and in persuading allies that this was in fact the world's fight (Bush 2005, 553–554).

Collaboration with the law-enforcement community was an integral part of the process of policy and administrative change. Law-enforcement agencies had naturally been focused on crime control and engagement with communities, and now the crisis required a new emphasis on intelligence collection. There would also be a heightened need for bilingual analysts at many levels (J. White 2002, 288). The law-enforcement community lacked a "standard operating model for law enforcement" in order to deal with the new threat. If officers were to continuously keep an eye open for intelligence related to national defense, would they sacrifice their other core missions such as combatting crime? Local police units had little jurisdiction over such matters, and the new policies did not formally provide for much more (J. White 2004, 1–7). But the coordination of a meaningful domestic network of terrorist control would not work without their engagement and assistance.

Parallel reactions to terrorism by the Russian and American leaderships

There were parallel features in the two nations' responses to terrorism. Probably, that parallelism paved the way for a brief window of understanding about their common front in the global struggle.

Both nations had in very different ways become embedded in a struggle against Osama bin Laden and al Qaeda. Bin Laden was located in Afghanistan during Soviet troops' near-decade-long engagement of there in the 1980s. He was part of the resistance that the Soviet military was attempting to stamp out, as it was a threat to the puppet regime that the USSR was seeking to support. Further, the followers of bin Laden carried out suicide bombings against Russians stationed in Chechnya in 2000 during the second war there (J. White 2002, 167). Of course, bin Laden had targeted U.S. interests in the 1993 attack on the World Trade Center, the 1998 hits on the American embassies in Kenya and Tanzania, the explosions on the U.S.S. *Cole* off the coast of Yemen in 2000, and, finally, the 9/11 attacks.

Al Qaeda's cultural war against the West incorporated both Russia and America as enemy forces. In calling for expression of extreme Islamist views that were allegedly related to the beliefs of the Prophet, bin Laden was following the teachings of his modern inspiration, Sayyid Qutb. It was not only that they rejected what the West was doing in the late twentieth and early twenty-first centuries but that they also dismissed the Enlightenment and the emphasis on reason and rationality that its philosophers expressed. While the terrorists certainly rejected the role that the Brezhnev regime had played in Afghanistan in the 1980s, as well as the wars of Yeltsin and Putin in the Caucasus, they concluded that Western interventions in Saudi Arabia at the time of the Persian Gulf War in 1990–91 and the warm-up to the Iraq War of 2003 were more offensive. After all, Saudi Arabia was the location of Mecca and Medina, the spiritual centers of the Muslim faith and the location of the Prophet's teachings. Further, America had been the strongest supporter of Israel and its control of East Jerusalem, the site of Islam's third-holiest mosque (J. White 2002, 290–293).

Other parallel points emerged between the two nations in developing responses to the threat of terrorism. Both worried about the terrorists getting control of Weapons of Mass Destruction (WMD), for Russia and America had both produced many of these. In addition, in both countries the terrorists had hit vulnerable targets of great symbolic value. For the U.S. these included the center of its military capabilities as well as two structures that represented its economic strength (Jenkins 2004, 131, 136). On the Russian side the targets had included apartments where innocent civilians lived, a theater where people were simply watching a play, and an educational institution at which children and their parents were celebrating the beginning of the school year.

The 9/11 attacks stiffened the backbone of Russia as well as that of its counterpart across the Atlantic. While the Bush administration developed a series of administrative and policy responses to the terrorists, opinion in Russia intensified against the Chechens as a result. The rebels had been anticipating negotiations with Moscow to end the Second Chechen War, but Moscow refused after watching the horrifying events in America (Gakaev 2005, 36). In fact, the attacks in both nations increased public support for the two respective presidents (Pain 2005, 71).

Administrative centralization was also a by-product of the terrorist attacks

President Bush had campaigned in 2000 on a platform that called for less centralization in Washington, but the events of September 2001 led him to push through four administrative changes, such as the creation of the Homeland Security Department and the Transportation Security Agency. In addition, there was a great need to include local law enforcement officials in intelligence gathering about future planned attacks. Prior to the attacks, the local police had never played a "cohesive role in national policy" (J. White 2004, 5).

In Russia, centralizing decisions of equal consequence were made. For example, in January 2001, the government switched control over the counter-terrorist campaign from the military to the Federal Security Service (Baev 2005, 120). It also recruited top generals from the two campaigns to fill top military positions and in the administration of the republics. Further, Putin enacted a major change in the way governors for the republics were chosen. Election was the process outlined in the 1993 constitution, but in a law of December 2004 the changed procedure to appointment by the office of president. Most observers interpreted this change as a tactic for controlling separatist tendencies or even possible terrorist activities in other republics (Pain 2005, 74–77).

During the Iraq War in particular, reliance on defense contractors was part and parcel of most military missions. These contractors were often former military officers and enlisted men who had gone to work for private contractors after leaving the military. They took on many construction projects such as building housing for American troops and installing electricity and plumbing services. They also played a role in combat missions. In March 2004 four men working for the contractor Blackwater were killed in an ambush in Fallujah and their bodies were then suspended from a bridge. They worked alongside military units and troops, but were often paid several times what the individual soldiers received. This use of contractors partially privatized the war in Iraq. In a parallel way, the Russian military introduced contractors to work alongside its conscripted soldiers. Often these people were demobilized soldiers who had joined private security companies and ended up on the battlefields of Chechnya. Just as the American contractors often aroused suspicion over financial matters, so also some of the Russian contractors were viewed by some as mere crooks. As they worked with Special Forces in sweeps through communities, some may have engaged in torture or other criminal acts. Some observers noted that their *zachistka* or cleansing operations were similar to those of the Serbs in the Bosnian War (Van Herpen 2014, 189–192).

To conclude, there was one parallel point that reflected a basic disagreement between the United States and Russia. Prime Minister/President Putin moved quickly after the 1999 Moscow apartment bombings to commence the bombing of terrorist sites in Chechnya. In part, the American-led NATO bombing campaign in Kosovo provided a convenient precedent for that tactical decision. If America could inspire a bombing campaign to protect a republic in Yugoslavia that was not part of the NATO alliance, then Russia was justified in punishing a terrorist group that was active on its own territory (Pain 2005, 69–70).

The impact of terrorist attacks in stimulating mutual understanding between America and Russia

After the 9/11 attacks there was a sense that Russia and America were now "natural allies on this issue." President Putin expressed the hope that President Bush now understood the challenge that Russia had been facing from terrorists throughout the previous decade (Jenkins 2004, 140). Western leaders began to perceive how the Russian and American battles were now inextricably linked in a new "frontier in the war on terrorism" (Russell 2005, 244). These close moments generated a mutual understanding for at least the next year. The two sides signed the Treaty of Moscow, which would reduce the number of nuclear weapons on each side to 1,700–2,200 by 2010. Interestingly, Russia was relatively quiescent about the American decision to withdraw from the ABM Treaty. After the American invasion of Iraq, Russia was still willing to write off some Iraqi debt and provide a certain amount of economic assistance to promote stability in a very troubled nation. In turn, the United States was less critical of Russian military activities in Chechnya and also encouraged Russia to move closer to NATO (McCormick 2010, 225).

Russia was also willing to offer substantive assistance to the United States in the upcoming battle in Afghanistan. For instance, it was the first allied nation to offer information sharing to American leaders, as well as use of Russian airspace for humanitarian missions (McCormick 2010, 217). It was also willing to permit the former republics Kyrgyzstan and Uzbekistan to offer bases for American use in the war in Afghanistan. Thus, Manas base in Kyrgyzstan and Khanabad in Uzbekistan were available to the Americans for transferring both troops and supplies to the theater of operations (Terzuolo 2006, 95). This concession by President Putin was a significant one, for Russian influence in the former Soviet republics was a matter of continuing importance and sensitivity. That willingness to work with the United States on the consequences of the 9/11 attacks revealed an understanding of the two states' mutual challenges and a readiness to reach out in partnership.

The mutual apprehensions of the new partners against terrorism

There were three points of contention between the two nations and their reactions to the terrorist onslaught. First was the divisive factor of Osama bin Laden and his impact on both powers. Second was the general Western reaction to the way in which Russia prosecuted the First Chechen War, and third was the Bush administration's interpretation that the invasion of Iraq was a meaningful follow-up to the 9/11 attacks.

A principal enemy of the Soviet Union during its occupation of Afghanistan in the 1980s was al Qaeda and its leader Osama bin Laden (J. White 2002, 162–163). America designated that group as the source of terrorist actions directed against the United States from at least 1993 until 2001. On the surface, the common foe should have been a force that created a common understanding between the United States and Russia. However, the twist in the policy issue was the role of the Carter and Reagan administrations during the Afghan War of the 1980s. The United States led a Western effort to support the opposition to the Soviet occupation, and on February 3, 1980 President Carter's National Security Advisor Zbigniew Brzezinski actually aimed a rifle down the Khyber Pass in the direction of the Soviet military. It was a symbolic move on his part, but the financial and military support that the United States provided to the opposition was not. As a result, al Qaeda benefited from Western assistance and American aid helped to strengthening the group that would become its main terrorist foe a decade later.

The United States and other Western powers had sharply criticized Russia for the brutality of its military tactics during the war in the Caucasus from 1994 to 1996. The attacks on the Chechen capital, Grozny, were particularly vicious and forced 300,000 refugees out of the city. Losses among the civilian population were particularly severe, and in April 1996 the Russian military killed the designated Chechen leader, Dudayev. There was a certain cynicism in the way in which that first war ended, for it was clearly a necessity to assure the re-election of President Boris Yeltsin. Russia eventually signed the Khasavyurt Agreement on August 31, 1996, which many depicted as sealing a Russian military defeat, as the Chechen soldiers were able quickly to slip back in and retake Grozny (Gakaev 2005, 28–29). Overall, American opinion focused on the excesses of the Russian military action and did not precisely relate the Chechnyan threat to the global, post-9/11 al Qaeda-based terrorist movement.

It is also true that the decision of the Bush administration to commence war in Iraq in March 2003 soured the warming relationship with the Russian leaders who surrounded President Putin. Those leaders had understood the need for America's military forces in Afghanistan to use two bases located in the nearby Eurasian states. However, they did not support the decision to spread the battle against terrorism from Afghanistan into Iraq. After all, in the past the Soviet Union had provided military assistance to the Iraqi leader, Saddam Hussein. Toppling Saddam would not have been a Russian priority, and there was no solid evidence that the Iraqi leader was linked to al Qaeda. No doubt, Russian leaders were not at all interested in watching American interests grow and develop in several nations that were geographically within the Russian orbit.

Conclusion: analytical components of the wars against terrorism

The more settled and concrete models and theories do not seem to fit the Russian wars fought in Chechnya, the American battle against al Qaeda, and the shifting relationship between the two nations on what the appropriate moves were in containing such threats. This ambiguity is related to the sudden emergence of terrorist attacks as a major characteristic of the post-Cold War world. After awakening to the new realities of the transformations of 1991 and onwards, both Russian and American leaders expected to see progress in building democracies and free-market economies, but the reality turned out to be profoundly different. Therefore, the two models that help in clarifying the new realities are the Multipolar Model and the Chaos/Complexity Model. The first model factors in the new forces that began to compete for attention on the world stage, while the second calls attention to the frustrations that both sets of leaders encountered as they tried to react in a way that protected their nations. In terms of the available theories, the Theory of Critical Junctures can be useful in outlining one of the unexpected transitions in post-Cold War times. However, one could properly ask: "A transition to what?" Perhaps Realism Revised can provide at least a partial answer. One of that theory's hallmarks is the intangibility of state borders and the resulting ability of non-state actors to penetrate them with apparent ease. A brief consideration of these analytical components can cast light on the dilemmas that surrounded the two sets of leaders.

Multi-polarity was in evidence across several dimensions and sectors. On the one hand, there were additional states that played a role in the calculations of both Russia and America. After several years of support by the West for their democratic reforms, Russian leaders were unprepared for the sharp criticism that leaders of the same Western states brought to the table during the First Chechen War. By the same token, there was virtually unanimous support from America's allies after the terrorist attacks on U.S. territory. Thus, collective responses from many states constituted a kind of pole of power that affected the calculations of both of the countries afflicted with terrorist attacks. On the other hand, non-state actors constituted a new pole of power that had a powerful impact. The Chechen rebels made up one republic in the vast Russian Federation but had an outsized impact on its policy. In a very different way, al Qaeda terrorists had virtually no territorial base but operated cells within and across many states in several hemispheres.

The Complexity/Chaos Model was in evidence throughout the period of intense preoccupation with terrorism. It is possible to consider both the Chechen and al Qaeda attacks as chaos events that forced their targets to develop unexpected and creative solutions to the new and violent set of challenges. It was inevitable that there would be an evolution of sorts to a new order. Evidence of the new order in both Russia and America was the increasing centralization of political power in order to obtain the necessary controls to set up a process for preventing future violent challenges. In the Russian case, this entailed co-optation of military top brass from the Chechen campaign to serve at the top levels of administration in Moscow. It also included the division of Russia into seven large districts, with presidential appointees in charge of each one, as well as the replacement of the elective principle with an appointive one for republican governors. The Bush administration set in motion the passage of four sets of organizational change, each of which pointed toward the consolidation of power at the national level, and particularly in the hands of the executive. The creation of the Department of Homeland Security was very visible evidence of this process, for it pulled together under one roof previously independent organizations such as the Coast Guard, the Immigration and Naturalization Service, and the new Transportation Security Agency.

The transition into the new age of global terrorism also constituted a critical juncture for the United States, the Russian Federation, and many other nations. America in the 1990s had been devoted to building the conditions for greater economic security, following the end of the Cold War and the mobilization for Operation Desert Shield and Desert Storm in the Persian Gulf region. Considerable military demobilization took place, and writers described the possibility of an era of "democratic peace." In Russia, the building of a democratic framework was the key project, as so many groups and political parties clamored for a part in the action after the collapse of communist control. Observers noted that the 1993 constitution contained a rather lengthy exposition of presidential powers, and that became a harbinger of things to come in the next century. However, the emergence of uncontrolled terrorism disrupted those patterns in both countries and constituted a juncture at which new directions and emphases were mandatory. The world would no longer look so peaceful, but it was unclear what would replace the hopes and aspirations of the early 1990s.

The Realism Revised Model, with its emphasis on the power of globalization forces to overwhelm political and organizational leaders provides insights into the new era. That model reveals the apparent impotence of national leaders in Russia and America to control what happens within their territorial borders. How is it possible to prevent the breakdown of governance procedures in one of the Russian Federation's republics, especially if that territorial unit has already declared its independence? How could the open social order of the United States, a land of immigrants, keep a close eye on all who meant it harm and managed to enter the country? At the same time, the increasing sophistication of non-state actors enabled them to cross borders and create damage in ways that were heretofore unanticipated. The terrorist groups included numerous cells that were organized in a very independent and decentralized manner. In that regard they were totally different from the hierarchies of power that had characterized previous enemies, such as the regimes of Hitler and Stalin. Terrorist groups operated freely across territorial lines. Chechen terrorists moved easily into Dagestan in 1999, and al Qaeda suicide bombers operated freely across European borders as they made their way to Logan Airport in Boston.

In conclusion, these softer models and theories are the ones that are most useful in evaluating the impact of the new age of terror on both America and Russia. To many American citizens, the world did seem more chaotic after September 11, 2001. Old expectations of security in airports, and indeed on all modes of transportation, disappeared. Safety in locations where crowds gathered to attend athletic events, to enter huge shopping malls, or to enter routine transportation hubs could no longer be guaranteed. A nearly invisible and constantly moving pole of power had emerged that did not fit at all into the existing state system, with its reliance on national leaders who were in control. It was clearly a critical juncture, but the path to the other side was unclear. In a similar way, the Russians also were dealing with a chaotic situation that included not only war in Chechnya but also severe economic difficulties in 1998, a strengthened Communist Party in the 1996 elections, and a physically weakened President Yeltsin. For their leaders, an enlarged NATO alliance constituted a new pole of power that could constrict their regional and global movements. Irritatingly to them, the expansion included those very states that Moscow had led or directed during the Cold War. It was unclear to them too what the path would be to the other side of this critical juncture, and the extremely long Russian border invited incursions of many sorts that are anticipated by the Realism Revised theory. At least the United States had the protection of the Atlantic Ocean in the east and Pacific Ocean in the west.

7

The wars in Afghanistan (2001), Iraq (2003), and Georgia (2008): a mixed set of perceptions

Introduction

Following the initial shock and surprise of confronting the qualitatively new challenges from the Chechens and al Qaeda, both America and Russia moved to a new plateau, with wars fought on the territory of other nation-states in the first decade of the new century. While Russia's war in Georgia lasted only a few days, its roots in the past were deep and its impact on relations with other states in the near future was considerable. America's wars in Afghanistan and Iraq were brief in terms of achieving the initial objective of dislodging the Taliban from power in the former and Saddam Hussein from his position in the latter. As in the Russian case, the quick victories did not solve the deep-rooted problems, for the wars opened up a host of challenges that required the United States to keep its troops there well into the Obama administration.

In each of the three cases there was a central and common problem that the larger power sent its military forces into a much smaller and weaker country. The territorial integrity of the targeted states was thus compromised, as the invading nations claimed that unusual reasons required their presence. In the case of Georgia, Russian leaders pointed to the alleged threats made by the Georgian government to its two separatist enclaves of Abkhazia and South Ossetia, and it is likely that the Georgian military did move into those areas prior to the Russian incursion. The Bush administration warned both the Taliban and Saddam that they needed to step down from power very shortly, otherwise an American invasion would ensue. The Taliban had harbored bin Laden, while Saddam's regime had not been open and forthcoming about the kinds of weapons that it possessed. Neither backed down, and the invasions were then inevitable.

However, the three situations and wars were very different in their appearance, as well as in their reception by the international community. Russia had
entered the territory of a bordering state that had been an important republic
in the former Soviet Union, and and this invasion symbolized in part Russia's
reduced territorial reach after the collapse of the Soviet Union.. In contrast,
the United States was not in the neighborhood of either Afghanistan or Iraq.
In the case of the former, there was overwhelming evidence that the 9/11
attacks had been possible due to the protection that the Taliban provided to
bin Laden and his group of terrorists. In that instance, the geographic distance
from American shores did not matter very much. Iraq was equally distant from
America, but there was a history between the two states, as the George H.W.
Bush administration had orchestrated a military operation against Iraq that had
resulted in the liberation of Kuwait in 1991. Thereby, the two wars took on
a very different cast from each other. Further, reactions by the international
community were very supportive of the operation in Afghanistan but quite
critical of the move into Iraq, as well as of the brief Russian war against
Georgia.

It is important to outline the key features of all three of these wars so as
to comprehend more fully both what they implied for America and Russia
individually and what their impact was on the relationship between the two
states. The conflict in Afghanistan lasted officially from 2001 until the end of
2014, but a considerable contingent of U.S. personnel remained after that to
help train indigenous forces and to help keep the nation together. In the Iraqi
case, Americans fought from 2003 until the end of 2011, but the rise of ISIS
brought a contingent of Americans back several years later. Russia's war in
Georgia lasted for only a few weeks in August 2008, but Russia's eventual
recognition of Abkhazia and South Ossetia put it at odds with the leaders in
Georgia for a long time after that. Therefore the residue of each of the wars
was long lasting.

Given the continuing echoes of each war, they all were bound to influence
American–Russian relations in significant ways. It is clear that the Afghan War
brought the two together, while the Iraq and Georgia wars drove them apart.
To Russia, the 9/11 attacks resembled very much the Chechen attacks on
key civilian gatherings in Russia, and in that light it was willing to work with
the Bush administration in controlling Afghan-based terrorism. However, the
attacks on Iraq seemed to President Putin to have less justification and to be
either excessive or an example of the new American unilateralism. Georgia's
vulnerability to the larger military power to the north made it seem to be a
real victim and thus placed a wedge between Moscow and Washington.

Another component of the Russian–American relationship was the matter
of NATO involvement, given Russian anxieties about the expansion of
that alliance. NATO eventually took over most of the allied military forces
in Afghanistan. While the alliance refused to play a similar role in Iraq, its

members did take over a training mission for Iraqi police officers and military personnel. The NATO connection in the Georgia War was interesting but less direct. At its Bucharest Summit in April 2008, NATO had refused Georgia's petition to start the process that would result in its membership. That factor may have been one of many that prompted the Russian leadership to send its forces into the embattled nation. While NATO involvement in all three battles was not a factor that visibly drove Russia and America apart, it was a tremor that reverberated through all three conflicts.

It is also useful to assess parallel features of the Russian and American experiences of war on the territory of other nations. The different characteristics are very clear and center primarily on the length of the two wars that the Bush administration began and the brevity of Russia's battle in northern Georgia. Differences in outcomes are also apparent, for the American engagement seemed to many to be never-ending, while the Russian one had an end point in terms of military operations but long-term consequences in terms of the incursion into Crimea six years later, in 2014. However, there were similarities among all three, for the struggle against terrorism set the stage for each of them. In the American wars, the connection was the very direct in terms of al Qaeda's launching of four commercial airliners in attacks against important economic and military targets. Chechnya was in the background of Russian sensitivities about troubled border tensions, and the fear that those terrorists might find a safe haven in the remote areas of Georgia had some impact.

The War in Afghanistan and American resolve

America did not march into Afghanistan alone, for support from nations in all regions of the globe was immediately forthcoming. Given the reach of the terrorists and their presence in so many allied nations, there was a common fear of who would be the next victim and how extensive the damage would be to people and national psyches. NATO Secretary-General George Robertson decided that the alliance should invoke Article 5 for the first time in its five-decade history, as that provision required all members to support a partner whose territorial integrity had been violated. This was the case on 9/11, and so America received much collective support from the beginning of the conflict. Eventually, the United States' leadership decided not to take advantage of all the troops that partners had offered. This decision was based on America's confidence in the superiority of its own military capabilities, but it did put some distance between Washington and European members of the alliance (Hendrickson 2006, 120–126).

In spite of the initial lack of actual participation by NATO partners, the American military did invite the British to join the invasion, and British naval vessels launched cruise missiles against Taliban and al Qaeda forces. American weaponry was advanced even beyond the capabilities utilized during the

Persian Gulf War a decade earlier. The weapons now used included Joint Direct Attack Munitions, Daisy Cutters, Thermobaric Bombs, and different Unmanned Aerial Vehicles (UAVs). UAVs now included Global Hawks that gathered information and Predators that constituted air-to-surface missiles. In addition, Air Force planes dropped propaganda messages to dissuade the Afghan population from responding to the call of the extremists. For example, and February 3, 2002, planes scattered 300,000 leaflets throughout the country.

Collaboration with neighboring countries assisted in maximizing the U.S.-led efforts. For example, both Uzbekistan and Kyrgyzstan permitted the use of their air bases, while Turkmenistan opened up a land corridor to the troops and permitted over-flights that carried humanitarian supplies. In return for the cancellation of a considerable amount of its debt, Pakistan permitted the use of selected bases as staging areas, as well as granting over-flight rights. In light of the porous nature of its western border with Afghanistan, the sympathetic Pakistani leadership also directed its own army to do all possible to keep Taliban soldiers from fleeing into Pakistan in search of sanctuary. There were also indigenous power centers with which the American units worked. One key partner was the Northern Alliance, which consisted of minority Uzbeks and Kyrgyz. After the quick defeat of the Taliban, American forces and political leaders worked with President Hamid Karzai as he set up an interim government. An important victory occurred at Tora Bora in December 2001, but key leaders, including perhaps bin Laden, escaped from the allied network (Papp *et al.* 2005, 469–470). The year of 9/11 ended with about 16,500 troops deployed in a successful effort to overthrow the Taliban (Papp *et al.* 2005, 219).

In the fall of the following year, the Bush administration announced a new National Security Strategy that could guide decision making. Reflecting on the lessons learned in the previous year, the strategy call for a renewed emphasis on containing regional conflicts through which the new enemy moved in very elusive ways. A high priority was placed on denying WMD capabilities to terrorists and on combatting rogue states. Other power centers that could be of assistance included strong Asian players and the EU, as well as the already engaged NATO structures. As a harbinger of the future, the document also endorsed the notion of pre-emptive action against an enemy, if there was a considerable threat to U.S. interests and people (McCormick 2010, 216–217).

The International Security Assistance Force (ISAF) had been formed in December 2001 and it coordinated operations in Afghanistan under American leadership. However, NATO took formal control of ISAF and its Operation Enduring Freedom five years later, in 2006, by which time there were 40,000 troops in Afghanistan. All twenty-six NATO partners were performing some tasks within the country by then, and associated with them were personnel from another eleven countries. The coalition had divided Afghanistan into twenty-five Provincial Reconstruction Teams (PRTs), and the allied nations took part in the rebuilding effort within the PRT framework. Allied countries often had particular missions in which they specialized. For instance, Italy provided assistance with judicial reform, Germany with training police, and the United Kingdom on counter-narcotics. American efforts centered on helping the Afghan National Army to prepare itself for the day when it would carry on the battle by itself. The UN also had an Assistance Mission in the country, and some of its foci included the construction of clinics and road building.

At the end of 2006 there was an important NATO summit in Riga, Latvia. As so many countries had become part of this broad-based struggle, some had wished to reduce the possibility of taking casualties. They did not want to risk the lives of their soldiers or to receive pressure for a pull-out from their home front. Thus, they added caveats to their commitments that might locate their soldiers in relatively quiet provinces. At the Riga Summit, alliance planners requested that they lift these caveats and play more central roles in the main battle of defeating the enemy. In the following year, 2007, there was a further attempt to coordinate efforts through the formation of the Afghan Compact. With NATO officers as a liaison force, there would be more formal coordination with ISAF itself, the Afghan government, international organizations, and neighboring countries (Peterson 2011a, 81–88).

It would seem that the situation should have been under control six years after 9/11. However, in 2007 the Bush administration decided to shift many troops from Afghanistan to Iraq as part of a "surge" there, for the battle in Iraq was not going well. When Barack Obama took over the White House in early 2009, the drain of military forces from Afghanistan was having a visible negative impact there on the struggle against the Taliban. Therefore, President Obama ordered 21,000 more troops into Afghanistan in the spring of 2009 and a parallel "surge" in Afghanistan of a further 30,000 at the end of the year (Hook 2014, 68). Interestingly, the same General David Petraeus who had supervised the earlier surge in Iraq moved to the Afghan setting to manage that surge in 2010. He had been commander of U.S. Central Command located in Tampa, Florida between those two vital missions. Helmand province in the south of Afghanistan was a key hotbed of Taliban strength, and 80,000 soldiers were located there during the surge. At that time NATO commanded all troops, with the exception of 20,000 Americans who operated under their own leadership. In March 2010 all of those U.S. troops were taken under NATO command as well (Peterson 2011a, 107–108). That shift was not such a pronounced one, for the top NATO commanders were also Americans.

During the first term of the Obama administration the war in Afghanistan continued in a draining and punishing way. New issues emerged, such as "green on blue" shootings in which apparently Afghan allied soldiers turned their rifles on their American partners and killed them. This reality certainly complicated the making of the planned transition to control by the Afghan National Army, and it undercut support from the American public for this unexpectedly long and costly military engagement. There was also continuing controversy over the prisoners at Guantanamo Bay. President Bush had initially ordered use of that prison to house those captured in the fighting, and it held 7,000 such prisoners overall. To President Bush, internment at Guantanamo Bay was preferable to either the captives' classification as prisoners of war or their trial on American soil. Barack Obama had promised in his 2008 election campaign to shut down the prison, but that had not happened. At the beginning of his second term Obama announced the eventual pull-out from Afghanistan for December 2014. That event did happen, but there were lengthy debates about how many troops to leave there under NATO command, and the decision was to leave about 12,000 into 2015 and after.

The war in Iraq and the American gamble

The post-9/11 enunciation of a doctrine of pre-emption provided for the possibility of intervention in Iraq in 2003, and no doubt that is what President Bush had in mind when he articulated that policy theme in late 2002. Earlier in 2002 he had listed Iraq as one of the three nations on the "Axis of Evil" in his State of the Union Address, with Iran and North Korea being the other two. Technically, Saddam Hussein's hostility to UN inspection of Iraq's potential nuclear capacities was what led to the decision to invade Iraq. Prior to May 1, 2003, Hans Blix had worked as the UN's chief inspector in Iraq, and his mission had mixed results. The Iraqi president permitted the inspectors to come in at that time but did not permit them access to all the desired sites (Papp *et al.* 2005, 225). For President Bush, that was the culmination of twelve years of uncertainty with regard to Iraq's potential possession of the wherewithal to manufacture nuclear weapons. Following Iraq's defeat in the Persian Gulf War of 1991, the UN Security Council had passed Resolution 687 requiring both a report from Iraq within thirty days and an open door to the UN inspectors. However, there were other factors that prompted the American-led invasion. Saddam's provocative role in the Iran–Iraq War of the 1980s, his use of chemical weapons in that war as well as against the Kurds in the Iraqi north, and his continued harsh measures against the majority Shiites in the south were among the causes for the intervention.

President Bush mentioned several of those motivations when he presented his case for war to the American public. Since the UN had not lived up to its duties, "we will rise to ours." While not attempting to link Saddam's threat to the al Qaeda attacks on the U.S. specifically, he did conjure up a picture of Saddam being willing to make surprise attack from the air that would devastate the American people. In his view, American force need to take action before Saddam's weapons "suddenly appear in our skies and cities."

He also brought World War II imagery to bear on the case by reminding that appeasement of Saddam could lead to devastating consequences. Taking action might prevent that horror, but waiting could be suicidal (Bush 2005, 555–557).

After American-led forces entered Iraq, they searched carefully to locate the nuclear weapons or the work on such weapons that had been the presumption behind the war. However, they were unable to find them, and it is probably the case that the Iraqi regime had abandoned such work at some point in the 1990s. Thus, it was necessary to present other rationales for the decision to go to war. Regime change was necessary, due to Saddam's oppressive regime and his record of action against his own population as well as against neighboring nations. The "Shock and Awe" military campaign was very quickly successful in achieving the goal of regime change, as Saddam and his associates left their positions and went into hiding. The invading forces toppled statues to the dictator and began mopping-up operations against the remaining enemy forces.

After the deposition of the regime in May 2003 the American surrogate leadership decided to dismiss all members of the Iraqi military as well as all public employees who had joined the Ba'athist political movement. This resulted in the creation of massive unemployment as well as fodder for future radical movements such as ISIS. For example, at least one refugee from Iraq moved to Belgium as a consequence of that American decision. He had lost his pension rights and seen three brothers die in the civil war that engulfed Iraq soon after the American-led invasion. In 2016 he decided to return to Iraq from Belgium, as his hopes for a better life in the West had died (*New York Times*, 2016a). In August 2003, suicide bombings commenced and even the UN Special Representative in Iraq was killed. Brutal enemy attacks in Fallujah took many lives in March 2004, and the Shiite Mahdi Army led by the cleric Muqtada al-Sadr became aroused. With 60,000 soldiers, al-Sadr caused much damage in the next few years. Internecine warfare among Shiites, Sunnis, and Kurds continued. In the month of October 2006 alone, 3,709 Iraqi civilians died (Pelletière 2007, 67–101).

Elections had taken place in 2005 and the twenty-five-member council that had governed in tandem with seven well-known expatriates was replaced. Prime Minister al-Maliki from the Shiite majority emerged as the dominant leader. The new rules required that the ceremonial president be a Kurd and the Speaker of the legislature be a Sunni. However, the internecine struggle continued to grow in the two years following the elections, and the American leadership decided to increase troop numbers and execute a "surge" in the military effort in 2007. There was an injection of five military brigades totaling 21,000 soldiers, and the violence subsided somewhat (Hook 2014, 68). However, the simultaneous siphoning of off of troops from Afghanistan weakened the military presence there.

Allied support and involvement were certainly less than they had been in Afghanistan. The UN did not give its blessing, nor did NATO sponsor the invasion. This gave rise to a problem in 2003, because the American strategists had worked with Turkey so that the invading forces could cross over from there into northern Iraq. Turkish leaders feared retaliation from Iraq and sought to invoke NATO's Article 4, which would have promised alliance consultations if there had been a threat to Turkish territorial integrity. NATO vetoed that request, with the result that the Turkish route was unavailable and entry into southern Iraq from Saudi Arabia became the only military reality. The key powers vetoing the Turkish route were Germany, France, and Belgium. Germany and France had been vocal in their doubts about the desirability of an invasion at all. However, other allies from the "new Europe" played a central role as part of the "Coalition of the Willing." Poland administered a broad swath of territory south of Baghdad, and Germans were in fact part of that operation so as to maintain some control over the delicate situation. Ukrainian troops worked with the Poles, and 100 Czechs trained 12,000 Iraqi police officers (Peterson 2011a, 115–118). Finally, from 2004 on, NATO set up training missions for Iraqi police and military forces under the heading of NTM-I.

There were an assorted range of issues that undermined the success of the war effort, as well as support for it, both within America and among its alliance partners. Scandals such as the mistreatment of prisoners at Abu Graib by American military personnel raised questions about America's control over its military operations and personnel. Along with the United Kingdom, Spain had been a partner in the original plan to intervene in Iraq. Al Qaeda attacked Spain's train system in 2004, just before national elections. As a result, the Spanish withdrew from the scene in order to focus on issues at home (Jentleson 2007, 383). Heavy reliance on National Guard and Reserve forces weakened domestic support in America for the continuation of the struggle, while the role of defense contractors in the battle and reconstruction of Iraq became controversial. In spite of all these difficulties, American military forces stayed the course until their political leaders called for troop withdrawal by December 2011.

The war in Georgia: Russia enters the fray

Georgia's link to the West after the end of the Cold War contributed to its alienation from Russia and the 2008 war. For example, in 2002 American military personnel trained Georgian anti-terrorist personnel. The U.S. leadership was concerned about the neighboring Chechens using the inaccessible parts of Georgia as a route to join the Taliban or al Qaeda (Papp *et al.*, 219–221). In this instance, the American and Russian wars against terrorism were linked.

There is also evidence that Russia's posture towards Georgia in the years prior to 2008 in part prefigured its aggressive response at the time of the brief war. In December 2000, during the Second Chechen War, the Russian leadership imposed new visa requirements on Georgian citizens in an effort to prevent Chechen rebels from getting home from Russia through Georgia. In 2002, Moscow provided passports to persons living in Abkhazia and South Ossetia, and this seemed to signal that President Putin had more in mind for these two Georgian enclaves. The emergence of Georgian President Mikheil Saakashvili after the Rose Revolution in 2003 further alienated Russia, and the Russian police retaliated by raiding places frequented by Georgian migrant workers in Russia. Ironically, Kosovo's declaration of independence in February 2008 also put distance between Georgia and Russia. If Kosovo could be independent from Serbia, why could Abkhazia not have more independence from Georgia? Thus, Russia lifted some sanctions that it previously had imposed on the enclave. Prior to the war, Russia held the Kavkaz-2008 military exercises in North Ossetia, near its border with Georgia. These military activities utilized the 58th Army, the Russian Air Force, and the Black Sea Fleet. Cossack forces were also mobilizing in case of a need to defend South Ossetia (Van Herpen 2014, 206–221). In light of these overtures by Russia, the war itself should not have been a complete surprise.

Much evidence points to the fact that Georgian troops actually initiated the war with a surprise attack on South Ossetia on August 7. Russia responded immediately by sending it military forces into the enclave to push the Georgian troops back, and then penetrated into the territory of Georgia beyond South Ossetia. To the dismay of much of the world, the Russian response was excessive, especially since word about the initial penetration in Georgia did not spread immediately. Why would Russia have overreacted with such a powerful military thrust? The answer may reside partly in Russian sensitivity to NATO's serious consideration that of Georgian membership in April of that year. The economic crisis of 2008 hit Russia particularly hard, and only a few years had passed since the so-called "color" revolutions of 2003–5 in Georgia, Ukraine, and Kyrgyzstan (Tsygankov 2013, 237). However, the war was a short one, and the Russian troops pulled back to the enclaves quite soon.

Russian reactions to the outcome of the war were multi-faceted. Russia walked out of the NRC in protest and stayed away for a full year. It located 3,000 troops in Abkhazia to prevent another invasion by Georgia, and also placed tanks and long-range missiles in the enclave. In March 2011 Russia announced plans to locate three more submarines in the Black Sea Region. Plans to maintain Abkhazia's 90% dependence on trade with Russia also proceeded apace (Peterson 2013, 113–115). In 2011 Russian leaders also proposed a Eurasian Union that would inject broader regional stability into the fragile region (Tsygankov 2013, 248). President Medvedev developed a number of principles after the war to guide future decision making and let the West know more fully about Russian protectiveness in the Caucasus and Eurasia. One point pertinent to the Georgia War was the acknowledgement that Russia shared special links with close neighbors with whom it had a shared history and culture. Medvedev went so far as to characterize those ties as "privileged interests."

There was much discussion in the West and elsewhere of the significance and outcome of this war. Surprisingly, the war in Georgia actually had an impact on the prosecution of the war in Iraq. Due to the crisis at home, the Georgian government withdrew 2,000 troops from Iraq so that they could take part in defense against Russia. Georgia had maintained a large number of troops in Iraq nation, and the decision impacted the decisions of General Petraeus, because British and German troop withdrawals had already depleted the ranks of the allies (*Los Angeles Times* 2008). American Defense Secretary Robert Gates asserted that the Russian move into Georgia called the whole relationship between Russia and America into question. Secretary Gates also stated that the leader behind the aggression was Prime Minister Putin, who desired to take another step toward restoring Russian greatness. Gates cancelled two forthcoming exercises, one with Russia that involved both navies and another that brought in Canada as a third partner (*Washington Post* 2008a). Importantly, it was the EU that mediated the crisis and proposed the terms for a ceasefire that called on the Russians to pull their troops back to pre-war positions (*Washington Post* 2008b). A refugee emergency also arose, because 150,000 persons were uprooted by the crisis; there were 30,000 refugees in South Ossetia alone (*Christian Science Monitor* 2008).

Important discussions took place within the Russian political scene. Former Soviet leader Mikhail Gorbachev raised questions as to why Russia should take part in global institutions if its views counted for very little. He noted that the Russian perspective was ignored through the declaration of independence by Kosovo, the American withdrawal from the ABM Treaty, the American-proposed Missile Shield program and the "unending expansion of NATO" (Gorbachev 2008). Abkhazia also had its say, as it requested Russia to recognize its independence, and Moscow responded that it was prepared to do so (*iDnes* 2008a). Russian leaders warned other nations such as Moldova to avoid replicating the disastrous decision of Georgian leaders to send military forces into an enclave that leaned towards Russia. With 1,500 Russian troops stationed in Moldova's Trans-Dniestr, Moldova should not consider escalating its own internal conflict (*USA Today* 2008a). American Vice President Richard Cheney visited Tbilisi in the month after the crisis, and this was accompanied by a Russian effort to connect the travails of Georgia to the American political campaign. President Medvedev escalated his rhetoric by suggesting that the United States may have prompted Georgia to start the war in order to underpin the presidential candidacy of John McCain (*USA Today* 2008b). At about the same time, the Russian Duma passed a 2009 defense budget that called for a 25% increase in allocations and spending (*USA Today* 2008c). In addition, two months after the war President Medvedev travelled to Evian, France and proposed at a conference there that Europeans should join with Russia to establish a new transatlantic organization in which the U.S. would not play such a prominent role (*USA Today* 2008d). All of these responses by Russia paralleled the heightened rhetoric that was emanating from Western capitals.

As a kind of footnote to history, Georgian leader Saakashvili re-emerged as a political force in Ukraine in 2015–16. First, he served as regional governor in the Odessa region and then as the main fighter against corruption in Ukraine (*New York Times* 2016a). Thus, his populist resistance to Russia while in Georgia was now transferred to another former Soviet Republic that had experienced a Russian invasion!

The Russian–American relationship in the three wars

In terms of the war in Afghanistan, Russian–American relations were positive. President Putin expressed Russia's frustration with the lack of understanding that Western leaders had demonstrated towards its struggles with the Chechen separatists and terrorists. The 9/11 attacks on the U.S. seemed to him to be a partial vindication, and he thought that now American leaders would understand what the source of Russian suffering had been. He did not protest when the United States gained access to two bases in the former Soviet Republics of Kyrgyzstan and Uzbekistan, although Russia did express a desire for a time limit on the American residency. Over-flights of Russian territory were permissible, and in 2012 Russia approved the transit of goods through the airport at Ulyanovsk en route to Afghanistan. The American battle against the Taliban and al Qaeda did resemble the Russian struggle with its own Republic of Chechnya. The parallel was even strengthened by subsequent terrorist events on Russian soil. While the explosions in the Moscow apartments in 1999 preceded the 9/11 attacks, the terrorist onslaughts on Nord Ost Theater in Moscow and the school in Beslan came later.

Relations between the powers were not so amicable or full of understanding on the matter of the American invasion of Iraq. Putin described that operation as a mistake that would generate additional international instability (Jentleson 2007, 377). Russia joined with France and Germany in leading the opposition in the UN to any endorsement of the Bush decision to move into Iraq. With America tied down by a two-front war in far-off places, Russia could move more aggressively at a time when oil prices were strong and the Russian economy was stronger than it had been five years earlier (Peterson 2011a, 119). There was also some touchiness with regard to Iraq, for Russia had been supplying it with weapons in the middle of the Cold War. At that time, American support for the shah of Iran had put the U.S. on the opposite side, in alliance with Iran (Peterson 2014, 153–157).

Of course, there was considerable tension between Russia and America over the war in Georgia. Georgia had become a PfP member of NATO in 1994, and the 2003 Rose Revolution put in power leaders who developed "Security Concept 2005," which would link Black Sea security to the Euro-Atlantic security system. There was also generalized concern about the security of the new Baku–Tbilisi–Ceyhan oil pipeline in the event of a crisis. Georgia had also been a very active contributor to Western military operations and peacekeeping missions. It had worked with German and Turkish troops under KFOR in Kosovo from 1999 to 2008, and had been willing to dispatch 750 soldiers to the dangerous Helmand province of Afghanistan, where it took 170 casualties by summer 2008. In addition to its several thousand troops in Iraq, Georgia had also been willing to send seventy soldiers in a medical unit and engineering platoon.

The Bucharest Summit of NATO in spring 2008 had entailed serious consideration of Georgia for full membership of the alliance. NATO did declare that Georgia could eventually become a member, but alliance planners did not issue it with a Membership Action Plan that would have provided a path from PfP status to full membership. Following the August 2008 war, Georgia issued a Minister's Vision in 2009 that outlined the inter-dependability of its military within the NATO structure (Peterson 2013, 86–91). Early Russian efforts to repair relations with the West came to naught. In 2009, President Medvedev's proposal for a Security Treaty with the U.S. and Europe fell on deaf ears, and the West chose not to take part. In particular, the new East Central European members of NATO were disinterested in working in a setting in which Russia could veto alliance initiatives (Tsygankov 2013, 42–243). Clearly, the Georgia War led to more stress and tension between Russia and America than did the Afghan and Iraqi wars.

Parallels between the Russian and American approaches to war in the first decade of the new century

There were several commonalities between the Russian and American approaches to war between 2001 and 2008. Both powers were willing to enter territory in which there were sharp ethnic divisions, even though neither nation had a permanent or significant attachment to the group with which it allied. In Afghanistan, the United States worked with all ethnic groups that were willing to take the fight to the Taliban. In Iraq, the consequence of the American involvement was support for the Shiite majority that had been the victim of Saddam Hussein's policies over several decades. When Russian troops entered Georgian territory they acted as a protective force for the Abkhazian and South Ossetian minorities. The ethnic consequences of the invasions were very clear in each case. In Afghanistan, non-Taliban groups came to power under the presidency of Hamid Karzai, while the elected Shiite leader al-Maliki came to power in Iraq. The two enclaves in Georgia both received the protection of Russia's sponsorship of their declarations of independence.

A second common feature was the willingness of both powers to take action in spite of outside reactions. While many nations supported Operation Enduring Freedom in Afghanistan, American chose to begin the war with only British involvement, in spite of the fact that NATO had invoked its Article 5. With no official endorsements for intervention in Iraq, the Americans moved forward with the Coalition of the Willing that principally included the United Kingdom and Spain. Other allies soon joined in with military forces and peace-keeping missions in both settings, but there was a unilateralist flavor to each operation at the outset. The Russian intervention in Georgia was a complete surprise and initially appeared to be a manipulation of a weak nation with which Russia shared a border. With no meaningful alliance memberships at the time, Russia was truly on its own.

A final parallel centers on the costs of these operations to both America and Russia. The costs of the war in Afghanistan primarily related to the length of the war, the repeated duty postings for many soldiers, the amount of money spent, and the loss of lives that might have made significant contributions after their military service to families and professions. In Iraq, many of the costs were the same, but to those were added the United States' loss of stature, due to the unpopularity of the war and the questions that many allies posed about its rationale. For Russia, the surprise involvement in Georgia alienated most Western nations and created a temporary sense of isolation for the nation and its leaders. Its formal role in the NATO–Russian partnership was postponed, and desired Western cooperation on other noteworthy matters was likewise delayed.

Conclusion: asserting and adjusting great-power initiatives

The period was one of disjuncture in light of the implications for models of behavior and explanatory theories. The Unilateral Model that had been power-ful in the first two decades after 1945 emerged for the United States on the global scale in the period after 9/11, but also for Russia on the regional stage. Both countries took firm action with little consultation of their allies and managed to get away with the results. At the same time, pursuit of the Balance of Power was a constant across these three wars as pressures converged upon both America and Russia to frame their overtures within global norms. Further, the theory of Realism was a powerful driving force behind the actions of both nations, for they sought to defend national interests and security in a world that was filled with cross-border pressures that were hard to contain. Legacy Theory was also a prominent reality of the three wars, for American and Russian interests were luminescent throughout the events that led up to the wars. Legacy Theory probably led to a Realistic assessment of the threat scenario, and the results were unipolar actions that eventually faced the limitation of the reality that most Western nations preferred the maintenance of a balance of power.

Unipolarity was most in evidence with the decision of President Bush to invade Iraq, for the stakes were much higher than they were for Medvedev and Putin in Georgia. When the plan failed to receive the endorsement of the UN and NATO, the president came up with the novel concept of the Coalition of the Willing that included several traditional European partners and most of the new NATO and PfP partners from Central Europe. There was also a hint of Unipolarity in the decision to invade Afghanistan, for the 9/11 attacks had taken place on American soil only, and the assistance offered by the NATO partners was initially set aside, due to the single-mindedness of the American leadership and its desire to rely on the technological superiority of U.S. weaponry. Lacking any meaningful community of alliance partners, Russian leaders decided alone to resolve the conflict in Georgia with an incursion to protect Russian allies in the two enclaves. The isolation of unipolar decision making had consequences, but it may have seemed inevitable to leaders in Moscow and Washington.

The achievement of a strong and stable Balance of Power was a desired result for the regional partners of both prominent actors in the regions in which the wars took place. A natural balance emerged once the United States brought all NATO members, its PfP, and other allied countries into the equation. Allies imposed caveats on the locations of their contributions to Operation Enduring Freedom in Afghanistan, and American leaders had to be responsive to their ideas about the direction of the war and the hoped-for end of involvement and casualties. In Iraq, many nations assisted in the reestablishment of stability after the fall of Saddam, and American leaders needed to listen to their perspectives in order to accomplish a collective operation in the best interests of the Iraqi nation and its peoples. Eventually, Russia pulled back into the enclaves and reestablished its connections with the West in a gradual way. The initial isolation was not a situation that the Russian leaders had planned for in the long run.

The theory of Realism guided each nation as it calculated the needs for moving into another country with force. Protection of national interests in an era of porous borders and globalization was a prime necessity for both. American airspace had been hijacked by four planes flown by al Qaeda pilots rather than by their designated American flight personnel. Just as President Franklin Roosevelt had ordered an attack on Japan right after the Pearl Harbor attacks, so President Bush sent troops into Afghanistan in short order. While the rationale for the invasion of Iraq is more difficult to depict in terms of straightforward national interests, the fear of another attack from the air was foremost in the minds of American leaders, as well as the long history of Saddam's resistance to UN efforts to discover what his plans were for the future development of WMD. Russia is a much more powerful state than Georgia, but its decade-long struggle with terrorists on its own territory made it particularly sensitive to the perceived strong-arm tactics of regional actors on its borders. Was Russia's national interest at stake in Georgia? It was, if one considers the number of nations nearby in which a Russian or Russian-friendly minority was seemingly victimized. Standing firm in Georgia would send a message to Ukraine, Moldova, and the Baltics.

Legacy Theory was prominent in each case study, for the Cold War and immediate Cold War heritage were prominent throughout the crises. The attacks that led to the Afghan invasion were the virtual straw that broke the camel's back, for America had watched bin Laden and al Qaeda take lives in the World Trade Center bombing in 1993, the attacks on two American embassies in Africa in 1998, and the sacrifice of seventeen American military personnel in the attack in 2000 on the U.S.S. *Cole*. The invasion of Iraq was rooted in several decades of state-based terrorism executed by the Ba'athist regime, which included the use of chemical warfare against the Kurds and Iran, wars against two neighbors, and stonewalling of the UN in reference to charges that Iraq sought to develop nuclear weapons. The legacies that generated the Russian invasion of Georgia were long lasting and powerful. They included the fact that Georgia had been a Soviet republic for a full seven decades, the rapid movement of Georgia toward NATO membership, and the problematic nature of the Georgian leadership that emerged after the Rose Revolution. After all, Saakashvili replaced Edward Shevardnadze, a Georgian leader who had led the republic in the time of the USSR and also had been Soviet Foreign Minister.

In sum, America and Russia both sought in a realistic way to protect themselves against national security threats that they perceived in other nations. The main difference was the proximity of Georgia to Russia and the distance between America and its two battle zones. Neither nation was impervious to the efforts of allies and neighbors to criticize the aggressive moves of Moscow and Washington, and a certain type of responsiveness emerged in each case. Significant legacies affected the reasoning of both nations, but that heritage did not predetermine all components of the decisions to invade. Current needs, connected with economic strength and with the threat of terrorism, were motivating factors as well. There may have been a unipolar moment for each central actor at the time of the invasions, but considerable regional and global pressures limited their staying power.

8

The Missile Shield proposal by the U.S. in 2007–9 and the Arab Spring of 2011: contrasting priorities

Introduction

Two main events that took place in the five-year period 2007–12, and both touched the nerves of the American–Russian relationship. The three wars in Afghanistan, Iraq, and Georgia accompanied these two phenomena, but the wars had only an indirect consequence on the dynamics of their evolution and outcomes. The United States proposed a Missile Defense System against the possibility of an attack from an unpredictable or rogue state. Russia was continuously critical of that plan, interpreting it as directed against its own nuclear capabilities. Eventually, the Obama administration cancelled the plan in the fall of its first year in office, and the immediate crisis ended. While the Missile Shield proposal was a plan that American leaders developed to deal with the residue of the 9/11 attacks and fears, the explosion of the Arab Spring was unplanned and unexpected. Both Russian and American leaders paid careful attention to its evolution, but two of the affected nations generated questions that Russia and America answered in quite different ways. American intervention in the Libyan civil war was another example, to Russia, of aggressiveness by on the part of the United States and NATO. Syria was another case entirely, for the United States threatened action on behalf of the opposition to President Assad, but it was Russian leaders who proposed compromises at the critical time. Their leanings were clearly toward the Alawite leader whom the Americans had seen as expendable. Controversy continued when ISIS entered the Syrian War and the two powers came up with different ways of containing and destroying that savage force. Thus, both sets of events pushed Russia and America apart but became issues that were not overwhelming and were subject to debate and compromise.

Controversy over the Missile Shield proposal

The American proposal

After withdrawing from the 30-year-old ABM Treaty in 2002, the Bush administration decided to set up a new Missile Defense Agency and to house it in the Department of Defense. Its purpose was creation of a defense system that could be "layered" in order successfully to intercept missiles from lift-off stage to re-entry stage. With an initial financial commitment of $10 billion, American defense planners hoped to incorporate recent discoveries in research projects connected with missile defense. It was also the case that both Russia and China possessed ICBMs, and there were also unpredictable rogue states that had pursued nuclear capability. Concerns about rogue leaders such as the Serbian Slobodan Milošević and Iraq's Saddam Hussein had set much of the foreign policy agenda in the 1990s. However, the 9/11 attacks heightened concerns about rogue movements and states that might someday acquire nuclear capabilities.

The proposed protective system very soon acquired critics who pointed to the unworkability of such a system in the best of scenarios. It would be unable to stop missiles delivered on the ground in a suitcase or other protective cover. Psychologically, leaders in other nations might be concerned that the system would give the U.S. such an advantage with that it might use nuclear blackmail to achieve its objectives. Testing of the evolving system was proceeding apace, and only seven of the first fourteen ground-based missile defense tests were successful (Hook 2014, 336–337). Other critics pointed out that the defensive system would not be able reliably to distinguish between nuclear missiles and non-nuclear ones (Garwin 2008, 41). Further, some observed that a clever enemy might be able to enclose a nuclear missile in a balloon that missile defense could not detect (Lewis and Postol 2008, 38). With such critiques, political leaders would need to present a very persuasive case in order to bring the complicated system into being.

The proposed defensive system would cover and protect the United States, Europe, and the western and eastern sectors of Russia. However, it would not shield from danger the central and southern portions of Russia or adjoining states. Where would the components of the project be located? The Bush administration decided to emplace the radar detection system in the Czech Republic, and ten anti-missile interceptors in Poland. In a sense, the choice of these two nations was a logical consequence of their early admission to NATO, although the alliance was not a sponsor of the planned new program. Given the amount of instability in the 1990s in the Balkans, and continuously in the Middle East, the two Central European nations would be closer to the source of challenges and somewhat better positioned than Western European nations.

Both President Bush and Secretary of Defense Robert Gates visited Central Europe in 2007 in order to discuss the project with allied leaders in the involved countries. Secretary of State Condoleezza Rice also visited, and pointed out the value of such a system to the whole Euro-Atlantic region (Peterson 2011a, 2–6). America viewed Central Europe as a kind of buffer against trouble that might arise from points to the east and south (Terzuolo 2006, 107–110). In particular, the Czech leaders were quite responsive to the inclusion of the radar site at the town of Brdo near Prague. Czech leaders such as the esteemed former President Václav Havel noted that the American President Woodrow Wilson had led Western efforts in the 1918 creation of Czechoslovakia. Others pointed out that the United States had not gone along with the appeasement approach taken during the Munich Agreement of 1938. Hitler's violation of that agreement with British Prime Minister Neville Chamberlain had resulted in the invasion and temporary break-up of the new Czechoslovak state. It is also true that Czechs were willing to rely on American protection instead of building up a military capacity of their own. The Warsaw Pact invasion of 1968 had made them cautious about locating large military forces in their nation again, and so soon after the end of Soviet occupation in 1989. The leading political party in the Czech coalition government was the Civic Democrats (ODS) and it too went on record as supporting the proposal.

However, there was opposition also. The two other principal parties were the Socialists (ČSSD) and the Communists (KSČM), and both were opposed to the project. Opinion polls revealed a very divided public, with a majority also in opposition. Further, there were continuing protests at the proposed site in Brdo as well as in Prague (Peterson 2011a, 8–10). The opposition did not agree that the Czechs would benefit from once again being swept into great-power politics and plans. Others worried that such prominence for the Czech Republic would serve as a kind of invitation to terrorist attacks as the nation became more visible and vulnerable in global defense strategies.

Key American leaders came to Prague and Warsaw in summer 2008 for signing ceremonies to kick off the program, but legislative approval would also be necessary. Interestingly, the idea of the Missile Shield program had first received official attention in discussions at the 2002 NATO Summit that was held in Prague. The summer meetings of 2008 were also preceded by the NATO Summit at Bucharest in April. At that time, the alliance offered its support for the American concept and plans, and said that it expected the project eventually to become a NATO project. In July, Secretary of State Rice signed the agreement in Prague with Czech Minister of Foreign Affairs Karel Schwartzenberg. Other supportive Czech attendees included Prime Minister Mirek Topolánek and President Václav Klaus. In September 2008, Defense Secretary Robert Gates came to Prague and signed the Status of Forces Agreement (SOFA) with Minister of Defense Vlasta Parkanová. This latter agreement set out the details of construction at the site, and it was important that it would be mainly Czech workers who would construct the facility and, of course, receive salaries (Peterson 2011a, 18–20). Although legislative approval was necessary, it seemed to be the case that the agreement was concluded and the project would be built. Parallel events took place in Poland, and so the second part of the system was moving forward as well.

The Russian response

However, Russian leaders were mystified and angered by this effort to insert an American system into Central Europe very close to their own borders. The American proposal came forward after a decade and more of disruptive challenges both within their borders and in nearby states. The Russians had fought two wars in Chechnya and been hit by at least three major terrorist attacks from that same region on elements of their civilian population. The "color revolutions" had taken place in three former Soviet republics just a few years prior to the emergence of the Missile Shield concept. All of these popular uprisings had undermined the dreams of President Putin to make the new century into a fresh start for Russia by moving back to its distinguished position in the region and strong role in global politics. Part of the plans of the Russian leadership had been to restore strength in the area of nuclear capabilities. From that perspective, the American effort to establish a protective layer over its own nation and that of its allies was startling and perhaps a setback for Russian interests (Peterson 2011a, 11).

Animated discussion in Russia was immediate, and persisted throughout the next few years. In 2007 President Putin addressed the Duma and described the American Missile Defense plan as a threat to Russian interests. He noted that his nation was at the time reducing conventional weapons under the 1990 CFE Treaty, while Western nations had ceased implementation of the promises explicit in that Treaty. After discussions in Istanbul in 1999, Western nations had stopped complying with CFE, due to the fact that Russia had not yet pulled its troops out of its protected enclaves in Georgia and Moldova. In response to the Missile Shield plan, President Putin decided that Russia also would no longer comply with CFE. Moscow also raised its objection to the failure of the three Baltic states as well as Slovakia to ratify CFE. The Baltics had not done so because they were still part of the Soviet Union in 1990. In a parallel way, Slovakia was still part of Czechoslovakia at that time (White 2011, 285).

Further, the Russian leader pointed out in the fall of 2007 that the INF Treaty of 1987 also had a number of loopholes that the new Bush proposal brought to mind. For example, it only limited land-based short- and medium-range weapons that could be used in Europe and western Russia. However, it did not include American cruise missiles carried on naval ships, and the preponderance of American missilery was sea based, while the Russians' was land based. INF also did not include the British and French nuclear arsenals or the capabilities of China, India, and Pakistan. The last two had "joined" the nuclear club in 1998, a decade after the passage of the INF Treaty. The Russian president even went so far as to compare the burgeoning set of tensions to the Cuban Missile Crisis (White 2011, 286).

Other top figures in the Russian political elite chimed in with supplementary arguments and proposed retaliatory measures. For example, First Vice Premier Sergei Ivanov spoke in May 2007 and pointed out that Russia had just tested a new ICBM that could counteract any defensive provisions of the planned American program. After his inauguration as president in early 2008, Dmitry Medvedev gave a speech near the end of the year in which he outlined concrete retaliatory steps that Russia was now planning to take. First, it would put short-range Iskander surface-to-surface missiles in Kaliningrad, with the result that Russia would then have a nuclear presence on the Russia–NATO border. Second, Russia would keep three rocket divisions in readiness, and third they would deploy radio-electronic suppression systems in order to neutralize the new American technology. Both Putin and Medvedev called for discussions at broader levels such as the OSCE, even NATO, or within the framework of a proposed European security treaty (White 2011, 286).

Additional counterproposals emerged on the Russian side as well. If Iran was the intended target rather than Russia, then Putin asked for the location of the site closer to Iran, perhaps at Gabala in Azerbaijan, to be considered. At another point Belarus proposed a joint space defense system with Russia that would include the Iskander rockets (Peterson 2011a, 12). Russia also asked if its own soldiers could be in residence at the Missile Shield sites in Poland and the Czech Republic. However, the agreements struck between the United States and the two Central European nations that would have the sites on their territory only permitted Russians to stay at their embassies in Prague and Warsaw, although they would have the right to visit the military facilities (Peterson 2011a, 14). The Czechs had already undergone the experience of hosting Russian soldiers on their territory for two full decades, while the Poles had been the recipients of Russian military pressure on a number of momentous occasions.

Personnel from the Russian military and Foreign Ministry also chimed in, with the result of presenting a united front against American aggressiveness. In fall 2008, Colonel General Nikolai Solovstov threatened to aim Russian strategic missiles at the Czech and Polish facilities once they were completed. Since the SOFA had been signed just after the war in Georgia, the general charged that this was another example of revenge on Russia. Key leaders in Moscow would never buy in to the American statements that Russia was not a target of the Missile Shield. Solovstov called for the American assumption of legal obligations in that connection, rather than mere empty-sounding promises. In the same week, the Russian Foreign Minister Sergei Lavrov went to Poland and spoke with Prime Minister Donald Tusk. Lavrov complained that Poland was simply taking revenge on Russia for its very recent military defense of South Ossetia (*USA Today* 2008e). Clearly, echoes of the Georgia War haunted discussions of the recently completed Missile Shield Agreement.

Cancellation of the Missile Shield

On September 17, 2009 President Obama suddenly cancelled the proposal that the Bush administration had signed the preceding year. There had been hints early in his administration that he had doubts about its wisdom and workability. However, his phone calls to Prime Minister Jan Fischer in Prague and Prime Minister Donald Tusk in Warsaw were surprises to them. The president said that U.S. intelligence indicated that Iran was no longer working on long-range missiles. The Czechs talked with the Americans about playing a role of some kind in the plan's replacement, while the Poles expressed their concern that cancellation would lead to more uncertainty about future Russian moves toward them. Lithuanian leaders expressed disappointment, for they felt more exposed as a small state on the border with Kaliningrad. However, there was a Russian response or concession, for it cancelled plans to locate the Iskander missiles in the Kaliningrad enclave. President Obama then announced a new tentative plan to put SM-3 missiles on eighteen Aegis cruisers that would principally operate in the Mediterranean Sea (Peterson 2011b, 21–22). Later on, the Obama administration came up with a more fully fledged plan to locate the radar sites in Turkey and twenty-four interceptors in Romania. Both nations were closer to the main sources of concern in terms of the development of nuclear capabilities (Hook 2014, 337).

It was clear that Russia wanted to be a full partner in discussions of Western security, and that it did not feel comfortable as NATO "military infrastructure" moved closer to its borders (Tsygankov 2013, 241). In early 2010, with cancellation of the missile program in progress, it came forward with a new military doctrine that was critical of any sort of missile defense plans in any location. However, there was also progress on limiting long-range nuclear missiles. START I had expired in December 2009, and the Russians took part in discussions to put its successor in place. In April 2010 presidents Medvedev and Obama came to Prague and signed the replacement treaty (White 2011, 287). In light of Czech participation in the planning for the Missile Shield, the choice of the city was symbolic.

The Arab Spring of 2011

The breathing spell for America and Russia lasted for just a year after the cancellation of the Missile Defense program, for in December 2010 revolts began in Tunisia that would set off uprisings in many countries of the Middle East. A marketplace vendor named Mohamed Bouazizi lost his cart, due to pressure from the police. His large family depended on his income, and he committed suicide on the spot. Within a short time, massive demonstrations occurred that drove President Ben Ali from office and out of the country. There had been little evidence of the success of democratization movements in the region prior to that event. In 2005, Iraq had held relatively free elections for the first time, and the majority Shiites came to power after long years of rule under the minority Sunnis and Saddam Hussein. However, that transition had been as a consequence of the American invasion that drove Saddam from power. In contrast, the protest movements that the Tunisia demonstrations sparked were spontaneous.

Arab Spring revolts in Egypt, Libya, and Syria

The uprising in Egypt followed closely on the Tunisian revolution. As Tunisia had, so too Egypt had labored under authoritarian leadership since the assassination of Anwar Sadat three decades earlier. His defense minister had somehow survived the shootings at a celebratory parade, but his rule became exclusive and, over time, it paid little heed to democratic norms. Those who began the protests on January 25, 2011 issued complaints about the corruption of government officials, persistent poverty within the population, and too-frequent explosions of violence. In a little over two weeks President Mubarak left the Egyptian state, tried to flee the country through his estate in northeastern Egypt, and then finally returned as a captive to Cairo. It took a long time to plan elections, as there were so many groups vying for political positions and a share in power. Legislative elections were held at the end of the year, but presidential elections were not held until June 2012. Surprisingly, the winner was Mohammed Morsi of the Muslim Brotherhood, a group that had not been central among the democratic activists who overthrew Mubarak.

The military had been a powerful interest or ruling group under Mubarak, and continued to play a leading role in the next year through the National Defense Council. Morsi acted as a conventional elected president in fall 2012, but in the spring he launched into a more authoritarian direction, severely limiting the orbit of the judiciary and not being particularly observant of human rights protections. On July 13, 2013, the military overthrew Morsi and put its top general, Abdel Fattah al-Sisi, in power. Western leaders were disappointed by these results, and Secretary of State John Kerry announced the cancellation of $260 million in economic aid and military supplies for Egypt (Peterson and Kuck 2015, 22–24).

The revolt in Libya was both similar to and different from the revolutions in Tunisia and Egypt. On the one hand, the principal target was the dictatorial regime of President Gadhafi. His regime had been as insensitive to popular views and aspirations as had been those of Ben Ali and Mubarak. However, the case differed in the sense that the West played a role in the outcome of the Libyan civil war through an allied bombing attack that offered protection to the opposition.

Muamar Gadhafi had been in power for about four decades and his record was similar to that of Saddam Hussein in Iraq. He buttressed his own authority by fragmenting society and playing one group off against another. He had a continual suspicion of institution building and so kept the media, private businesses, and the police under his control (Peterson and Kuck 2013, 9–10). Through his *Green Book* he advertised his Ba'athist view of society that was close to socialism but included elements of other systems as well. He had struggled vigorously with the West and had responsibility in the killing of two American servicemen in West Berlin. When the Reagan administration had sent Air Force planes near Libya, he had declared a line of death off the coast and challenged the aircraft to cross it. He also covered up those Libyan perpetrators of the shooting-down of a Pan American commercial plane in the late 1980s. Thus his unpopularity at home matched condemnations that came in from abroad.

Very soon in the Arab spring, a revolt developed in the northern part of the country near the city of Benghazi. The disparate groups formalized themselves into an organization called the Libyan Transitional National Council. In response to the high number of civilian casualties, Western allies commenced protective air strikes on March 19, 2011. The leading powers in those strikes were the United States, and United Kingdom, and France. Through Resolutions 1970 and 1973, the UN Security Council provided them with a mandate to protect civilians who were in harm's way. Eventually, NATO pulled the Western military strikes together under Operation Unified Protector. The alliance capabilities consisted of 8,000 troops, 260 air assets and 21 naval assets. On the ground, the allies destroyed 600 tanks and 400 artillery pieces. Eventually, the rebels captured territory to the west and surrounded Gadhafi's home base of Tripoli. The rebels eventually killed him, following a tip from NATO about his location in a drainage ditch.

In the following year, 2012, there were mixed results in Libya from the Arab Spring revolt. Elections took place in July and Ali Zidan became the new prime minister. However, the hatred of Gadhafi that was the glue that enabled the rebel groups to stick together until they achieved victory loosened very quickly after his death. The groups had little in common, and a civil war of sorts cast doubt on how meaningful the democratic elections had really been. A few months later one of the groups attacked the American embassy in Benghazi and four U.S. personnel were killed, including Ambassador Chris Stevens (Peterson and Kuck 2015, 20–21). The construction of a stable state out of all the pieces remained a formidable challenge.

At first glance, the Syrian revolt appeared to be part of the seamless fabric of the Arab Spring upheavals that were sweeping across the region. However, the revolt turned into an unending civil war that took far more casualties than did any of the other uprisings. The crisis began with a heavy-handed crackdown by President Assad's military forces on some teenage boys who had written complaints in graffiti on a wall. Protestors eventually demanded an end to government corruption, attention to the problems connected with economic inequality, the release of political prisoners, and the end of a forty-eight-year-long Emergency Law (Kuck and Peterson 2014, 20). Part of the problem stemmed from the fact that Sunnis were a majority within Syria, but President Assad belonged to the Alawite sect of Shia Islam. That complicated the international picture, for it made Iran more supportive of an embattled fellow Shiite.

As the civil war developed in its early years, the United States imposed sanctions on the Assad regime for its brutal crackdown on centers of opposition strength. There was support for the objective of the Free Syrian Army in seeking the overthrow of Assad, but the diversity of the opposition created problems for outside involvement. The rebels included secular nationalists, Kurds, democratic activists, but also Al Qaeda units. Therefore, non-lethal aid was the only viable option for the United States, and this included medical kits, uniforms, food, and night-vision goggles (Peterson and Kuck 2015, 11). In late summer 2012, President Obama responded to evidence that President Assad had chemical weapons at his disposal in this war. Obama that said he would draw a "red line" around chemical weapons, which meant an American military response if they were used. One year later, photographs and additional evidence emerged that indicated that some people had died as a result of the use of chemical weapons. Since the evidence pointed toward the weapons' probable usage by government forces, President Obama declared that there would be a military strike against chemical weapons factories. Instead of acting immediately, he decided to check with Congress on the matter first. At that point, President Putin came up with a compromise plan that all parties accepted.

Russian reactions to the Arab Spring

Russian leaders were not nearly as engaged in the Arab Spring uprisings as were their American counterparts. After dealing with the Chechen revolts within their own federation, and after having nervously watched the "color revolutions" near their own border in the southwest and Central Asia, they were wary of sudden and undirected revolts. They did not strike out with sharp criticism of the Western acceptance of the Egyptian revolts, but they were at odds with the American-led responses to the Libyan and Syrian versions of the Arab Spring.

The Russians were critical of the U.S.-led NATO operation that brought a halt to the Libyan conflict and an end to the Gadhafi regime. It was not their view that the Western alliance should have "regime change" as an objective. Their opposition was consistent with the criticism they had registered at the time of the NATO air attacks on Serbian forces in Kosovo in 1999. Again, the West was challenging the ability of a regime to control matters within its own territory. However, the Russians merely abstained when the UN Security Council voted to authorize air strikes against centers of Gadhafi's power in Libya.

In the Syrian case, Russia again did not support Western plans and hopes to remove President Assad from power. When such resolutions came up for a vote in the UN Security Council, both Russia and China vetoed the proposals. When the matter of chemical weapons and their use came up in fall 2013, President Putin criticized American plans to strike the facilities in Syria. Instead, the Russian leader proposed that outside powers should exercise leverage on Assad to give up control of his suspect weapons. As a result, the Organization for the Prohibition of Chemical Weapons took control of the situation and set a deadline for their full withdrawal (Kuck and Peterson 2014, 21–23). While the civil war and suffering continued, this put a halt to significant outside involvement until the intervention of ISIS in the war occurred a little less than a year later.

Comparing the case studies through the Russian–American lens

As American leaders looked into the lens of the Arab Spring, the Middle East was an overwhelmingly significant region into which they had poured significant assistance and resources in the past. Of course, long-standing support for Israel had been a central thread following its creation after World War II. Following the conclusion of the 1967 Middle East War, Egypt under President Sadat was willing to make at least a partial peace with Israel. Its reward for doing so was considerable American economic assistance. For a number of years, Israel ranked first on the list of American aid recipients, and Egypt second. Centering on American dependence on oil from the region, the close relationship with Saudi Arabia was a significant one. Further, the United States itself had fought two wars against Iraq, one to push it out of Kuwait and the other to depose Saddam Hussein from power. In light of those past commitments, the explosion of the Arab Spring created great uncertainty in a region that had become a "permeable membrane" touching other areas of significance to the United States (Pollack 2011, 280–281). It is also true that America was linked to a number of key alliances that could bring pressure to bear on the most difficult situations that resulted from the Arab Spring revolts. America was the lead partner in NATO and had a working relationship with the Arab League and Gulf Cooperation Council, two organizations that were in the process of developing military capabilities for collective response in precisely defined situations. This reality encouraged American leaders to conclude that they were part of an "informal multilateral arrangement" that could promote stability (Jones 2011, 309).

Russia's lens revealed a very different picture of how its national interests fitted into the changes that the Arab Spring was fomenting. Russian leaders were cautious about popular demonstrations in general and had watched them take place even in Moscow as a warm-up to the 2012 presidential elections. They were also cautious about promoting regime change of the type that America had accomplished in Libya and Iraq, and they opposed similar efforts in the Syrian situation. While they had provided military assistance to nations in the Middle East, their depth of involvement over the decades had not been nearly as extensive as that of the United States. In addition, their own military alliance had collapsed and their connection to NATO through the NRC had not been very active after the 2008 Georgian War. Finally, they probably saw the Western overtures in the region and involvement in two civil wars as similar in intention to the NATO expansion process of the previous decade. The West's involvement in the wars of the Middle East once again brought its military organizations closer to the Russian border.

Conclusion: theoretical implications for the Russian–American relationship

The Balance of Power and Chaos/Complexity Models cast light on these crises in the five-year span from 2007 to 2012. They may appear to be contradictory models, but each can explain one or more threads of the Russian–American relationship in the period under review. In terms of the explanatory theories, Systems Theory and Realism Revised are the most useful, for the latter highlights the pressures that flared nearly out of control in the period, while the former offers the beginnings of a plan for bringing about future stability. In sum, the Balance of Power Model and Systems Theory offer blueprints for moving in the direction of stability. In contrast, the Chaos/Complexity Model and Realism Revised Model fit the evidence of a tumult that generated the need for enhanced security.

Clearly, both the United States and Russia pursued Balance of Power in both of these situations. American promotion of the Missile Shield was intended to check the power of rogue states that might gain access to nuclear weapons and use them to obtain an advantage over the stronger powers. However, this display of American power in Central Europe required checks and balances, from Moscow's perspective. Thus, the Russians countered with plans to upgrade their own military capabilities in Kaliningrad. The Arab Spring demonstrations again brought American power onto the scene, once genuine civil wars had broken out. While Russia only criticized the use of allied air power to bring down the Gadhafi regime in Libya, it checked American plans in Syria to push Assad from power and to strike chemical warfare sites.

The Chaos/Complexity Model presumes that a chaos event sets in motion creative responses by players who work towards a new order in a turbulent situation that is continually evolving. The Arab Spring was such a chaos event that spread so rapidly that it also acquired the name "Twitter Revolution."

Memory and feedback from the past certainly influenced the American response, for the two Assads (father Hafez, and now his son Bashar) and Gadhafi had been stumbling blocks for some time. The decision to push for the removal of Gadhafi and the younger Assad was an instinctive response. For Russia the complexity of those upheavals was reminiscent of recent turmoil from three locations: Chechnya, neighboring states, and election-year demonstrations. Thus, the Russians avoided direct involvement in the political responses within the various countries and chose to react only when the West moved too forcefully. The Chaos/Complexity Model was in the shadows during the debate over the Missile Shield. After 9/11 there was fear about situations in which extremists would be able to gain access to nuclear capabilities. In that light, it is interesting that Russia did not critique the idea of missile defense in principle but confined its reactions to the questions of why it was left out of the plans or even, possibly, considered to be one of the targets.

It is tempting to refer to the main features of Systems Theory in order to guide future decision making in the two areas of missile defense and the Arab upheavals. Both crisis areas generated new inputs to the international system, in the one case in factoring in terrorists or rogue states that might actually deploy nuclear weapons, and in the other in understanding how many authoritarian leaders reached the end of the road under popular pressure at the same time. At the same time, each of the two areas of ferment demanded new outputs or policies from both Russia and America. America presented a new policy option in the form of the Missile Shield proposal, but what would be the Russian replacement, in light of the common understanding that there was a need for such a change? Further, how could Russia and America work together with allies to end the bloodshed in the worst of the civil wars that the Arab Spring had spawned? Outputs could be in the form of UN resolutions, bilateral agreements, or individual responses by each power.

The Realism Revised Model is a powerful one for analyzing the Arab Spring upheavals, for globalization pressures were central to that ferment. Leaders in the affected nations of the Middle East were unable to stop the Twitter Revolution from generating information overnight to their own populations. Rational responses by leaders in Syria, Egypt, or Libya were not possible, for they could no longer seal off the decision-making process from cross-border pressures to the extent that they had in the past. That generated similar pressures on Russia and America, for their leaders were also powerless to protect regional leaders with whom they had had stable relationships in the past. Similarly, the Missile Shield concept pulled in other nations whose leaders and populations might have preferred to remain detached from the politics of the nuclear powers. However, Czechs, Poles, Lithuanians, and Russian citizens of Kaliningrad were all made part of the discussion, and their future might have been quite different if the plan had not been cancelled.

Certainly, the Chaos/Complexity Model and Realism Revised Theory set the stage for important responses by the United States and Russia. The aspirations of Iran and North Korea to nuclear power status changed the game in which the two main nuclear powers had been engaged. It would no longer be possible to think only in terms of a successor to the INF, SALT, and START treaty processes to keep their regions and even the world free of the fear of nuclear weapons' usage. The problem had become more complex, and there was a need to revise the existing state-based plans. By the same token, and even with greater intensity, the chaotic nature of the Arab Spring uprisings created a whole new set of globalization pressures that neither Moscow nor Washington could ignore. It is reassuring that both Balance of Power and Systems Theory are still viable concepts in the midst of this global turmoil. The former has the power to encourage both American and Russian leaders that each can share in the power equation without constantly being preoccupied with the advantage that the other obtains. The latter can help not only in clarifying how new inputs can channel into the decision-making process but also in using existing policies as yardsticks for the next set of needed outputs.

9

America and Russia pivot towards Asia: political differences yield to economic rivalry

Introduction

Both Russia and America have made a purposeful and decided effort to direct foreign policy efforts towards Asia, and partly this is related to the growing economies and existing markets in that part of the world. For both nations, an emphasis on Asia would be a kind of welcome relief from the heavy commitments and preoccupations in the West. The United States fought two difficult wars in Afghanistan and Iraq, and their denouement offers an opportunity to set new foreign policy priorities. In addition, the Arab Spring presented a number of difficult challenges to the Obama administration, and the Syrian civil war has been particularly riveting. For Russian leaders, the Crimean annexation and ensuing crisis with Ukraine and, indeed, the entire West has been draining of energy and resources. A renewed focus on Asia can provide new opportunities and a chance to get somewhat away from the tug of the critics of that policy. The interesting question will be whether Russian and American policies will collide or mesh in that dynamic region.

As both powers look to Asia, their foci are partly similar and partly different. Both sets of leaders have been deeply involved in economic connections in the recent past, and there is now some breathing space and a golden opportunity to build on past successes. As India has boomed in recent years, both Russian and American leaders have increased the number of their visits there and have been building a foundation for a more concrete economic relationship. There is also common concern for both sets of leaders in the continuously shifting threat that North Korea and its leader, Kim Jong Un, present. However, in some respects Asia does present different preoccupations to each power. President Putin has an abiding interest in the five Central Asian nations that used to be republics in the Soviet Union. Some of them are rich in oil and natural gas, and so the Caspian Sea makes them continue to be important on the Russian agenda. President Obama placed less of a priority on those nations but more on Japan and South Korea. Both are countries that host a considerable American military force, and the saber rattling of North Korea and, occasionally, China means that near-term reductions in the force are unlikely. Other nations such as Pakistan and Vietnam claim attention from both Russia and America, but interest in them wavers according to what issues are on the table.

There is a certain symbolism wrapped up with the new emphasis of powers on the continent of Asia. America has looked both East across the Atlantic Ocean and West across the Pacific. Foreign-policy preoccupations often seem to vacillate from one side to the other. Both oceans offered a certain protection in the nation's early history, but with modern transportation and communications they now present opportunities. The Russian two-headed eagle looks in two sharply different directions, and some have concluded that within the Federation itself one head wins out for a period of time and then other becomes dominant. The head pointing east now seems to be on the ascent, while the Pacific-Ocean dreams of Americans are now on the rise as well.

The pivot towards Asia as a break from past history

What does it mean to "pivot" towards Asia? The term pivot is often used in describing a game of basketball, and is a positive statement about players' skills. A center may be able to move his or her feet quickly and sharply in order to take a needed rebound off the glass or dunk the ball into the basket with aplomb. A point guard may change direction quickly and open up a whole new set of options for a darting pass or dramatic three-point shot. The skills of foreign policy leaders are not unlike those basketball talents, for a pivot in a new regional direction will require speed, fancy footwork, and occasionally even a feint or fake of the opposition.

In comprehending what a pivot means in foreign policy, it is also important to look at past policy directions from which the pivot will be an abrupt shift.

Americans had a heavy preoccupation with Asia for a full quarter-century after World War II. They fought a difficult war on the Korean Peninsula for three years that ended with stalemate at the 38th parallel of latitude rather than outright victory. Storms began to brew in Southeast Asia soon after the Korean War ended in 1953. The long and anguishing wars in Vietnam and Cambodia took an entire decade and were ongoing through four presidential administrations. In 1975 the war ended with a victory by North Vietnam, which then absorbed South Vietnam, which the United States had been defending. This period and these wars were, then, huge burdens on America as it anticipated another move into Asia.

For Russia the weight of the past was quite different, for its preoccupation during the Cold War had been with the empire it had acquired in the West. Russia invaded Hungary in 1956 and Czechoslovakia in 1968, and it had a constant preoccupation with challenges from Poland in the years 1956 to 1981. In the east, its relationship with China was a troubled one after the emergence of the Sino-Soviet split in the early 1960s. From Russia's perspective there was no luxury of time or resources to explore possibilities in Asia during those decades. Certainly, a move into Asia in the twenty-first century was more likely to be achievable following the collapse of the Soviet Union and the end of communist rule by the Moscow-based party elite.

Thus, the points away from which both Washington and Moscow were pivoting were clear. For the United States, it was the history of past war and huge casualties in that region. For Russia, it was a lengthy troubled relationship with China as well as the steady drumbeat of challenges from the Warsaw Pact nations of Eastern Europe. New opportunities and threats presented themselves in the East, and a pivot in that direction would indeed require a particular set of skills and shifts of direction.

Russia: the two-headed eagle looks east

Central Asia

The first stopping point in an eastern strategy for Russia would be the five Central Asian nations. They are important since each of them was formerly a republic in the Soviet Union, and their populations mainly share the Muslim faith with people in surrounding nations. In communist times there was an official de-emphasis on the practice of religious faith in the face of communist ideology, but it was always unclear what the level of religious faith continued to be within the population. The region became strategically important after the Iranian Revolution of 1979, for a radical brand of Islam infused officialdom in the new Iranian government. From the point of view of Soviet leaders, they watched Iran move from being a U.S. ally under the shah to government by radical Islam under the Ayatollah Khomeini, with an indirect impact on the extreme Islamic movements in other regions. None of this had any direct bearing on Soviet rule in Central Asia, but the instability of the political system in nearby Afghanistan did catch the attention of Moscow. Fearing the possibility of the emergence of a second theocracy near their border, the Russians invaded Afghanistan at the end of 1979 and kept their military there for nearly a decade. Part of their concern was the possibility of two radical Muslim-led regimes that might have the capability to infect their own Central Asian populations.

During the period immediately after the 9/11 attacks, American interest in Central Asia was very high, due to the proximity of Central Asia to Afghanistan. With the agreement of President Putin, American forces got access to the air bases at Manas in Kyrgyzstan and Khanabad in Uzbekistan. Over-flight rights over Central Asian nations as well as Russia were also part of the agreement. However, Russian wariness about the U.S. military presence in the region was in the air at the September 2003 meeting in Washington between presidents Bush and Putin. Putin respected U.S. interests in the area, due to the Afghan conflict, but he also expected to lead or guide the process of permitting the American presence (Goldman 2009, 12–13). The intended American footprint in the area was deeper than simply nearby assistance in Afghanistan. In the 1990s, the Clinton administration had encouraged a certain independence from Moscow through the granting of PfP status to each of the five republics. After the beginning of the Afghan War, visiting American officials were often puzzled by the fact that all the leaders had an authoritarian governing style that approximated to the form of rule when each state had been a Soviet republic. In fact, some of these leaders had simply stayed on in the job after the 1991 transition. American officials were bold to criticize that pattern of rule in the new allies during the struggle against terrorism, and they often suggested that democratic reforms would be a fine idea. Such pressure nudged the Central Asian regimes back toward greater closeness to Russia, and the leadership in Moscow was thereby relieved (Goldman 2009, 25–27). However, a counter example occurred with the Georgia War of 2008. Although the Central Asian leaders were not overtly critical of the Russian moves, they did become somewhat more wary of Russian intentions in general (Goldman 2009, 197–198).

Of course, Central Asia is not a uniform monolith because of the common Muslim faith, and differences between the republics affected their orientation towards Russia, or even America. For instance, Nursultan Nazarbayev was the long-standing leader of Kazakhstan, and he sought a central regional role for his country. He employed terms such as "multivectorism" in foreign policy and acted as a spearhead for "Eurasian integrationism." Kyrgyzstan had fewer resources and less wealth than the other republics and pushed them toward a greater reliance on Russia. In light of its internal troubles, President Medvedev visited Kyrgyzstan in 2012 and offered Russia's assistance as the regional patron (Gleason 2013, 262–263). Uzbekistan had shown signs of independence from Russia even during the first decade after 1991. The Soviet leadership had assigned it the task of growing cotton during the Cold War, and this had not brought it economic diversification or much in the way of profits. It preferred to develop policy under its own guidance and actually withdrew from the CIS in 1999. Thus, Uzbekistan's responsiveness to America in terms of access to the base at Khanabad after 9/11 was not really a surprise (Cichock 2003, 265–267).

China

Russia, with its huge resources of oil and natural gas, was a natural partner for China, which, with its growing population and industrial infrastructure, had a great need for those resources. By 2005 Russia accounted for 11% of China's crude oil imports, and four years later the two powers made a concrete agreement that bound them even closer together. In the agreement of February 2009, China actually loaned large amounts of money to Russian oil conglomerates in order to further stimulate the Asian market. The loan from China to the oil giant Rosneft was $15 billion, and that to Transneft $10 billion (Sotiriou 2015, 184). The two powers also agreed on the building of a pipeline that would go from Skovorodino in Russia to Heilongjang in China, and that it would be completed by December 2010. In part, the Russian overtures to China and responsiveness to them were intended as a counter to the efforts of the EU to get involved more fully in some way in the Chinese market (Sotiriou 2015, 190–191). Russia had clearly come to envision China as the "gateway" to the global economy (Tsygankov 2013, 244).

The opening to China also entailed defense agreements, and the two powers signed a Russia–China Treaty for such purposes in 2001. During the following year they signed an arms agreement in which Russia would build two destroyers for China, and soon China was receiving of 40% of Russia's arms sales (Black 2004, 313). Another expression of their partnership was the holding of joint military exercises in August 2005. Both agreed that reduction of the U.S. military presence in Asia was a desired objective (Baev 2008, 75). China and Russia were both part of the six-party framework that dealt periodically with North Korea's challenge to regional security. The others included North and South Korea, Japan, and the United States (Tsygankov 2013, 245). In general, increasing defense connections between the two huge Asian geographic units had the promise of providing a balancing point in the continent, although they did place more defense equipment in the hands of a China that occasionally rattled a saber in the South China Sea.

India, Pakistan, and Turkey

During the Cold War the India–Pakistan rivalry intersected with the Sino-Soviet split, in the sense that Pakistan and China had a reasonably warm relationship. This outreach by China into South Asia opened up the opportunity for Russia to cultivate India through trade and periodic diplomatic visits. Arms sales continued to India after 1991, and by 2000 the profits to Russia were $3.8 billion (Black 2004, 315). A decade later, China and India were the purchasers of 90% of Russian arms sales (Tsygankov 2013, 245). Their burgeoning populations provided them with the economic means to make these purchases, and both had security challenges for which the weapons would provide a needed deterrent. China's border conflicts in the past had included those with Vietnam and Tibet, but the Uighur minority in the far west of China had committed violent acts in Beijing and were seemingly wrapped up with Islamic fundamentalist values that conflicted with the official atheism of the Chinese Communist Party. India's main defense needs included the constant focus on Pakistan. The mountainous Kashmir region that borders both was a periodic source of contention between them, and each nation maintained a military presence there. In 2009, terrorists from Pakistan invaded Mumbai from the sea and took 175 lives at such locations as the Taj Hotel. Also, Prime Minister Rajiv Ghandi was assassinated in the south of India in 1991, as conflict with nearby Sri Lanka flooded across the border.

Russia also developed links with Pakistan during NATO's military operations in neighboring Afghanistan. Visits and talks focused on Russian concerns about Taliban movements across borders and were aimed at reducing the impact of the group that Western countries had targeted in Afghanistan (Black 2004, 315). Taliban members found sanctuary in Pakistan, at times simply waited there until the weather permitted a return to the battlefields of Afghanistan.

Turkey was not an Asian nation, but it did impact Central Asian nations and thereby Russian interests. Turkey's desire for access to Central Asian energy supplies collided with Russian interests, in particular when the Baku–Tbilsi–Ceyhan pipeline by-passed Russian territory. Part of the motive was to avoid the troubled Caucasus republics of southwestern Russia, but Russia perceived Turkish interests as combining with U.S. objectives to limit Russia's influence in its traditional backyard in that area (Goldman 2009, 22). The fact that Turkey was a long-standing NATO member aroused Russian concerns even further.

Russia and Asian alliance networks

There are several regional alliances in which Russia has a part and aims to provide a guiding role. They include the CIS, the Asia-Pacific Economic Community (APEC), the BRICS (Brazil, Russia, India, China, South Africa), the Collective Security Treaty Organization (CSTO), the Shanghai Cooperation Organization (SCO), the Eurasian Economic Community, and a Customs Union.

The CIS was the immediate successor to the USSR, and its sweep had at one point included all five of the Central Asian states. Soon after Putin became president, he paid official CIS visits to Turkmenistan and Kazakhstan, and he made an agreement with the former about purchasing its natural gas. His visit to Uzbekistan resulted in discussions about how to control the extremists within its midst (Black 2004, 281–285). There was also a security component connected with this organization that became clear with the announcement of the Ivanov Doctrine in October 2003. Minister of Defense Sergei Ivanov stated that Russia would consider pre-emptive military strikes to guard the security of the Central Asian states (Goldman 2009, 29). Perhaps this was a way of countering the announcement of the Bush administration during the previous year that pre-emptive strikes were now on the American agenda. The Ivanov Doctrine followed President Bush's implementation of the similar doctrine in Iraq by only six months.

APEC was a large alliance that included all the nations bordering on the Pacific Ocean. Therefore it included Russia and many Asian nations, but also Canada, the United States, and a few Latin American countries. Its annual meetings provided a forum for discussion, and Russia had an opportunity at those meetings to meet with Asian partners for open discussions about future relationships. In 2012 Russia hosted the APEC meeting in Vladivostok, and part of the motivation was to get Siberia and eastern Russian elites to look east and south at a time when there was a preoccupation on the western flank with topics like EU expansion and the Missile Shield proposal. In addition, President Medvedev observed that Russia was deeply involved in developing its high-tech sector, a specialization that it would define as part of the Asia-Pacific market (Sotiriou 2015, 183).

Economic significance also played a large role in Russia's participation in the BRICS framework and meetings. Russia had an opportunity to discuss options with the Asian powers of India and China, but also with Brazil and South Africa. The main cohesive feature of this organization was the willingness of each partner to rely on a higher degree of central planning of the economy than most Western states such as the United States and is European partners would incorporate. Of course, there were exceptions, for Russia had moved to some components of a free-market system after 1991 and China had incorporated free-market principles after Mao's death in 1976. Coastal cities such as Shanghai were permitted to establish trade relations with Western nations, and this shift had much to do with the dramatic upsurge in the Chinese economy in ensuing decades.

Russia envisioned the CSTO as an eastern counterpart or balancing force to NATO, but it would require considerable time and development to get to that point. Through this organization, Russia is able to offer security guarantees to the Central Asian nations in return for access to their energy resources (Baev 2008, 72). The organization actually emerged in May 2002, after a founding meeting in Chisanau, Moldova, and there was a direct relationship between its founding and the regional turmoil that developed after 9/11. Through it, the Central Asian nations would have a protective barrier against violence that might spill over from Afghanistan, Iraq, and Iran (White 2011, 296). In that way, it could help to counteract the spread of extreme Islam, and it would serve the national interests of Russia as well as of its Central Asian partners (Goldman 2009, 15). That would be a better outcome for Russia than the results that it had feared, at the beginning of its own Afghan War, that Central Asia might succumb to the pressures flowing out of revolutionary Iran.

The SCO was born in 2001, and counter-terrorism was clearly one of its defining features (Gleason 2013, 261). The organization included Russia, China, Kyrgyzstan, Kazakhstan, and Tajikistan, and four years later, in 2005, it granted observer status to India, Pakistan, Iran, and Mongolia. Thus, it offered the potential to be a broad-based and heavily Russian influenced security organization in the region as well as a kind of Asian counterpart to NATO in the West. In 2007 the SCO held military exercises that sent a message that there existed a balancing force to the heavy NATO involvement in Afghanistan (White 2011, 304). After the 2008 Georgian War, Moscow requested that the SCO endorse Russian tactics in the battle. However, the organization voted for a neutral stand on the war, in part in order to stay on reasonable terms with the United States (Goldman 2009, 199).

Two organizations with a primary economic focus were also linked to the Russian pivot towards Asia. One was the Eurasian Economic Community, an organization formed in fall 2000 and very inclusive in terms of former Soviet space. Four of the Central Asian states (Turkmenistan was the exception) became members, as well as Russia and Belarus. Geographically, they comprised 99% of CIS territory, and the organization itself had a security as well as an economic role (White 2011, 294; Gleason 2013, 261). The Customs Union initially was a technique for knitting together the economies of Russia and Belarus, while its critics suggested that it was a forerunner to the recreation of the Soviet Union. Later, the organization took on an Asian aspect with the addition of Kazakhstan, Kyrgyzstan, and Tajikistan.

At times, personal diplomacy brought the Russian leadership together with a group of state leaders with a common interest in resolving a dilemma. One such meeting occurred in Astrakhan in southern Russia, close to the Caspian Sea. With the discovery of oil beneath the sea, it became very difficult for the littoral nations to agree on what constituted the territorial sea over which each had fundamental control. In the early fall of 2014 President Putin hosted the heads of government of Iran, Kazakhstan, Turkmenistan, and Azerbaijan. They discussed global conditions, relations among the nations bordering on the Caspian Sea, and demarking borders in the Caspian Sea. In the end, they agreed to establish an inner and an outer zone in the sea. The inner zone was under the control of the respective state that bordered it, and the outer zone each state had primary fishing rights of twenty-five nautical miles (*Izvestia* 2014).

In conclusion, the pivot to Asia assumed many faces rather than simply that of the single head of the eagle facing to the East. Engagement with Chinese economic success was a driving force behind the turn to the East. However, preserving carefully calibrated relations with the five Central Asian republics, India, and Pakistan played a significant role as well. The multiplication of political, security, and economic organizations over several decades provided the framework for Russia's extended connections. However, it would be difficult to predict how deeply those organizations would be involved in resolving key policy issues or how much of a management role Russia would play in them.

America: the single-headed eagle looks west

Even though America was preoccupied with Iraq, Afghanistan, and Ukraine in 2011, and again in 2014, President Obama called for a pivot to Asia. In part, there were renewed dangers such as that posed by North Korea, but there were also economic opportunities and expanded markets with the strengthening economies in China and India (Kay 2015, 155–156). With the strong American military presence in Japan, there was continued preoccupation with its policies and future challenges. Links to Taiwan were an inheritance from the Chinese communist victory on the mainland in 1949, while relations with Pakistan were under the heavy influence of unending challenges in the Afghan War. Conflict brewed in the South China Sea, and this brought the U.S. into a common front with Vietnam, the Philippines, Malaysia, and others. Thus, the American agenda in Asia bore some degree of commonality with Russian aims, but also differed in scope.

Conflict with North Korea

With American troops located in South Korea as a deterrent to North Korean aggression, any military tension between the two Koreas drew in the United States and required a show of solidarity with its southern ally. In 2010, forty-six South Korean sailors lost their lives after North Korea sunk one of their ships with a torpedo. The Kim Jong-il regime in the North claimed that the ship had violated its territorial waters, but proof for that assertion was uncertain. The response from Seoul later in the year entailed live-fire exercises in the direction of the North, and America sent more forces there in a show of force. The transition at the end of 2011 to the new North Korean dictator, Kim Jong-un, intensified the militancy of the north. For example, in 2013 North Korea tested long-range missiles that could reach the United States. By 2015 North Korea had the fourth-largest military in the world, with 1.9 million active troops. South Korea possessed only 655,000, and so the 28,500 from the United States helped to balance the power equation on the peninsula (Kay 2015, 152–154). President Bush had listed the regime in the North as one of the threats on the Axis of Evil in 2002, and probably that perception of the situation did not change much through the Obama administration.

In February 2016 South Korea decided to halt cooperative work on North Korean territory to construct a huge, jointly run industrial park. North Korea reacted quickly by declaring that it would turn over the entire site to its military. Earlier in the month the regime had fired a long-range rocket that seemed to be part of development of its missile technology. America responded somewhat later with low flights by four of its F-22 stealth fighters over South Korea and commenced discussions with its ally about deployment of the Terminal

High-Altitude Area Defense. Additionally, the joint military drills later in the spring were to be the largest ever (*USA Today* 2016a). Thus, the pivot to Asia was partly based on security needs, even though the Cold War threat from China had abated.

China and India

Beginning in the aftermath of the 9/11 attack on the World Trade Center, Chinese–American relations began to improve. China's leader, Jiang Zemin, visited the United States in 2002 and supportive public statements were made about their bilateral relationship by American leaders such as Secretary of State Colin Powell. China was willing to support the American invasion of Afghanistan, but not that of Iraq. China did not veto UN resolutions for the reconstruction of Iraq, and in 2007 it signed agreements with Iraq itself for cooperation in human resource training, economic cooperation, and technical cooperation. For its part, the Bush administration toned down criticism of China on the issues connected with Taiwan, Tibet, and its missile sales. President Bush also visited China in 2002, and that provided an opportunity for further discussions about the future of the relationship (McCormick 2010, 224–226). Of course, China has been forceful in its trade policy, and by 2005 the U.S. had a $200 billion deficit with China (Jentleson 2007, 326). A symbolic event occurred in 2015, when China surpassed Germany and Japan to become the second-largest global economy, behind only the U.S. Although China worked to build up its trade links with America beyond what they were, it also expanded trade ties to Japan, South Korea, and Australia. That resulted in making the U.S. pivot to Asia even more challenging (Kay 2015, 121–124).

American policy has also focused on India, in the hope that it will become a reliable anchor in an improving relationship with China. The mutual work with India has included projects that nurture it in the direction of peaceful nuclear development (Kay 2015, 150). However, support for India also include the U.S. role as chief arms supplier to India (Kay 2015, 168). It was the hope of the U.S. to build on this security relationship to develop expanded trade ties that would be of mutual benefit to both powers.

Japan, Taiwan, and Pakistan

Japan achieved enormous economic success with a dynamic trade policy in earlier decades, but its economic primacy in Asia suffered with the economic rise of China and India and their trade ties with the West. In 2015 there were still 38,000 American troops in Japan, mainly as a deterrent against a thrust from North Korea. However, in 2010 Japan enunciated a new defense strategy that focused more on the threat from China against islands that were contested between the two nations (Kay 2015, 123). There were also tensions with the U.S. over the presence of so many American troops in Okinawa, especially after scandals about crimes committed against Japanese youth by American soldiers. However, trade ties between Japan and the U.S. remained strong, and Japanese automobiles on every road in America were a reminder of that fact.

Taiwan was a small nation that America continued to treat in a protective way. Its leadership had come to Taiwan from the mainland after losing the civil war in China in 1949. Further, it had lost its position in the UN in the early 1970, since both Chinas still claimed rights to the territory of the other. It had been one of the Asian tigers that boomed economically in the 1990s, and thus trade relations with the U.S. remained robust and part of any American pivot to Asia. Although the risk of war between the two Chinas was remote, the warmth of their relationship depended heavily on the outcome of elections in Taiwan. After several years of overtures by the reformist leadership in Taiwan, the 2016 elections put leaders into power who were skeptical of such initiatives.

Pakistan was a critical but sometimes complicated partner of the United States in the regional war on terrorism. It had joined the nuclear club at the same time as India in 1998, and the result was the imposition of sanctions. After the 9/11 attacks, America lifted the sanctions on India and instead provided economic and security assistance that totaled $3.5 billion in the plan for 2009–14 (Hook 204, 381). However, there was considerable tension between the United States and Pakistan over prosecution of the war in Afghanistan. Taliban forces continued to find sanctuary in the northwestern corner of Pakistan, and the national government had never really been able to establish controls in that area. During the Obama administration drone attacks took place on the Pakistani side of the border and some civilian lives were lost. At one point, Pakistan raised the cost of transportation of needed goods and military equipment through its territory, such that America sought other routes. Finally, the discovery that bin Laden had been living in a relatively visible area of Pakistan for some time intensified American concerns about the reliability of ISI, the Pakistani intelligence service (Kay 2015, 150).

Trouble in the South China Sea

One challenge for America in the general overture to Asia has been continuing provocations from China in the sea off its coast. In the background to the recent expansion by the Chinese navy in "far sea defense" (Kay 2015, 126) are the examples of American military activities in other theaters. Chinese leaders were concerned that the American Missile Shield proposal would undermine China's nuclear deterrent, and so they expanded their own ICBM development. Having watched the use of American military capabilities in Kosovo and Iraq, China worked on expanding its MIRV capabilities as well. Its long-range missiles could hit U.S. cities, while short-range ones had Taiwan within their scope. In 2011, China sent a naval vessel to be stationed off the coast of Libya during the NATO air attacks on Gadhafi's forces (Kay 2015, 126–128).

Energy needs in part drove China's heightened interest having in more control in the South China Sea. In 2014 it moved a huge oil rig close to the Paracel Islands, which Vietnam claimed were over its continental shelf and exclusive economic zone. After protests and the dispatch to the site of thirty Vietnamese coastguard and fisheries vessels, China pulled the rig back in the summer of that year (*USA Today* 2014c). Partly in response to the new Chinese aggressiveness, President Obama portrayed the U.S. as a better partner for Africa on his four-day trip to that continent a year later. He indirectly portrayed China as seeking to exploit African resources while American efforts centered on contributions to continental development as well (*New York Times* 2015a). Later, in the fall, China's agenda shifted to military construction on reclaimed islands in the South China Sea.

At an APEC summit meeting in the Philippines, Obama called on China to stop that construction and submit the issue to arbitration among the nations of Southeast Asia (*New York Times* 2015b). Terrorism was also on the agenda of the Association of Southeast Asian Nations (ASEAN) summit two days later, due to the recent attacks in Paris, Lebanon, and Mali (*USA Today* 2015d). Shortly thereafter, the United States and Japan commenced a large military training exercise in the seas south of Japan. There were thirty warships and many planes involved in the exercise, and it was in part a message to China that there was sharp disagreement about Chinese claims to territorial control of those waters (*USA Today* 2015e). In December 2015 the Pentagon flew two B-52 bombers near contested islands, and this led China to call for an end to provocative actions (*USA Today* 2015f). Early in the new year, the U.S. sent the guided missile destroyer USS *Curtis Wilbur* near the islands under the label of a "freedom of navigation operation" (*USA Today* 2016b). President Obama hosted an ASEAN in southern California in mid-February 2016 and China was certainly on the agenda, although not represented there. The ASEAN leaders had become more suspicious of Chinese motives, due to the recent conflicts in the South China Sea. President Obama offered the alternative of his Trans-Pacific Partnership (TPP) as another choice on the table (*New York Times* 2016a). President Obama's opening-day speech called for the development of "accountable institutions," and he encouraged the others to work towards an international order in which global rules such as freedom of navigation were upheld (*USA Today* 2016c). Although the joint statement at the end of the summit did not mention the aggressive actions of China in the South China Sea (*USA Today* 2016d), China sent a message on the last day of the conference by deploying surface-to-air missile launchers on Woody Island in the contested Paracel Islands. That is an island that China, Vietnam, and Taiwan all claim as their rightful territory (*USA Today* 2016e).

Overall, hope dominated over fears in the projected pivot to Asia during the Obama administration. Prospects for expanded trade benefits were particularly high in the overtures to China and India, but they were also meaningful for ties with Taiwan, South Korea, and Japan. Security issues did exist with Pakistan, but they were likely to fade with the end of the war in Afghanistan. The biggest threat clearly was the one from North Korea, but an emerging threat existed in the tension with China over its claims in the South China Sea. However, multilateral diplomacy was occurring for each of those two threats, with six-party talks on the Korean issue and ASEAN discussions on China's hostile moves. In the background was the American–Russian rivalry and the question of how much their tensions on other issues would carry over to the Asian setting.

Conclusion: how the two Asian pivots are anchored in theory

Given how parallel American and Russian efforts are to develop a strong Asian policy focus, it is not surprising that Balance of Power Theory and Multi-Polar Theory are useful explanatory tools. The first theory underlines the competitive nature of both sets of initiatives toward Asia, as there would be a clear imbalance between them if only one moved in that direction. The second theory factors in all the new/old players that now become more significant. After fighting a long war in Southeast Asia, the American leaders now seek to cultivate a relationship with Vietnam. Russia finds itself more engaged with a number of medium-sized nations that are part of the new alliances that have formed in recent years. The Model of Critical Junctures is also pertinent, for each of the two major powers sought a fresh start in the East after much frustration and difficulty further west. The efforts of each set of leaders to direct the policy of their states in a changed direction reflect the Realist Model, for furtherance of national interests was at the heart of the two sets of strategies.

A new Asian-based Balance of Power between Russia and America would be an achievement in light of the sharp imbalance that existed at the time of the collapse of the Soviet Union. It may be that the struggles of America in Afghanistan and Iraq wore the edge off its temporary superiority, and it is possible that Russia's oil wealth enabled it to move up a few steps on the ladder of global power in the early years of the twenty-first century. It would be no small task to preserve a balance between the two in the East in future decades. What kinds of advantages would each obtain in their work with China to cultivate mutual relationships? Would alliances such as ASEAN for the U.S. and SCO for Russia become rivals that would enable both Russia and the United States to extend their influence through broader organizations?

Multi-Polar Theory in the Asian sense entails doing business with nations that may have been partners in the past but that may have declined in importance to the two powers during the heavy preoccupation with the consequences of 9/11, the Arab Spring, and the Ukrainian crisis. For both Russia and America, the heavy emphasis on more tightly knit relationships with both India and China was long overdue. Past experiences such as the Sino-Soviet Split and America's long-standing concerns about human rights protections in China yielded to the new reality of China's enormous economic prospects. Cold War rivalry between the Soviet Union and America for the cultivation of India now took on a new form in the economic arena rather than the political one. In light of their strategic location and energy resources, the five Central Asian republics have gained in importance for both powers. They have provided assistance to the United States in its nearby wars, and they draw Russia's attention as nations such as Turkey and India seek to establish trade ties in Central Asia.

The Model of Critical Junctures is a tempting choice in the sense that both nations sought to put troubles in the West behind them and have something of a fresh start in, or at least renewed emphasis on Asia. Economic successes in China and India were not likely to stagnate very much, and there would be a need to develop a meaningful strategy that worked to the benefit of both Russia and America. With the continued provocations by the North Korean regime, the six-party framework that included both Russia and America would remain vital and significant for regional stability. However, there was no guarantee that the western quagmires would disappear and release both Russia and America to do something entirely different. NATO mobilization to protect the Baltics, Poland, and Ukraine from unexpected future Russian moves would continue to require a sharp focus by Moscow. For America, there was a lingering obligation to assist Afghanistan in its pursuit of stability. For both Russia and America, the Arab Spring's outcome in Syria was very draining. Each was heavily involved in the military campaign against ISIS, but their different approaches and perspectives about who was the main enemy or ally did generate conflict between them.

The Realist Model offers a hopeful message to national leaders that it is still possible to design national policy in a controlled and rational way, even when pressures flow in across their borders in an uncontrolled way. For example, their policies in the West floundered in light of the massive movement of refugees from Syria across the national borders of many countries. How could both Russia and American help to defeat ISIS more quickly, so that the flow of refugees would begin to ebb? It was difficult to operate within the framework of the Realist Model in that setting. Would it be more possible in the Asian theater? Refugee movements, difficult civil wars, and Islamic extremist violence were less characteristic of Asia, and so the two states might have the chance to set and follow clear policies that would underpin their own national interests.

Overall, the pivot to Asia was promising for the political leaders of both countries. The conflict between them over NATO expansion, the Missile Shield proposal, the Russian take-over of the Crimea, and their sharply diverging strategies over the nature of the Syrian civil war did not have Asian counterparts. Both understood the dangers of the North Korean regime, and both could compete on even ground for a share of deeper trade ties with China and India. The latter two had such enormous populations that multiple trade partners were a realistic proposition. It is likely that the relatively new regional organizations would be a positive development as well, for Russia and America would need to negotiate with multiple smaller alliance partners and work to protect their interests as well. This would be as true for the American-inspired TPP as it would be for the Russian-initiated CSTO. There would undoubtedly be collisions between Moscow and Washington in Asia, but they might be less pronounced and engulfing that the unending challenges in the West.

10

The Ukrainian crisis to the center of the stage in 2014 and after: a game-changing earthquake in the relationship

Introduction

The eruption of the Ukrainian crisis and the associated annexation of the Crimea in 2014 marked a sharp setback in the American–Russian relationship. The 2014 Winter Olympics took place in the Black Sea resort of Sochi, in Russia, between the start of the Euromaidan demonstrations in Kiev that eventually deposed the ethnic Russian President Viktor Yanukovych on February 22, 2014 and the Russian annexation of the Crimea on March 18, 2014. The Russian government had allocated $50 billion to construction of the Olympic site, for Sochi had not previously been a winter sports venue. Prior to the opening ceremony, attention centered on threats from extremists to disrupt the games, and President Putin himself spent much time in Sochi to reassure all involved that the safety of all was guaranteed. As might be expected, the opening ceremony was replete with depictions of great events and personages from the Russian past. How did such a celebration give way to civil war in the Ukraine, and probably the most intense conflict between Russia and America since the Cold War?

First, it is important to look at the evolution of the Ukraine after independence in 1991, but it is also vital to examine the role and power of the Crimean Republic within that nation. Second, it is necessary to elucidate the main features of the double-barreled crisis that afflicted Ukraine throughout 2014. Third, Russia played a central role throughout the crisis, and it is necessary to understand and also to evaluate its policies. The fourth necessity is to outline and assess how the United States and other Western nations reacted to the perceived provocations in the East. While the shooting in the civil war died down in 2015, the unanswered questions and accusations did not.

The political development of the Ukraine and its Crimean Republic

Historically, the Ukraine was of great symbolic importance in the evolution of the Russian Empire. The small geographic area of Kievan Rus' was the seed from which the gigantic Russian Empire grew. Further, the area's conversion to Orthodox Christianity occurred in the Crimean Peninsula, when Prince Vladimir was baptized into Eastern Orthodoxy in 988 and declared that this would be a better religion for his people than the Jewish faith, Roman Catholicism, or Islam (Kalb 2015, 28–33). In 1791 Catherine the Great's forces wrested the Crimea from the Ottoman Empire and made it part of Russia until Khrushchev attached it to the Ukrainian Republic in 1954 (Kalb 2015, 57–58). General Suvorov (1730–1800) had defeated the Turkish fortress at Ismail, and the two empires signed the Treaty of Jassy in 1791. The Russians celebrated Catherine's conquests by adopting their first state anthem, "Let the thunder of victory sound!" in which they identified her as the "gentle mother of us all, the Brilliant Empress" (Giles 2016).

After gaining independence in 1991, the Ukraine had a number of key issues to settle with Russia, one of which was the distribution of military capabilities between the states. In the 1994 Budapest Agreement, Ukraine gave up its nuclear arsenal to Russia in return for cheap fuel sales from Russia for its nuclear power plants. In the 1997 Friendship Treaty or "Big Treaty," the Black Sea Fleet was divided up, with 82% going to Russia and 18% to Ukraine (Kalb 2015, 121–123). Ukraine did get sovereignty over all of the Crimea, but Russia kept its naval base at Sevastopol for the next twenty years. In return for the base, Russia lowered the price of natural gas sales to the Ukraine (Malgin 2014, 1).

In 1996, the Ukraine wrote a constitution that set up a federal system, but one that provided for an "asymmetric institutional autonomy arrangement in Crimea" (Sasse 2002, 70). There would be twenty-four republics in the Ukraine, but the status of Crimea would be that of a special republic. Sevastopol, in the Crimea would have the same special "republican jurisdiction" that the Ukrainian capital Kiev enjoyed (Sasse 2002, 73). The reality was that Kiev unexpectedly interfered with the Crimea's jurisdiction in several key episodes in the 1990s. For example, in March 1995 the Ukrainian secret services were unhappy with the Crimean President Meshkov and removed him from power. In 1998, President Kuchma of Ukraine reduced both the power of local authorities and local autonomy in the Crimea in an effort to stamp out criminal clans on the Peninsula (Malgin 2014, 1). Thereby, the Crimea's special rights appeared to be stronger on paper than in reality.

In 1996, the Crimea itself wrote a constitution for the Peninsula in which it identified its role as that of a special or autonomous republic within the Ukraine with its own representative assembly and executive branch. Following the elections of 1998, it revised that constitution and the new one came into effect on December 23, 1996 (Sasse 2002, 93–94).

On the one hand, the new constitution required that Crimean decisions must conform to those in Ukraine as a whole. The President of Ukraine had the power to suspend any acts of the Crimean Supreme Rada that did not conform to the Ukrainian constitution and its laws. Further, the Constitutional Court of Ukraine had the power to resolve any conflicts that emerged from such situations, while the Ukrainian president was empowered to repeal undesirable decisions that the Crimean Council of Ministers made.

On the other hand, the Crimean government had considerable powers as well. It controlled the protected city of Sevastopol, made any future territorial decisions through a referendum, and empowered the legislature to approve or disapprove referendum results. The Crimea had the right to decide what its emblem, flag, and anthem would be. In light of the fact that the majority of the Crimean population spoke Russian, that was the language used in all official communications. Birth certificates would be published in both Ukrainian and Russian, while each minority retained the right to educate its children in its own language. Legal documents would be in the state language, Ukrainian, but those who wanted to have them in Russian could obtain them in that language. With the return of so many Tatars from Central Asia, that people also received the right to receive documents in Crimean Tatar (Constitution of the Autonomous Republic of Crimea, July 10, 2014).

Ukrainian crisis of 2014

Ukrainian President Viktor Yanukovych had been narrowly elected in a close race with Julia Timoshenko in 2010, after losing to the Orange Revolution candidate Viktor Yushchenko in the problematic 2004–5 elections. Yanukovych, who was ethnically Russian, angered many by making one of his first visits after his inauguration to Russia. Soon he signed an agreement that gave the Russian Navy permission to use its base a Sevastopol for twenty more years after the expiration of the 1997 Treaty in 2017. In return the Russians agreed once again to reduce the price of natural gas deliveries to Ukraine. Pro-Russian policies such as this contributed to many Ukrainians lack of receptivity to one more economic deal with Russia when, in early 2014, Yanukovych negotiated with Russia for a $15 billion loan for use in economic development in difficult times.

Many Ukrainians had been hoping for an overture to the West and the EU instead of to Russia. During the Euromaidan demonstrations in Kiev the protestors made those expectations clear. Yanukovych responded by sending in the troops, with the result that one hundred people lost their lives. The results for Yanukovych were immediate, for he was forced from office, went into hiding, then escaped by helicopter into the Crimea, and eventually ended up in exile near Rostov in southwest Russia.

At the time of the Sochi Olympics there was much tension in the Crimea, for the 60% Russian majority were demanding a referendum that would ask citizens if they would be better off being part of Russia rather than the Ukraine. The newly appointed leaders in the Crimea permitted the holding of a referendum as allowed under the constitution. The new leadership in Kiev was only temporary, for an appointed president and prime minister had replaced the elected Yanukovych government. Troops from Russia entered the Crimea and worked with their counterparts at the base in Sevastopol to create the climate for a pro-Russian vote in the referendum, the result of which was that an overwhelming majority chose Russia over the Ukraine. Eventually, the Russian troops surrounded each of the Ukrainian bases in the Crimea and took them all under control. Some Ukrainian military personnel in the Crimea joined up with the Russian military, while others to relocate back to the Ukraine or to retire into civilian jobs in the Crimea. President Putin introduced legislation to make the Crimea into a Russian republic. A currency transition to the Russian ruble and other practical matters began soon thereafter.

Soon the separatist emotions spread to other cities in the predominantly Russian cities of eastern Ukraine. Battles raged in the Ukraine's industrial heartland in cities such as Luhansk and Donetsk. Russia engaged in a show of force along the Ukrainian border, and tens of thousands of troops massed in a show of support for their embattled Russian brethren in eastern Ukraine. Western leaders were chagrined by all of this and imposed economic sanctions on key businesses and individuals in Russia who were responsible for stirring up the buzzing hornets' nest. The Ukraine held formal elections in May 2014 and Petro Poroshenko became president (Kalb 2015, 183). He had been an independent businessman who had made considerable wealth in the chocolate business in a corruption-free way. He reached out to all sides in the Ukraine and continued to assert that the Crimea was justly part of the Ukraine.

In the summer of 2014, hostilities intensified to the point that the casualty count included several hundred deaths and more than 1,000 wounded. By fall of that year, the casualties had mounted to over 3,000. Russian militias took over government buildings in important cities, but Ukrainian troops moved in to free them. Russian rebels successfully shot down several planes used by the Ukrainian military. In the midst of all of this turmoil, nearly 300 people lost their lives when a surface-to-air missile brought down a Malaysian airliner on its way from Amsterdam to Kuala Lumpur. Evidence pointed to responsibility by Russian militias in eastern Ukraine, and the impact of the tragedy brought home to a global audience the importance of stopping the conflict in Ukraine. It took more than a year for a report to be issued about the evidence of responsibility for the incident. There had been many passengers of Dutch nationality on board the plane, and so it was the Dutch Safety Board that eventually issued its report on October 13, 2015. The report stated clearly that a Russian-made Buk missile was responsible for the downing of the airplane and the deaths of so many people (*USA Today* 2015g).

The crisis and civil war in Ukraine continued, even though the Crimea remained firmly in Russian hands. In mid-February 2015 there were clashes between the contested city of Debaltseve and the regime-controlled city of Artemivsk in Ukraine in which enough Ukrainian soldiers were wounded to require the dispatch of ten ambulances. These clashes had resulted from artillery shooting and small-arms fire from the Russian side (*Dagensnyheter* 2015c). A few days later there were charges and counter-charges. The Russian separatist troops claimed that they had pulled back their heavy weapons from eastern Ukraine, but the Ukrainian government stated that that was not the case. The February 2015 Minsk Summit, at which the leaders of Russia, Ukraine, Germany, and France all met, called for a pullback by all forces, but violations were clearly occurring (*USA Today* 2015h). A month later, in March, the Russian separatists in the east threatened to abandon the Minsk-inspired ceasefire, due to discontent over legislative amendments enacted in Kiev. Those amendments undermined the original promise of the Ukrainian government to grant special status to Donetsk and Luhansk. The issue between the two sides concerned the relationship between the law on autonomy and elections. The parliament in Kiev had passed the promised law providing for the autonomy of the eastern territories, but had added an amendment requiring them to hold elections approved by Kiev before receiving the special rights. The separatist leaders resisted such control by the central government, for it would give Kiev the right to approve of or disapprove their leaders (*USA Today* 2015i).

Evidence of violations of the Minsk Protocol surfaced again in May and June, for six Ukrainian soldiers died in the continuing conflict that should have ended after the Minsk meetings. Both sides should have pulled their forces back to an agreed-upon line of demarcation but certainly had not done so (*SME* 2015c). The governments in Moscow and Kiev then traded accusations about who was responsible for violating the ceasefire, while President Poroshenko stated that he was prepared for even more attacks (*USA Today* 2015j).

Prime Minister Arseniy Yatsenyuk of the Ukraine announced in the midst of all of this that the government had approved and sent to the president the Ukraine–NATO Annual National Program, and it included five key points. The Ukrainian military needed to meet the alliance's standards in communications modernization and exchange of information. There was also a focus on re-training activities and the socialization of military personnel. Physical rehabilitation of wounded soldiers was another priority, and modernization of logistics yet another. Cooperation between NATO and the Ukraine on cyber defense was the final pillar on which both parties should be active. In sum, the Program would buttress the military capabilities of the Ukraine and serve as a kind of deterrent against Russian separatists (Government Portal Ukraine, February 18, 2015). No doubt this link between the Ukraine and NATO would widen the split between Kiev and Moscow.

There were mixed signals in the fall of 2015 about prospects for stability in the Ukraine's relations with territories on it border. In September ethnic Tatars blocked roads into the Crimea and cut off supplies of food, electricity, and gas. The organizers said it was not in the Ukraine's interest to support Russian power. The impact was more symbolic than substantive, for the Crimea received only 5% of its supplies from the Ukraine (*USA Today* 2015k). Later discussions between the Ukraine and the Crimea did result in the partial restoration of electricity supplies to Crimea at the end of the year. The Cherson District in the Ukraine had been particularly hard hit and would benefit from the restored supply (*SME* 2015d). At the time of Vice President Biden's visit to the Ukraine in December 2015 discussions centered on the increase in small-arms fire in November and December. Observers noted that there had been a lull in the fighting in October, the month in which Russia was lobbying for support in its air campaign in Syria. The renewal of shooting at the end of the year put in jeopardy the fulfilment of the Minsk Accord, which called for an end to hostilities by the end of the year (*USA Today* 2015l).

Russian initiatives and responses in the crisis

Russian leaders played a central role in the origins and evolution of the Ukrainian crisis. President Medvedev welcomed the election victory of Viktor Yanukovych in 2010 and invited him to Moscow soon after his inauguration. It was President Putin who offered the $15 billion loan at the beginning of the crisis, in an effort to wean the Ukraine away from the temptation to move closer to the EU. Following the Maidan riots and the resignation and hasty departure of Yanukovych from Kiev in February 2014, the Russians assisted his escape into exile in southwestern Russia and enabled him to broadcast several messages back into the Ukraine from there. In terms of the Crimean referendum, even President Putin admitted that troops were sent from Russia to assist in the take-over of the Peninsula and to wrest the military bases away from Ukrainian troops. Following the Crimean referendum President Putin quickly presented a proposal to the Russian Duma to make the Peninsula into a new republic in Russia, and legislative agreement came very quickly. Certainly, part of Russia's motivation stemmed from its desire to hold on to the naval base at Sevastopol from which a number of ships had departed during the Russo-Georgian War of 2008 (Kalb 2015, xii–xix).

On March 18, 2014, President Putin gave a powerful speech in which he couched the absorption of Crimea in terms of the glory of Russian history. He cited the Kievan origins of the Russian Empire and remarked that Russia and the Ukraine were thus one with each other. He mentioned the role of Prince Vladimir in bringing the Orthodox faith to Russia, and the long battle against Nazi Germany in World War II. Not only was the church that commemorated Vladimir's conversion in the Crimea, but so also was the monument that celebrated the point at which Ukrainians began to push back the Nazis from their control in the Soviet Union. Much applause greeted his evocation of Russian historical themes, and he repeated many of them in a May 9 speech marking the victory over the Nazis.

A few days after the official annexation of the Crimea, fighting broke out in the ethnically Russian sector of eastern Ukraine. Russian insurgents took over government buildings in key cities such as Donetsk, Kharkiv, Slaviansk, Mariupol, and Odessa. Following the example of the Crimea, separatists declared the existence of the Luhansk People's Republic, the Donetsk People's Republic, and the Odessa People's Republic (Kalb 2015, 19–27). It is unclear how many troops from Russia took part in the battles with the Ukrainian military, but evidence pointed to a significant number. The leadership in Moscow claimed that these were loyal Russian soldiers who had chosen to use their leave time to fight alongside their fellow Russians in eastern Ukraine, but many assumed that Russia had a more direct hand in the fighting. In the midst of the budding civil war, combatants mistakenly shot down the Malaysian airliner, and the two sides traded accusations about which side was responsible. However, the tragedy would not have occurred had Russia not stoked the aspirations of the Russian separatists in eastern Ukraine.

During the following year, 2015, Russia continued to flex its muscles in order both to defend its role in Ukrainian policy outcomes and to extend its influence with other nations involved in the discussions. For example, Russian Foreign Minister Sergei Lavrov visited Slovakia in March to hold talks with President Kiska. It was unclear whether he would also meet with Prime Minister Robert Fico, who had criticized Russia for violating international law in the Crimea. Lavrov had originally accepted the invitation to visit and to help the Slovaks commemorate the seventieth anniversary of their liberation from the Nazis (*SME* 2015e). More commemorations of that anniversary were approaching, but President Putin did not issue an invitation to the Ukraine's President Poroshenko to attend the May 9 events in Moscow. A number of invited leaders such as Prime Minister David Cameron from the United Kingdom, EU President Donald Tusk, Slovak President Andrej Kiska, and German Chancellor Angela Merkel decided not to attend. Thirty leaders accepted invitations, and these included the leaders of Cuba, North Korea, China, South Africa, and the Czech Republic (*SME* 2015f). The Slovak Prime Minister Robert Fico did go to Moscow to attend the events, but the Slovak President did not..

Following new EU sanctions imposed on Russia in June 2015, President Putin visited Italy in order to test European unity on those penalties. He

pointed out that the sanctions had cost Italy one billion euros in defense contracts, and he also denied that it was Russia that had violated the Minsk agreements, and instead pointed the finger at the Ukraine. A visit to the popular
Pope Francis in Rome was also on Putin's agenda (*New York Times* 2015c).
At this time, a Russian naval warship appeared in the Baltic Sea off the
coast of Lithuania in a minor show of force. The ostensible goal was to
make it more difficult for Lithuania to free itself from dependence on Russian
energy supplies by constructing cables to the electricity grids in Sweden (*New
York Times* 2015d). As Russia prepared to commemorate the June 22 Day
of Memory and Sorrow, the EU announced additional sanctions that would
restrict the access of Russian corporations to Western capital markets. The
Russians reacted with great anger to the announcement on such an important
day (*New York Times* 2015e).

In July, Russian military exercises along the Ukrainian border had become
commonplace and undermined pronouncements by Moscow of a pullback.
The Russians stockpiled ammunition near the border and dispatched coal
trucks and stolen cars across the border at various points (*New York Times*
2015f). A little more than a year after the Malaysian airliner crash, the UN
brought voted on a resolution to set up a tribunal to prosecute those responsible for bringing down the airliner. Predictably, Russia vetoed that resolution
(*New York Times* 2015g). In spite of the veto, Russia emphasized the importance of spreading international cooperation (*Izvestia* 2015a). At about the
same time President Putin's press secretary, Dmitry Peskov, denounced new
American sanctions as a blow to the bilateral relationship and threatened asymmetrical counter-measures (*Izvestia* 2015b, 2015c).

The conflict in eastern Ukraine took another twist in August of 2015, for
there were bloody battles and disappearances of people in a struggle between
the Russian separatists and the Cossacks, who had sent many people into the
Ukraine to fight against the Ukrainian governmental forces. The Cossacks had
taken over three towns and labeled them as Cossack Republics. Their aspirations for an independent Cossack state surely collided with the goals of the
Russian separatist groups to form their own republics (*New York Times* 2015h).
A bizarre twist occurred in the Russian response to sanctions, for President
Putin had banned products from Europe and the United States from entering
Russian territory. As a result, government forces burned 350 tons of food that
had come in from those sources, and citizens in the poorer areas of Russia
were visibly disturbed (*USA Today* 2015m). At the end of the month, President
Poroshenko reported that in recent weeks 500 tanks, 400 artillery systems, and
950 Panser vehicles had entered eastern Ukraine to assist the rebels (*Dagensnyheter*
2015d).

Reports from UN officials in Geneva about the sacrifices made by people
during the Ukrainian civil war were grim. They reported that 8,000 people,
both soldiers and civilians, had lost their lives in the conflict, while the

wounded numbered about 18,000. The reports pointed also to the great need to restore rights and freedoms to the desperate Ukrainian population (*Izvestia* 2015d). One week later in September 2015 President Putin extended the scope of the conflict by signing an agreement for a Russian air base in Belarus. He also directed the personnel at the Russian Ministry of Defense to continue discussions about this plan with officials in Minsk (*Izvestia* 2015e). There was irony in this move as well, for two Minsk meetings had attempted to establish ceasefires in the Ukrainian war. It was an effort to strengthen Russian influence across the border, and also to stoke fears among the populations of Poland and the Baltic states (*iDnes* 2015b). Another sign of Russian purposefulness in the conflict included the announcement of the intention to construct a second base near the border with the Ukraine. There would be 5,000 soldiers at the base, with weapons, and it would serve as a hospital (*SME* 2015g). It was clear that the hostilities would continue and that Western responses to each Russian move would be forthcoming.

American responses to and initiatives in the crisis

While the United States was generally understanding of the situation in the Ukraine during and after the Maidan demonstrations and the departure from the country of President Yanukovych, there was dismay and an outcry against the enormous disruption in the Crimea and its rapid inclusion within the Russian Federation. The Maidan revolution was "an enactment of civil society," and it was an example of the value of free association and the rule of law (Snyder 2015, 705). With regard to the demonstrations, America called for adherence to democratic norms as it had been doing since the Orange Revolution of 2004. Those norms included reliance on elections, continued development of mass-base parties, and anti-corruption policies (D'Anieri 2007, 49–53). Russian positions were quite different, but they also emphasized elections by protesting that the Ukrainians had deposed the president who had been duly elected in 2010.

With regard to the take-over of the Crimea, President Obama both called on his Russian counterpart to undo that annexation and vigorously protested the escalation of the conflict by Russian nationalists in key areas of eastern Ukraine. America led a Western effort to impose sanctions on key elites in Russian society. Those groups included important industries, banks, oil companies, and individual leaders. The aim was to hit Russia's economic strengths at the top, but not ordinary citizens who were struggling in tough economic conditions. The Western partners of the U.S. also imposed sanctions but were more cautious about doing so, for they feared that Russia might retaliate by increasing the price to them of oil and natural gas.

America also led the NATO alliance to react to this new instance of Russian expansionism. It relocated 8,000 troops from southern Europe to

Poland and the Baltic states of Estonia, Latvia, and Lithuania. At their fall 2014 conference in Wales, NATO planners decided to create a Rapid Reaction Force, to be called the Spearhead Force, that could move very quickly to troubled spots in the region. Plans called for heavy British involvement in the make-up of the force, which would number about 5,000 persons. Eventually, that unit would be located in the three Baltic states and in Poland, Bulgaria, and Romania (Kalb 2015, 235). Clearly, the leaders of the alliance expected that there would be additional Russia provocations in the future and that a deterrent to them was absolutely necessary.

NATO's response in April 2014 included the suspension of civilian and military cooperation with Russia through the NRC. Practical activities that were affected included helicopter maintenance, a counter-narcotics initiative fund in Afghanistan, and counter-terrorism initiatives. NATO assistance to Ukraine centered on the provision of military trainers who would work with the local forces on the modernization of their procedures, as well as establishment of a trust fund to buttress military capabilities. Steps were also taken by the alliance to reassure and protect other allies in the region. For example, it upgraded the Baltic Air Policing Mission from four to sixteen fighter jets. In late March it also carried out daily over-flights of Ukraine, Poland, and Romania. Activities at sea were also an important part of the deterrent, as three maritime groups were on patrol by the middle of the summer. They covered the Baltic, Mediterranean, and Black seas, and the operation mainly included more senior alliance members along with Estonia. Additional military exercises were also on the agenda for Central and Eastern Europe, as well as a large one in the Ukraine in September. A full 6,000 NATO troops participated in Steadfast Javelin 1 in Estonia with replicated battles to fend off an attack on its territory. Rapid Trident was an additional U.S. Army exercise that was planned for the fall, and a combined U.S.–Ukrainian battalion would practice a peacekeeping operation. All of these new military activities came under the U.S. European Command's Operation Atlantic Resolve, and thus America played a leading and coordinating role in an alliance program of preparedness for any further Russian advances (*Congressional Research Service*, July 31, 2014).

During the years after the crisis year of 2014, the U.S. and additional Western nations continued to take responsive and preventive action with regard to the unknown question of what President Putin and Russia would be up to next. The EU had become involved in the conflict in September 2014 with a meeting in Minsk that gathered together the leaders of the EU, Russia, and Ukraine. The resulting Minsk Protocol required Russia to take away its support for the separatists in eastern Ukraine and to pull out of the Crimea. Early in the new year, it was evident that Russia had not met these conditions, and so the EU decided that it would not yet remove the sanctions that it had imposed on Russia (*USA Today* 2015n). NATO Secretary General

Jens Stoltenberg became involved at about the same time, as another violation of the Minsk Protocol occurred in Mariupol. Rocket attacks came from the direction of areas controlled by separatists, and the targeting of Mariupol made observers concerned about possible Russian intentions to use the city as the cornerstone of a land bridge from Russia to the Crimean Peninsula (*USA Today* 2015o).

With the unraveling of the 2014 Minsk Protocol there was much activity by Western leaders in early February 2015. German Chancellor Angela Merkel and French President François Hollande went to both Kiev and Moscow in order to get agreement on a new peace initiative that would assure the Ukraine of the intactness of its territory. The NATO Secretary General also proposed an increase from 13,000 to 30,000 in the NATO Response Force, which would be on top of the additional troops making up the new Spearhead Force. The Response Force had been in existence for some time, being a significant part of NATO capabilities since the Bosnian wars of the 1990s (*USA Today* 2015p).

American Secretary of State John Kerry went to Kiev for parallel talks with President Poroshenko. He announced assistance in the form of blankets, clothing, and counseling for people trapped in the fighting in Donetsk and Luhansk. At the same time, Vice President Joseph Biden went to Brussels to consult with European leaders there (*New York Times* 2015i). The aim of all this Western activity was the coordination of political, diplomatic, and military efforts to establish an effective deterrent policy in Central and Eastern Europe. Discussion about Ukraine also involved the matter of sending weapons to support the Ukrainian military. European leaders were very cautious about that prospect, and so was President Obama. However, in congressional hearings that accompanied his nomination as Secretary of Defense, Ashton Carter indicated a willingness to consider the provision of arms. In that sense, his view duplicated that of his predecessor, Chuck Hagel (*New York Times* 2015j).

The Merkel–Hollande trip to Kiev and Moscow drew much attention in Europe and the United States. Their two-fold objective included obtaining promises of a halt to the fighting in eastern Ukraine and preventing the Ukraine from becoming a flash-pan in the middle of Europe (*Süddeutsche Zeitung* 2015a). In light of the importance of the talks, EU foreign ministers decided to postpone the planned escalation of sanctions against Russia. These further sanctions included the addition of more people to the list of 130 Russians who were already the targets of economic restrictions, asset freezes, and travel bans (*New York Times* 2015k). After the Moscow discussions, the four leaders of Russia, Ukraine, France, and Germany converged once again on the Belarus capital of Minsk for further discussions. The atmosphere at the meeting was tense, for there was intense fighting at the time in eastern Ukraine. There were sixteen Ukrainian deaths after a rocket attack on the industrial city of Kramatorsk, and explosions also took place in Donetsk (*New York Times*

2015l). On the same day as the Minsk meeting and the fighting in Ukraine, officials in Latvia warned that the Baltic states might be the next target of Russian attacks (*Dagensnyheter* 2015e).

In the midst of all of this confusion and noise, the four leaders who met at Minsk did agree to a ceasefire, as they had done the previous September in the same city. Within two weeks of the ceasefire a buffer zone was to be established at a distance of between 31 and 87 miles from the front lines, depending on the caliber of the weapons. The agreement did contain an important compromise. The rebel regions needed to hold a new vote under Ukrainian law, while the Ukraine needed to enact a constitutional reform that gave significant powers to the eastern regions (*USA Today* 2015q). Surprisingly, the ceasefire held from the beginning, with the exception of firing in the first four days around the contested city of Debaltseve (*USA Today* 2015r). After a few more days, leaders such as the Swedish ambassador to America, Bjorn Lyrvall, expressed the hope that an effective ceasefire might take some of the pressure off Scandinavian countries as well as the Baltic states. In the recent past Russia had violated both their airspace and maritime territory (*USA Today* 2015s). In order to sound a note on the side of caution, a U.S. military parade took place in the Estonian coastal city of Narva. The Estonian leadership welcomed this NATO presence, while Lithuania announced that it would increase the size of its military force by 3,500 soldiers (*Süddeutsche Zeitung* 2015b).

U.S. Secretary of State Kerry went to Sochi in early March to meet with his counterpart, Sergei Lavrov. They discussed the Ukraine, and also the tensions connected with Syria and Iran (*USA Today* 2015t). Talks centered in part on the deployment of heavy weapons, as the flow of weapons east from Russia and west from Kiev had continued unabated after the ceasefire agreed at the Minsk meetings in February (*USA Today* 2015u). In light of the simmering tension even after this meeting, the American Vice President called again for the provision of anti-tank missiles to the Ukraine to be considered (*USA Today* 2015v). Obviously, the peace agreements had not stilled the voices of those who worried about future Russian moves and another outbreak of hostilities. As if to make Joe Biden's comments prophetic, OSCE monitors reported that they found four people wearing military uniforms with the insignia of the Russian Army in Petrivske, a little way south of Donetsk (*New York Times* 2015m).

In the middle of the summer America continued the pressure on Russia to hold to the agreements by imposing sanctions on twenty-six people and institutions that had been helping previously sanctioned entities to avoid the sanctions (*New York Times* 2015n). Russia continued the war of nerves by claiming that President Obama had launched a project in the Baltics to combat Russian propaganda (*Izvestia* 2015f). For its part, the Ukraine banned thirty-eight books published in Russia that were filled with propaganda (*SME* 2015h).

The Ukraine also announced that NATO would open a representative office in Kiev and would thereby be able to conduct discussions with the Ukrainian security office (*Izvestia* 2015g). The war of words and actions continued into the first days of 2016. Moscow decided to end the agreement with the Ukraine on the free movement of goods. This was apparently in punishment for the growing economic relationship between the Ukraine and the EU. Kiev reacted to the new sanctions by imposing a ban on forty Russian imports to the Ukraine (*SME* 2016a). The end to the massive shootings and killings was a welcome feature of the situation after the second Minsk Accord. However, echoes of hostility continued in the cultural, diplomatic, military, and economic areas.

Conclusion: theoretical explorations of the on-going Russian–American conflict over Ukraine

It is a challenge to apply models and theories to a searing and on-going case study of very recent vintage, but one also of enormous significance to both regional and global stability. The Bipolar Model that was an effective analytical tool during the Cold War deserves a dusting-off as it helps to explain at least the appearance of the Ukrainian conflict. Russia by itself was provocative in terms of both the annexation of the Crimea and the involvement in the civil war in eastern Ukraine. The American leadership of the response was singular in terms of the imposition of sanctions, and also in terms of leading NATO to a considerable shift in its capabilities and resources. On the other hand, the Chaos/Complexity Model is pertinent as well, for the desire of Russia to acquire a valued piece of a neighboring and very troubled nation was indeed a very new and unexpected event in the post-Cold War years. The theories that work in plausible ways are, first, Realism and then, Systems Theory. Realism is a reminder of how important state borders and violations of them still are. At a time when so many pressures make borders very permeable, Russia's violation of Ukrainian sovereignty over the territory within its borders was a shock to the West. Systems Theory raises hope of a way out of the troubled situation, for it contains within it the assumption that rational leaders can be responsive to public pressures as they design policies.

The Modern Bipolar Model is quite different from its Cold War ancestor, for in the late 1940s and 1960s most nations lined up either in the camp that America headed or the one that Russia had pulled together. In 2014 and after, associated nations were more independent. Although China and Russia had seen eye to eye on the Syrian crisis, the former did not particularly support the latter over the Ukraine. Further, the Minsk Accords were an exercise in soft power that primarily involved discussions between two partners from the western part of Europe and the two eastern nations that were at the heart of the struggle. However, America took the leading role in calculations about hard power and the deployment of military capabilities. Thus, the NATO Wales Summit was the location where the partners agreed on the development of a Spearhead Force, and troop redeployment to offer more protection for the nations of northern Europe was also completely in the hands of the American-led alliance. The Obama administration took the lead in imposing sanctions on Russia and took most of the heat from Moscow regarding their inappropriateness. Thus, global politics once again took on the appearance of bipolarity.

The newness and open-endedness of the conflict revealed a number of assumptions of the Chaos/Complexity Model. The take-over of the Crimea was a chaos event that forced the agents in the conflict to question old assumptions, with an eye on evolution towards a new type of order. It was not just that the Ukraine fell over the cliff into civil war, but it was also the case that a number of key Western nations perceived old certainties slipping away and felt vulnerable due to their small size or location. If Russia was willing to involve itself in two different incursions into the Ukraine on behalf of fellow ethnic Russians, would it do the same type of outreach to the Russian minorities in the three Baltic states? Might Moscow make a similar move on behalf of its ethnic brothers and sisters in the Trans-Dniestrian sector of Moldova? Would long-standing contention between Poland and Russia lead to a new frigidity, or even conflict between them? The glue that had held nations and allies together in the early decades of post-Cold War was loosening, and pieces were beginning to break off from their traditional centers.

State-centered Realist Theory also experienced a new life, as leader after leader attempted to impose rational control over the loosened variables within their political systems. It was a pattern that was unlike the futility experienced by European nations and the EU in the face of the refugee outflow from Syria in 2015–16. It was a situation quite different from the immediate aftermath of 9/11, when terrorist movements across state lines were seemingly unstoppable. President Poroshenko thought in traditional ways about steps that could strengthen the eastern border with Russia and offer more chances for self-rule in the many troubled cities of eastern Ukraine. Autonomy for an ethnic minority was still in tune with realist assumptions linked to national sovereignty, while the recent refugee flows and the earlier terrorist freedom of action presented much more serious challenges to state-centered controls that national leaders could evoke with effect.

The familiar Systems Theory applies to very set situations in which there is no profound and disruptive change and in which a democratic framework for policy making is a given. In the language of Systems Theory, countless new inputs to the policy process cropped up in the eastern sector of Europe during and after the events of winter and spring 2014. They included politicians, demonstrations, revolts, military interventions, the crash of a civilian airliner, and heavy involvement by outside powers and leaders. However at the heart of the theory is a "black box" in which all kinds of inputs can receive a kind of blessing and be converted into sensible policy outputs and policies. From that perspective, conversion forces included the two Minsk Accords, the NATO Wales Summit, the bargaining over economic sanctions between the West and Russia, and troop movements by Russia into eastern Ukraine and by NATO from the south of Europe into its north. What was missing was coordination of effort among all the players, headed by America and Russia, into a settled set of concrete agreements that would create more predictable policy paths for the future. Systems Theory also includes a feedback loop in which uncertain policy decisions can become the framework and source of new outputs in a future day. Perhaps, that was happening in the region, as the unsettled state of affairs acted like a whirlpool that sucked in the leaders of the affected countries and encouraged them to think anew about future outputs and outcomes.

Considered as a package, the two proposed models and two theories pull in different directions, but that has been the nature of the continuing crisis as well. If the re-emergence of bipolarity pulls both Russia and America into new difficulties but also new discussions, it can act as a sort of centerpiece for the crisis. In part it is again up to Washington and Moscow to take the lead. The stakes in doing so are higher than in previous post-Cold War battles, for the complexity of the situation and its apparently chaotic nature unsettle many populations as well as their leaders. Pressure is heavy on the leaders of all concerned states to think in creative and rational ways about what the realistic path out of the crisis looks like, and the path should be one that maintains both territorial intactness and state sovereignty. It may also be that the system that has been evolving since 1991 is now yielding to another whose parameters will look quite different than its post-Cold War predecessor. Many would think that it is about time that it should do so!

Conclusion: theoretical approaches and a path from the Crimea to stability

Theoretical approaches

From an examination of Table 1 it is apparent that three of the ten Models/ Theories were helpful in explaining the political dynamics in more than half of the chapters (five or more of nine). Balance of Power was the most frequently cited model (in seven chapters), and it reflects the extent to which Russia and America strove earnestly after the end of the Cold War to establish some sort of equitable continuum between them. The Multipolar Model and Realism Theory were also quite useful, as they worked in clarifying the situation in five of the chapters. Many new power centers had emerged, such as the post-communist states in Central Europe, and they reinforced the ascendant multi-polarity. Further, America and Russia struggled to contend with all kinds of non-state actors that threatened the boundaries of their nation-states, and these strivings reflected the realist beliefs of their leaders that rational control and planning were possibilities.

The Chaos/Complexity Model and Critical Juncture Theory assisted in the analysis of less than half of the chapters (four), and yet each cast some light on features of the relationship between the two global powers. Explosions such as the collapse of the Soviet Union, the 9/11 attacks, and the annexation of the Crimea did create a sense of chaos for many global players, and both Russian and American leaders floundered in attempting to understand and cope with them for a number of years. Similarly, the overall period under review here did not share the consistency of its Cold War predecessor in many ways, and there were several critical junctures at which new policy departures, such as the mutual pivots to Asia after 2011, offered the opportunity for new American and Russian beginnings after a series of troubled years in other settings.

Table 1   Classification of models and theories by chapter number

Chapter	Model					Theory				
	Balance of Power	Bipolar	Unipolar	Multipolar	Chaos/Complexity	Systems	Legacy	Critical Juncture	Realism	Realism Revised
2	X			X			X		X	
3	X				X			X		X
4	X			X		X		X		
5	X			X			X		X	
6				X	X		X	X		X
7			X						X	
8	X				X	X				
9	X			X				X	X	
10		X			X	X			X	

Systems Theory, Legacy Theory, and Realism Revised Theory played a role in the analysis of one third of the chapters (three of nine). Since there was so much flux in this time frame, it is not surprising that the somewhat rigid assumptions of Systems Theory did not cast as much light on the constantly changing Russian–American relationship as did other theoretical approaches. Legacy Theory was probably very instructive in exploring how the vestiges of the Cold War lingered into the period after 1991, but it may not be as informative in the period after 1991, since new patterns were so slow to solidify and reappear as legacies later on. Realism Revised Theory, with its heavy emphasis on the power of globalization pressure to overwhelm national leaders and their plans, may explain much about nations in the Middle East and developing world, but both Moscow and Washington had the where-withal to channel at least some of those waves in directions that served their national interests.

The least frequently cited theoretical approaches in this study were the Bipolar Model and Unipolar Model, for each helped to pull together the material in only one chapter. Bipolarity conjures up an image of the United States and Russia bestride the globe and able to penetrate their influence into many regional corners of it. That kind of dominance may have contributed to the picture only during the Ukrainian conflict in 2014 and after. Further an appearance of unipolarity helped to clarify the picture only during the years when America was fighting in Afghanistan and Iraq at the same time, for many believed that America was marching to its own drumbeat, in a unilateral way.

Taken together, these models and theories help in explaining both convergence and erosion in the American–Russian relationship. The three most frequently applicable approaches were the Balance of Power Model, the Multipolar Model, and Realism Theory. Each of them points toward convergence of interests between the two strong powers, while they can also be barriers against the erosion of relationships along many policy axes. One problem is that some of the other approaches poke through at inconvenient times and erode the convergence of interests that may have been underway. This is very much the case with the Bipolar and Unipolar Models. Fortunately, in this analysis they played the smallest role in the evolving Russian–American relationship. The key challenge is to construct a foundation that makes the three convergence models resistant to the waves of the two erosion models. That challenge will require commitment from both sets of leaders.

A path from the Crimea to stability

The Crimea and the American–Russian relationship
Responses to the destabilizing series of events in the Ukraine were not confined simply to separate actions by the United States and Russia. They also included interactions between the Obama and Putin administrations that aimed

to clear the path out of the wilderness of trouble but sometimes had the effect of putting more branches in the way.

Presidents Putin and Obama were at least at the same ceremonial event in Normandy for the seventieth anniversary of the D-Day invasion in June 2014. However, they did not plan to meet, and speculation circulated as to whether they might informally "bump into each other." The event was scheduled at the same time as the twenty-fifth anniversary of free elections in Poland, as well as the G-7 summit in Brussels. In view of the take-over of the Crimea, the site of the summit had been changed from the planned location of Sochi to Brussels. Further, it was no longer the G-8 group, for the other members had pushed Russia out after the spring aggression (*USA Today* 2014d). At the first of those three events, in Poland, President Bronislaw Komorowski greeted the American leader symbolically, at an airplane hangar in front of F-16 fighter jets. Simultaneously, Obama announced plans to spend $1 billion on military equipment and more American troops in the region. There would be additional military exercises and training missions, and the special focus would be on the Ukraine, Georgia, and Moldova (*Associated Press*, June 3, 2014). Phillip Breedlove, Commander of U.S. forces and NATO units in Europe, stated that the Russian take-over of the Crimea taken Europe to the most decisive point since the end of the Cold War. American leaders decided to call the planned military activities in Europe "Operation Atlantic Resolve" (*iDnes* 2014c). Reports were also circulating that Russia would have access to a base in Cuba for use in spying on the United States (*SME* 2014).

Throughout 2015 there were mixed signals over the Ukraine between Russia and America. In April, a Russian fighter jet made a very unsafe move in the direction of a U.S. reconnaissance plane over the Baltic Sea. The plane's maneuver was part of Russia's expanded air activity towards the West (*USA Today* 2015w). Commander Breedlove issued a stern warning to Russia to stop underestimating the more intense shooting episodes in eastern Ukraine (*SME* 2015i). Public surveys by the Pew Research Center were revealing about attitudes towards the significance of the crisis. In general, the data indicated that allies were reluctant to aid a nation attacked by Russia, since they expected that the U.S. would act as a shield in defense of an ally. More than half of the Ukrainians surveyed favored the entry of their nation into both NATO and the EU (*USA Today* 2015x).

The Russians were correspondingly upgrading their military capabilities, and they put on a high-tech military demonstration in a park outside Moscow. President Putin's opening remarks included the announcement that Russia would be adding forty ICBMs to its nuclear capabilities that year (*New York Times* 2015o). On the following day the EU agreed in preliminary fashion in Brussels to extend economic sanctions against Russia beyond their planned expiration date of July 2015, until January 2016 (*New York Times* 2015p). Soon afterwards the American Secretary of Defense, Ash Carter, announced the dispatch of 250 tanks, armored vehicles, and additional military equipment to seven European nations. Ostensibly, the equipment would assist in military training, but it could also help NATO's new rapid-reaction or Spearhead Force (*USA Today* 2015y). A more promising occurrence at the end of the year was a meeting between Secretary of State John Kerry and President Vladimir Putin in Moscow (*Izvestia* 2015h). However, that did not prevent NATO Secretary General Jens Stoltenberg from announcing in early 2016 the strengthened air, naval, and land capabilities along the alliance's entire eastern border from the Baltic Sea to the Black Sea (*iDnes* 2016a).

Russia expands its range of activities in the wake of the Ukraine
The outreach of the Russian leadership in other directions had the aim of broadening the base of its support system on a selected set of policy topics. For example, in the summer of 2015 President Putin hosted the Greek Prime Minister, Alexis Tsipras, in St. Petersburg. The two agreed that over the next few years they would jointly plan a gas pipeline that would go to Europe through Turkey (*USA Today* 2015z). St. Petersburg was also the location of a summit that included leaders from a dozen European far-right parties. They heard about President Putin's values and his strong style of leadership. Their opposition to the EU and NATO fitted Russia's efforts to push at the cracks in the Western alliance (*USA Today* 201aa). Even though it was a long way from the troubled border with the Ukraine, Russia announced the creation of a new army specialized in air defense for deployment in Siberia along its long eastern border (*SME* 2015j).

Egypt also received overtures from Russia. This occurred after the emergence of a military figure as Egyptian president put some space between that nation and the United States. President Abdal Fatah al-Sisi visited Moscow for a third time in mid-2015 in an effort to persuade it to play a bigger role in the fight against terrorism in the Middle East (*SME* 2015k). The Russian press depicted the meeting as one that fostered cooperation and would deepen trade relations between the two states (*Izvestia* 2015i). Iran was also on President Putin's agenda, for before the major agreement on Iran's nuclear ambitions had been completed he lifted a ban on the sale to Iran of an S-300 surface-to-air missile defense system (*New York Times* 2015q).

There were additional Russian efforts to make a dent in opinion at home and abroad. For instance, plans were moved forward to build an 82-foot-high statue to St. Vladimir on a Moscow hill to commemorate the fact that Kiev was the birthplace of the Russian Empire (*New York Times* 2015r). Russia had had big plans to spend money on hosting the 2018 Football World Cup. When scandal hit FIFA (the International Federation of Association Football), the sport's international governing body, and officials were arrested in Zurich in May 2015, Putin described these events as an effort by the United States to deny Russia's right to host the competition (*New York Times* 2015s). He also announced further plans to improve the readiness of the Russian military for action in a broad area that stretched from the Urals to Siberia (*SME* 2015l). In Scandinavia, it was major news that Russia had decided to establish a new air base in Belarus (*Dagensnyheter* 2015f). Scandinavia also reacted strongly to Russia's plans to considerably modernize its nuclear weapons arsenal by 2020 (*Dagensnyheter* 2015g).

As the year 2015 neared an end, President Putin visited Iran after world powers had signed the Iran nuclear deal. Just prior to the visit he announced that Russia would import enriched uranium from Iran, dilute it, and then export it back to Iran. This gave Russia a specific role in the implementation of the nuclear accord and also linked it more closely to Iran (*USA Today* 2015bb). A crisis that involved Russia in Turkish matters occurred at the end of the year, after Turkey shot down a Russian warplane that it claimed had entered its airspace. Russian leaders retaliated by denying new contracts in Russia to Turkish construction companies (*New York Times* 2015t). Plans emerged in early 2016 for the Serbian, President Tomislav Nikolich, to visit Moscow to meet with both President Putin and Russian Orthodox Patriarch Kirill. The two presidents would work on a plan to tie the two nations more closely in a trade zone linked to the Eurasian Economic Union (*Izvestia* 2016a).

While much of the expanded activity emanated from Moscow, there were several moves by the West to work in other directions too. For example, NATO decided to send ships to the Aegean Sea in order to prevent people smugglers from moving across the water from Turkey to Greece, as they became invisible in the refugee flow from Syria into the EU sphere. NATO would pass on to the EU any information that it picked up so that action could be taken (*New York Times* 2016b). NATO Secretary General Stoltenberg also announced that the alliance was making progress in its work with Georgia on prospects for eventual membership. Work with Georgia on its defenses was important, and that was a message to Russia, who had invaded Georgia in 2008 (*USA Today* 2016f).

The Syrian civil war and Russian–American relations

Both the United States and Syria became heavily involved in the Syrian civil war in 2015 and after. Earlier there had been differences in attitude towards President Assad, for the United States favored his removal from power, while Russia twice vetoed resolutions in the UN to do so. Those differences intensified after ISIS became a huge threat in Syria and the region. America led a coalition to weaken and destroy ISIS, while President Putin eventually sent in the Russian military, mainly to back up President Assad. The result was damage to some of the anti-Assad forces that the Western nations had been seeking to support (*New York Times* 2015u; *USA Today* 2015cc). Eventually, Russia began to supply Syria with military capabilities as well, and including equipment, advisors, and humanitarian assistance (*USA Today* 2015dd). These decisions prompted President Obama to consider one-on-one talks with Putin in order to clarify the situation and coordinate actions to some extent (*New York Times* 2015v). A follow-up to that planning about people smugglers in the Syrian conflict was a telephone call between American Secretary of Defense Ash Carter and Russian Minister of Defense Sergei Shoygu. Their discussion focused on preventing conflict between the Russian and American military forces, given their tactical differences over the prosecution of war efforts in Syria (*USA Today* 2015ee). Another meeting of significance took place in London between Secretary of State Kerry and United Arab Emirates Foreign Minister Abdullah bin Zayed (*Dagensnyheter* 2015h).

However, President Putin pulled a surprise with the announcement of an agreement with Iraq, Syria, and Iran on coordinating intelligence about ISIS. Russian military officers had actually gone to Baghdad to discuss the details (*New York Times* 2015w). The common feature was that two leaders were Shiites and the third was Alawite/Shiite. Russian initiatives also included the dispatch of the submarine *Rostov on Don*, carrying winged rockets, to the coast of Syria and (*iDnes* 2015c). President Putin claimed that the ship was on its way to another location, but he issued a stern warning to Turkey that tough action would be taken against any nation that attempted to weaken the Russian role in Syria. Turkey's downing of the Russian warplane in late 2015 was the immediate source of his concern (*iDnes* 2015d). Sergei Lavrov, the Russian Foreign Minister, followed up with a warning that it might be necessary to close the Syrian–Turkish border (*Izvestia* 2015j). Russia also issued a clarification that the *Rostov on Don* was targeting ISIS terrorists while on its way home to its base with the Northern Fleet (*Izvestia* 2015k). After several months of Russian attacks in Syria, it was unclear whether they had really reduced the power and capabilities of the terrorists by very much. On the other hand, Russia's involvement had led to a loss of Russian lives and equipment, as well as the embittering of relations with Turkey (*New York Times* 2015x).

Early in 2016 the dramatic news emerged that President Assad's forces had encircled Aleppo and were about to take it, with the result that many more refugees were on the move (*USA Today* 2016g). Probably the Russian air strikes near the city had strengthened Assad's forces to the point that their plan was coming to fruition (*New York Times* 2016c). American strategists began to speculate as to whether it was necessary to think in terms of a military solution rather than the political solution that had been on their agenda for some time (*New York Times* 2016d). Better news emerged from Munich, where key foreign ministers had been meeting. John Kerry and Sergei Lavrov announced that a temporary ceasefire would allow the air to clear and consideration to be given to what the next steps should be (*USA Today* 2016h). One important feature of this agreement was the provision of food and medicine to victims of the war on the ground in Syria (*New York Times* 2016e). This was a positive step, but aid groups and the UN Secretary General warned that humanitarian assistance must not be used as a bargaining chip.

Clearly, for a time the events in Syria pushed the Ukrainian conflict into the background. Whereas the latter had pitted America and Russia against each other on countless occasions and revealed an impasse on literally every possible solution, the war in Syria offered more hope for relations between Moscow and Washington. There was sharp disagreement over the role of President Assad in taking the fight to ISIS, but the common and barbaric enemy at least pulled Putin and Obama towards one another. It was hoped that this pattern on the Syrian war would continue, and spill over into other future conflicts between the two powers.

Continued erosion, occasional convergence, and a hope for stability
In 2016 actions by both Russia and America included increases at some times in military preparedness, and at other times in actual provocations. Both types of activities were erosive, in light of jangled nerves since the commencement of tensions over the Crimea. NATO joint exercises in the Black Sea in mid-April were a signal of the alliance's readiness to defend the three Baltic States as well as Poland. In response, Russian warplanes buzzed the USS *Donald Cook*, a guided missile destroyer. President Putin had earlier identified NATO's approach to the Russian border as a threat, in a formal decree that became part of Russia's National Security Strategy (*USA Today* 2016h). The American response consisted of reminders about similar incidents earlier in the year and the ways in which they had escalated tensions (*USA Today* 2016i). In the following month of May, the United States began to introduce elements of its missile defense system into Romania, and President Putin warned that this would upset the strategic nuclear balance between the two powers (*Izvestia* 2016b).

Military provocations in other theaters took place and contributed to the erosion of relationships. For example, Russia's pivot to Asia took on the unexpected form of parallel flights with the Chinese military along the American West Coast. Whereas Russia had been intent on a higher-profile policy in the Asia-Pacific Region, China's activities were perhaps related to its intention to assert its rights in the South China Sea and beyond (*USA Today* 2016j). In June, America sent the USS *Porter* into the Black Sea, where it docked at the port of Varna, Bulgaria. This was not the first time that U.S. ships had entered the Black Sea, but the Russians' response was vociferous as they warned that retaliation might be forthcoming (*USA Today* 2016k).

In early July, NATO held its summit meeting in Warsaw, Poland and the symbolism in holding it there was accompanied by concrete policy commitments. President Obama announced that the United States would dispatch 1,000 troops to Poland to serve with the Polish military. They would serve on a rotating basis, and an armored brigade would also move its headquarters

to Poland (*USA Today* 2016l). Also at the summit, Obama expressed his sat-
isfaction that alliance partners had halted their decline in defense spending.
The NATO target for each had been to spend 2% of their gross domestic
product on defense, and at the time of the Warsaw Summit only five of the
twenty-eight members were meeting that standard (*USA Today* 2016m).
Russian provocations occurred in that time frame as well, for in August there
was skirmishing along the Ukrainian–Crimean border. President Poroshenko
of Poland reported that Russian troops in the Crimea had moved closer to
that border, and so he decided to increase the level of military readiness to
the highest level (*iDNES* 2016b).

All of this skirmishing between the United States and Russia clearly spread
into other nations and regions that were affected by the conflict and made
it more difficult to halt the erosion of relations. At the same time there were
some signals that pointed to a potential convergence of interests. As the United
States assisted the Ukraine in increasing its military preparedness, it continued
to confine that assistance to defensive skills rather than offensive ones. For
example, it turned down a Ukrainian request for sniper training, as that skill
clearly fitted into the offensive rather than the defensive category (*USA Today*
2016n). In September the U.S. and Russia negotiated another ceasefire in
Serbia. All parties agreed to this new venture, but it was not a move that
protected the al-Nusra Front or the Islamic State in Syria (*USA Today* 2016o).
The agreement did have the result of providing Russia with more standing in
the region and contributed to a kind of balance of power with the United
States, at least on this major issue (*USA Today* 2016p). Finally, American and
Russian interests had converged in endeavoring to control a civil war in Syria
that had taken so many hundreds of thousands of lives. Such agreements did
not end Russian–American confrontation over many issues, but they did hint
at the possibility of greater stability in their relationship in the coming few
years.

Postscript: two eagles

What is the path from the Crimea to stability? There has obviously been considerable conflict between Russia and America over the Balkan wars, NATO expansion, the Iraq War, the Missile Shield proposal, the Georgia War, the Arab Spring, the Ukraine/Crimea, and the Syrian civil war. It is mandatory to look at this key global relationship from another angle, for it is much too easy to speculate on what the next conflict between the two strong nations is likely to be. The mutual imagery of two eagles suggests that it may be best to look in another direction. Since eagles soar through the skies, perhaps it is better to look upwards towards ideals rather than always downwards at earth-borne and often sad realities. An emphasis on ideals may highlight the importance of cooperative postures replacing nationally defensive ones; of mutual appreciation of each other's cultures rather than a fixation on constant reminders about historical betrayals by the other side; and of interpreting signals by one state as meaningful efforts to promote humanitarian values rather than as reminders about absorption with national pride and self. Their two state anthems remind us that both Russia and America inherited huge territories with a rich mixture of peoples and a belief in a special destiny and path in the world. Both the single-headed bald eagle of America and the double-headed Russian imperial eagle have the capacity to soar together through the heavens and offer protection and inspiration to those below.

References

Aron, Leon. 2002. "Structure and Context in the Study of Post-Soviet Russia: Several Empirical Generalizations in Search of a Theory." *Demokratizatsiya*. 10/4: 429–461.

Almond, Gabriel A. and G. Bingham Powell, Jr. 1978. *Comparative Politics: System, Process, and Policy*. Boston: Little, Brown and Company.

Andrusyszyn, Walter E. 2015. "Interview by James W. Peterson." October 13.

Asmus, Ronald D., Richard L. Kugler, and Stephen Larrabee. 1997. "NATO Enlargement: A Framework for Analysis." In: *NATO's Transformation: The Changing Shape of the Atlantic Alliance*, edited by Philip H. Gordon. New York: Roman & Littlefield Publishers, Inc., 93–120.

Associated Press. 2014. "Obama: US to Boost Military Presence in Europe," *The Morning Report*, June 3.

Baev, Pavel. 2005. "Chechnya and the Russian Military: A War Too Far?" In: *Chechnya: From Past to Future*, edited by Richard Sakwa. London: Anthem Press, 117–130.

—— 2008. *Russian Energy Policy and Military Power: Putin's Quest for Greatness*. New York: Routledge/Taylor & Francis Group.

Balmaceda, Margarita M. 2000. *On the Edge: Ukrainian-Central European Security Triangle*. Budapest: Central European Press.

Berger, Samuel. 2005. Oral History at the University of Virginia's Miller Center, "Sandy Berger's Washington," *The Atlantic*, 2015/12.

Bialer, Seweryn. 1986. *The Soviet Paradox: External Expansion, Internal Decline*. New York: Alfred A. Knopf.

Billington, James H. 1966. *The Icon and the Axe: An Interpretive History of Russian Culture*. New York: Alfred A. Knopf.

Black, J.L. 2004. *Vladimir Putin and the New World Order*. New York: Rowman & Littlefield Publishers, Inc.

Book Review. 2011. *American Foreign Policy Interests*. 33: 49–51.

Brown, J.F. 1988. *Eastern Europe and Communist Rule*. Durham: Duke University Press.

Brown, Michael E. 1997. "The Flawed Logic of NATO Enlargement." In: *NATO's Transformation: The Changing Shape of the Atlantic Alliance*, edited by Philip H. Gordon. New York: Rowman & Littlefield Publishers, Inc, 121–139.

Carter, Ralph G. and James M. Scott. 2014. "Hitting the Russian Reset Button: Why is Cooperation So Hard? In: *Contemporary Cases in U.S. Foreign Policy: from terrorism to Trade*. Washington, D.C.: Sage/CQ Press.

Christian Science Monitor. 2008. "Russia-Georgia Conflict: Why Both Sides Have Valid Points." August 19. www.csmonitor.com.

Cichock, Mark A. 2003. *Russian and Eurasian Politics: A Comparative Approach*. New York: Longman.

Congressional Research Service. 2014. "NATO: Response to the Crisis in Ukraine and Security Concerns in Central and Eastern Europe," July 31.

Constitution of the Autonomous Republic of Crimea. 2014. Available at: www.rada.crimea.ua/en/bases-of-activity/konstituciya-ark (accessed on July 10, 2014).

Constitution of the Russian Federation. 1994. Edited by Vladimir V. Belyakov and Walter J. Raymond. United States of America: Brunswick/Novosti.

Cocozzelli, Fred. 2009. "Critical Junctures and Local Agency: How Kosovo Became Independent." *Southeast Europe and Black Sea Studies*. 9/1–2: 191–208.

Dagensnyheter. 2015a. "Analys: Tvksamt om Nato kan leverera det Erdogan begär." July 28. Accessed in www.dn.se.

—— 2015b. "Bedömare: Anfallen mot IS en ursäkt för att bomba PKK." July 26. www.dn.se.

—— 2015c. "DN:s reporter: Kaotiska scener med skadade soldater." February 18. www.dn.se.

—— 2015d. "Ryska stridsvagnar i Ukraina." August 24. www.dn.se.

—— 2015e. "Varningen: Baltiska Länderna kan bli Putins nästa mål." February 11. www.dn.se.

—— 2015f. "Ryssland vill etableera flygbaser i grannländerna." September 9. www.dn.se

—— 2015g. "Ryssland rustar – byter ut alla kärnvapen." September 22. www.dn.se.

—— 2015h. "USA och Ryssland i möte om Syrienkrisen." September 18. www.dn.se.

D'Anieri, Paul. 2007. *Understanding Ukrainian Politics: Power, Politics, and Institutional Design*. Armonk, New York: M.E. Sharpe.

Donnelly, Paul and John Hogan. 2012. "Understanding Policy Change Using a Critical Junctures Theory in Comparative Context: The Cases of Ireland and Sweden." *Policy Studies Journal*. 40/2: 324–350.

Downing, Wayne A. 2004. "The Global War on Terrorism: Focusing the National Strategy." In: *Defeating Terrorism: Shaping the New Security Environment*, edited by Russell D. Howard and Reid L. Sawyer. Guilford, Connecticut: McGraw-Hill/Dushkin, 146–157.

Fuchs, Christian and John Collier. 2007. "A Dynamic Systems View of Economic and Political Theory." *A Journal of Social and Political Theory*. 113: 23–52.

Gaddis, John Lewis. 2007. "End of the Cold War: The Unexpected Ronald Reagan." In: *American Foreign Policy The Dynamics of Choice in the 21st Century*, Third Edition, edited by Bruce W. Jentleson. New York: W.W. Norton & Company, 251–253.

Gakaev, Dzhabrail. 2005. "Chechnya in Russia and Russia in Chechnya." In: *Chechnya: From Past to Future*, edited by Richard Sakwa. London: Anthem Press, 21–42.

Garwin, Richard L. 2008. "Evaluating Iran's Missile Threat." *Bulletin of the Atomic Scientists*. May/June, 40–44.

Gel'man, Vladimir. 2015. *Authoritarian Russia: Analyzing Post-Soviet Challenges*. Pittsburgh: University of Pittsburgh Press.

Giles, Thomas. 2016. "Wartime Allies in Harmony: When Britain and Russia Shared a National Anthem." In: *Russia Beyond the Headlines*. May 13. Special to *RBTH*. Also YouTuve, January 29, 2017.

Gleason, Gregory. 2013. "Relations with Central Asia." In: *Return to Putin's Russia: Past Imperfect, Future Uncertain*, edited by Stephen K. Wegren. New York: Rowman & Littlefield Publishers, Inc., 257–275.

Goldman, Minton. 2009. *Rivalry in Eurasia: Russia, the United States, and the War on Terror.* Denver, Colorado: ABC CLIO.

Gorbachev, Mikhail. 1987. *Perestroika: New Thinking for Our Country and the World.* New York: Harper & Row Publishers.

—— 2008. "Russia Never Wanted a War." In: *New York Times.* August 20. www.nytimes.com.

Government Portal Ukraine. 2015. "Arsenij Yatsenyuk Says Gov't to Approve Ukraine-NATO Annual National Program." February 18. www.kmu.gov.ua.

Haas, Mark L. 2014. "Ideological Polarity and Balancing in Great Power Politics." *Security Studies.* 23/4: 715–753.

Hendrickson, Ryan C. 2006. *Diplomacy and War at NATO: The Secretary General and Military Action after the Cold War.* Columbia: University of Missouri Press.

Hook, Steven W. 2014. *U.S. Foreign Policy: The Paradox of World Power*, Fourth Edition. Washington, D.C.: Sage/CQ Press.

Howard, Russell D. and Reid L. Sawyer. 2004. *Defeating Terrorism: Shaping the New Security Environment.* Guilford, Connecticut: McGraw-Hill/Dushkin.

Huntington, Samuel P. 1997. *The Clash of Civilizations and the Remaking of the New World Order.* London: Simon and Schuster UK, Ltd.

Huskey, Eugene. 1999. *Presidential Power in Russia.* Armonk, New York: M.E. Sharpe.

Hutchings, Robert L. 1997. *American Diplomacy and the End of the Cold War: An Insider's Account of U.S. Policy in Europe, 1989–1992.* Washington, D.C.: The Woodrow Wilson Center Press.

Hyland, William G. 1988. "East–West Relations." In: *Gorbachev's Russia and American Foreign Policy*, edited by Seweryn Bialer and Michael Mandelbaum. Boulder, Colorado: Westview Press.

iDnes. 2008a. "Požádáme Rusko o uznání nezávislost, rozhodl parlament Abcházie." August 20. www.idnes.cz.

—— 2014a. "ČR po posílení vojsk NATO v Evropě nevolá řekl Sobotka. Schytal kritiku." June 3. www.idnes.cz.

—— 2014b. "Rusové pořádají manévry u Baltu do Kalinigradu vyslali sochoje." June 12. www.idnes.cz.

—— 2014c. "Kvůli ruské agresi spouštíme operaci Atlantické odhodlání,oznamily USA." July 1. www.idnes.cz.

—— 2015a. "Ankara nás žene do slepé uličky, varuje Putin po sestřelení bitevníku." November 26. www.idnes.cz.

—— 2015b. "Putin se sešel s Lukašenkem. Plánuje ruskou vojenskou základnu v Bělorusku." September 19. www.idnes.cz.

—— 2015c. "K pobřeží Sýrie dorazila ruská ponorka Rostov na Donu." December 8. www.idnes.cz.

—— 2015d. "Putin: Jakýkoliv cíl ohrožující naše activity v Sýrii musí být zničen." December 11. www.idnes.cz.

—— 2016a. "Najděte posily pro východní křídlo, nařídili ministři plánovačům NATO." February 10. www.idnes.cz.

—— 2016b. "Porošenko nařídil nejvyšší bojovou pohotovost u Krymu a v Donbasu." August 11. www.idnes.cz.

Izvestia. 2014. "Vladimir Putin along with Leaders of the Caspian Sea Nations Releases a Sturgeon into the Volga" (translated). September 26. www.izvestia.ru.

—— 2015a. "Russia Blocks U.N. Security Council Resolution on a Tribunal for Boeing" (translated). July 29. www.izvestia.ru.

—— 2015b. "Peskov: 'The Response of Russia to Sanctions of the United States May Be Asymmetrical'" (translated). July 31. www.izvestia.ru.

—— 2015c. "Peskov: "The Sanctions of the United States Disturb the Atmosphere of Reciprocity with Russia" (translated). August 7. www.izvestia.ru.

—— 2015d. "U.N.: About 8,000 Persons Have Died in the Course of the Conflict in Eastern Ukraine" (translated). September 8. www.izvestia.ru.

—— 2015e. "Putin Orders the Signing of an Agreement for an Aviation Base in Belarus" (translated). September 19. www.izvestia.ru.

—— 2015f. "The United States Launches a Baltic project to Combat Russian Propaganda" (translated). August 10. www.izvestia.ru.

—— 2015g. "Ministry of Defense of Ukraine: NATO Opens a Representative Office in Kiev" (translated). September 7. www.izvestia.ru.

—— 2015h. "Vladimir Putin Wishes John Kerry a Good Night's Sleep" (translated). December 15. www.izvestia.ru.

—— 2015i. "Russia and Egypt Broaden Cooperation" (translated). August 26. www.izvestia.ru.

—— 2015j. "For the Fight Against Daesh it is Necessary Quickly to Close the Syrian-Turkish Border" (translated). December 13. www.izvestia.ru.

—— 2015k. "The Submarine Rostov-on-Don Entered the Black Sea after the Attack on Daesh" (translated). December 14. www.izvestia.ru.

—— 2016a. "Presidents of Russia and Serbia to Meet in Moscow on March 9" (translated). February 12. www.izvestia.ru.

—— 2016b. "Russia Responds to the Launching of PRO (Anti-Rocket Defense) into Romania." (translated). May 13. www.izvestia.ru.

Jenkins, Brian Michael. 2004. "Countering Al Qaeda." In: *Defeating Terrorism: Shaping the New Security Environment*, edited by Russell D. Howard and Reid L. Sawyer. Guilford, Connecticut: McGraw Hill/Dushkin, 127–145.

Jentleson, Bruce W. 1997. "Who, Why, What, and How: Debates over Post-Cold War Military Intervention." In: *Eagle Adrift: American Foreign Policy at the End of the Century*, edited by Robert J. Lieber. New York: Longman, 39–70.

—— 2007. *American Foreign Policy: the Dynamics of Choice in the 21st Century*, Third Edition. New York: W.W. Norton & Company.

Jones, Bruce. 2011. "The International Order and the Emerging Powers: Implications of the Arab Awakening." In: *The Arab Awakening: America and the Transformation of the Middle East*, edited by Kenneth M. Pollack *et al.* Washington, D.C.: Brookings Institution Press, 305–310.

Jones, David Martin and M.L.R. Smith. 2015. "Return to Reason: Reviving realism in Western Foreign Policy." *International Affairs.* 91/5: 933–952.

Kalb, Marvin. 2015. *Imperial Gamble: Putin, Ukraine, and the New Cold War.* Washington, D.C.: Brookings Institution Press.

Kay, Sean. 2015. *Global Security in the Twenty-First Century: The Quest for Power and the Search for Peace.* New York: Rowman & Littlefield.

Kissinger, Henry A. 1969. *Nuclear Weapons and Foreign Policy*, Abridged Version. New York: W.W. Norton & Company, Inc.

Kotkin, Stephen. 2016. "Russia's Perpetual Geopolitics." *Foreign Affairs.* 95/3, 2–9.

Krauthammer, Charles. 2007. "Unilateralism: The Unipolar Moment Revisited. In: *American Foreign Policy: The Dynamics of Choice in the 21st Century*, Third Edition, edited by Bruce W. Jentleson. New York: W.W. Norton & Company, 556–560.

Kuck, Sarah and James W. Peterson. 2014. "Pulling Back from the Brink in 2014: Case Studies of the Civil Wars in Syria and Ukraine." Presented at the Annual Convention of the Georgia Political Science Association, November 13–15.

LeDonne, John P. 1997. *The Russian Empire and the World, 1770–1917: The Geopolitics of Expansion and Containment.* New York: Oxford University Press.

Lewis, George N. and Theodore A. Postol. 2008. "Why Countermeasures Will Defeat National Missile Defense." *Bulletin of the Atomic Scientists.* May/June, 38–39.

Lieber, Robert J. 1997. "Eagle Without a Cause: Making Foreign Policy Without the Soviet Threat." In: *Eagle Adrift: American Foreign Policy at the End of the Century*, edited by Robert J. Lieber. New York: Longman, 3–25.

Light, Margot. 1989. "Restructuring Soviet Foreign Policy." In *Gorbachev and Perestroika*, edited by Ronald J. Hill and Jan Åke Dellenbrant. England: Edward Elgar, 171–193.

Los Angeles Times. 2008. "Georgia Fallout Felt in Iraq." August 15. www.latimes.com.

Lukyanov, Fyodor. 2016. "Putin's Foreign Policy." *Foreign Affairs*. 95/3: 30–37.

McCormick, James M. 2010. *American Foreign Policy and Process*, Fifth Edition. United States: Wadsworth/Cengage Learning.

Mahnke, Dieter. 2004. "The Changing Role of NATO." In *Redefining Transatlantic Security Relations: The Challenge of Change*, edited by Dieter Mahncke, Wyn Rees, and Wayne C. Thompson. New York: Manchester University Press, 52–83.

Malgin, Andrei. 2014. "The Crimean Knot." Available at: www.eng.globalaffairs.ru/The-Crimean-Knot16713 (accessed on June 7, 2014).

Mandelbaum, Michael. 2007. "America as the World's Government: The Case for Goliath." In: *American Foreign Policy: The Dynamics of Choice in the 21st Century*, Third Edition, edited by Bruce W. Jentleson. New York: W.W. Norton & Company, 568–570.

Mansbach, Richard. 2005. "Is Balance of Power Relevant in Contemporary Global Politics?" *Naval War College Review*. 58/3: 141–142.

Michta, Andrew A. 2006. *The Limits of Alliance: The United States, NATO, and the EU in North and Central Europe*. New York: Rowman & Littlefield Publishers, Inc.

Naughton, Barry. 2013. " 'Concert-Balance' as US Grand Strategy Option: Global Necessity but with Domestic Obstacles." *Journal of International Affairs*. 67/5: 675–680.

New York Times 2015a. "Obama, on China's Turf, Presents U.S. as a Better Partner for Africa." July 29. www.nytimes.com.

—— 2015b. "Obama Calls on Beijing to Stop Construction in South China Sea." November 18. www.nytimes.com.

—— 2015c. "Vladimir Putin, on Visit to Italy, Criticizes Ukraine Sanctions." June 10. www.nytimes.com.

—— 2015d. "Intrusions in Baltic Sea Show a Russia Challenging the West." June 10. www.nytimes.com.

—— 2015e. "Russia Assails Extension of E.U. Sanctions in Ukrainian Crisis." June 22. www.nytimes.com.

—— 2015f. "Russian Town Near Ukraine, Once Quiet, Now Buzzes with Military Activity." July 20. www.nytimes.com.

—— 2015g. "Russia Vetoes U.N. Resolution on Tribunal for Malaysia Airlines Crash in Ukraine." July 30. www.nytimes.com.

—— 2015h. "Cossacks face Reprisals as Rebel Groups Clash in Eastern Ukraine." August 4. www.nytimes.com.

—— 2015i. "U.S. Joins Europe in Efforts to End Fighting in Ukraine." February 5. www.nytimes.com.

—— 2015j. "Ukraine Insists Any Pact With Russia Must Adhere to Terms of September Accord." February 6. www.nytimes.com.

—— 2015k. "European Foreign Ministers Postpone Russia Sanctions to Allow Talks." February 9. www.nytimes.com.

—— 2015l. "World Leaders Meet in Belarus to Negotiate Cease-Fire in Ukraine." February 11. www.nytimes.com.

—— 2015m. "Monitor in Ukraine Reports Seeing 4 in Russian Insignia Near Donetsk." May 29. www.nytimes.com.

—— 2015n. "U.S. Names New Targets of Sanctions Over Ukraine." July 30. www.nytimes.com.

—— 2015o. "As Vladimir Putin Talks more Missiles and Might, Cost Tells Another Story." June 17. www.nytimes.com.

—— 2015p. "E.U. Agrees to Extend Economic Sanctions Against Russia." June 17. www.nytimes.com.

—— 2015q. "Putin Lifts Ban on Russian Missile Sale to Iran." April 13. www.nytimes.com.

—— 2015r. "Another Huge Statue in Russia? Not Rare, but Hugely Divisive." May 28. www.nytimes.com.

—— 2015s. "Putin, on Guard for 2018 World Cup in Russia, Denounces FIFA Arrests." May 28. www.nytimes.com.

—— 2015t. "Russia Expands Sanctions Against Turkey After Downing of Jet." December 30. www.nytimes.com.

—— 2015u. "New Diplomacy Seen on U.S.–Russian Efforts to End Syrian Civil War. August 11. www.nytimes.com.

—— 2015v. "Obama Weighing Talks with Putin on Syrian Crisis." September 15. www.nytimes.com.

—— 2015w. "Russia Surprises U.S. With Accord on Battling ISIS." September 27. www.nytimes.com.

—— 2015x. "Putin Gambit Over Syria Proves to Be Dual-Edged Sword." December 15. www.nytimes.com.

—— 2016a. "U.S. Drawing Southeast Asia Closer With California Summit." February 13. www.nytimes.com.

—— 2016b. "NATO Will Send Ships to Aegean Sea to Deter Human Trafficking." February 11. www.nytimes.com.

—— 2016c. "Syrian Forces Press Aleppo, Sending Thousands Fleeing." February 5. www.nytimes.com.

—— 2016d. "Russian Intervention in Syrian War Has Sharply reduced U.S. Options." February 10. www.nytimes.com.

—— 2016e. "Syria Truce Deal Makes Aid a Political Tool, Critics Say." February 12. www.nytimes.com.

Northam, Stephen W. 2013. "The Birth of a University Center at the University of North Georgia: The Use of Complex Adaptive Systems theory as a Research Model in the tudy of a Complex Policy Implementation." Dissertation: Valdosta State University.

Nye, Joseph S. 1988. "Gorbachev's Russia and U.S. Options." In: *Gorbachev's Russia and American Foreign Policy*, edited by Seweryn Bialer and Michael Mandelbaum. Boulder: Westview Press, 385–408.

Orvis, Stephen and Carol Ann Drogus. 2015. *Introducing Comparative Politics: Concepts and Cases in Context*, Third Edition. Washington, D.C.: Sage/CQ Press.

Ovie-D'Leone, Alex Igho. 2010. "The Shifting Global Power Balance Equations and the Emerging Real 'New World Order.'" *Alternatives: Turkish Journal of International Relations*. 9/2: 72–87.

Pabst, Adrian. 2009. "Central Eurasia in the Emerging Global Balance of Power." *American Foreign Policy Interests*. 31/3: 166–176.

Pain, Emil. 2005. "The Chechen War in the Context of Contemporary Russian Politics." In: *Chechnya: From Past to Future*, edited by Richard Sakwa. London: Anthem Press, 67–78.

Papp, Daniel S., Loch K. Johnson, and John E. Endicott. 2005. *American Foreign Policy: History, Politics, and Policy*. New York: Pearson/Longman.

Paterson, Thomas G., J. Garry Clifford, Shane J. Maddock, Deborah Kisatsky, and Kenneth J. Hagan. 2005. *American Foreign Relations, Volume 2, A History since 1895*, Sixth Edition. Boston: Houghton Mifflin Company.

Pelletière, Stephen C. 2007. *Losing Iraq: Insurgency and Politics*. Westport, Connecticut: Praeger Security International.

Peterson, James W. 2011a. *NATO and Terrorism: Organizational Expansion and Mission Transformation*. New York: Continuum.

—— 2011b. *European Security, East and West: The Significance of the Missile Shield Proposal*. Pittsburgh, Pennsylvania: The Carl Beck Papers in Russian and East European Studies, Number 2102.

—— 2013. *Building a Framework of Security for Southeast Europe and the Black Sea Region*. Lewiston, New York: The Edwin Mellen Press.

—— 2014. *American Foreign Policy: Alliance Politics in a Century of War, 1914–2014*. New York: Bloomsbury.

—— and Sarah Kuck. 2013. "American Foreign Policy after the Arab Spring." Presented at the Annual Convention of the Georgia Political Science Association, November 14–16.

—— and Sarah Kuck. 2015. "The Role of Outside Players in Civil Wars during the Last Five Years: Syria, Libya, Egypt, Ukraine, and Yemen." Presented at the Annual Convention of the Georgia Political ScienceAssociation, November 12–14.

Petrovic, Milenko. 2014. *The Democratic Transition of Post-Communist Europe: In the Shadow of Communist Differences and Uneven Europeanisation*. New York: Palgrave Macmillan.

Pollack, Kenneth M. 2011. "External Powers: Riding the Tsunami." In: *The Arab Awakening: America and the Transformation of the Middle East*, edited by Kenneth M. Pollack *et al.* Washington, D.C.: Brookings Institution Press, 277–284.

President Bush Makes the Case for War on Iraq." 2005. In: *Major Problems in American Foreign Relations, Volume II: Since 1914*, edited by Dennis Merrill and Thomas G. Paterson. New York: Houghton Mifflin Company, 555–557.

President William J. Clinton Applauds America's Globalism and Warns Against a New Isolationism." 2005. In: *Major Problems in American Foreign Relations: Volume II: Since 1914*, edited by Dennis Merrill and Thomas G. Paterson. New York: Houghton Mifflin Company, 510–512.

Rees, Wyn. 2004. "Emerging Security Challenges." In: *Redefining Transatlantic Security Relations: The Challenge of Change*, edited by Dieter Mahncke, Wyn Rees, and Wayne C. Thompson. New York: Manchester University Press, 161–207.

Remington, Thomas F. 2004. *Politics in Russia*, Third Edition. New York: Pearson/Longman.

Robinson, William J. 1998. "Beyond the Nation-State Paradigms: Globalization, Sociology, and the Challenge of Transnational Studies." *Sociological Forum*. 13/4: 561–594.

Russell, John. 2005. "A War by Any Other Name: Chechnya, 11 September and the War Against Terrorism." In: *Chechnya: From Past to Future*, edited by Richard Sakwa. London: Anthem Press, 239–264.

Sakwa, Richard. 1990. *Gorbachev and His Reforms1985–1990*. Englewood Cliffs, New Jersey: Prentice Hall.

—— 2005. "Introduction: Why Chechnya?" In: *Chechnya: From Past to Future*, edited by Richard Sakwa. London: Anthem Press, 1–20.

Sartes, Tönis. 2016. "The Ethnic–Colonial Communist Legacy and the Formation of the Estonian and Latvian Party Systems." *Trames: A Journal of the Humanities and Social Sciences*. 20/2: 115–143.

Sasse, Gwendolyn. 2002. "The 'New' Ukraine: A State of Regions." In: *Ethnicity and Territory in the Former Soviet Union: Regions in Conflict*, edited by James Hughes and Gwendolyn Sasse. Portland, Oregon: Frank Cass Publishers.

Schneider, William. 1997. "The New Isolationism." In: *Eagle Adrift: American Foreign Policy at the End of the Century*, edited by Robert J. Lieber. New York: Longman, 26–38.

Silvius, Ray. 2016. "The Embedding of Russian State-Sanctioned Multipolarity in the Post-Soviet Conjuncture. *Globalizations*. 13/1: Abstract.

SME. 2014. "Rusi budú znova špehovať USA cez základnu na Kube." July 16. www.sme.sk.

—— 2015a. "Pred 16 rokmi ich bombardovali. Teraz Čierna Hora vstupuje do NATO." February 12. www.sme.sk.

—— 2015b. "NATO podporuje tureckú vojenskú akciu proti Islamskému štátu." July 28. www.sme.sk.

—— 2015c. "Situácia v Donbase je napätá, o život prišlo šesť ukrajinských vojakov." May 6. www.sme.sk.

—— 2015d. "Ukrajina čiastočne obnovila dodávky elektriny na Krym." December 8. www.sme.sk.

—— 2015e. "Kiska sa stretne s Lavrovom, hlavnou témou bude ukrajina." March 25. www.sme.sk.

—— 2015f. "Putin nepozval Porošenka na oslavy konca vojny do Moskvy." March 26. www.sme.sk.

—— 2015g. "Moskva plánuje pri hranici s Ukrajinou druhú veľkú vojenskú základňu." September 23. www.sme.sk.

—— 2015h. "Moskva krítizuje Ukrajinu za zákaz kníh porporujúcich separatistov." August 11. www.sme.sk.

—— 2015i. "Veliteľ NATO vyzval Rusko, aby nepodnecovalo krízu na Ukrajine." April 15. www.sme.sk.

—— 2015j. "Nová armada bude chrániť 22-tisíc kilometrov východných hraníc Ruska." August 7. www.sme.sk.

—— 2015k. "Egypt dúfa, že Rusko pomôže v boji proti terorizmu na Blízkom východe." August 26. www.sme.sk.

—— 2015l. "Putin nariadil preveriť bojaschopnosť jednotiek na Sibíri." September 7. www.sme.sk.

—— 2016a. "Začala platiť dohoda medzi EÚ a Ukrajinou i odvetné sankcie Ruska" January 4. www.sme.sk.

Snow, Donald M. 2004. *National Security for a New Era: Globalization and Geopolitics*. New York: Pearson/Longman.

Snyder, Timothy. 2015. "Integration and Disintegration: Europe, Ukraine, and the World." *Slavic Review*. 74:4 (Winter): 695–707.

Sotiriou, Stylianos A. 2015. *Russian Energy Strategy in the European Union, the Former Soviet Union Region, and China*. New York: Lexington Books.

Soviet Reformer Arbatov Explains the 'New Thinking' in the Soviet Union." 2005. In: *Major Problems in American Foreign Relations, Volume II: Since 1914*, edited by Dennis Merrill and Thomas G. Paterson. New York: Houghton Mifflin Company, 505–508.

Stent, Angela. 2016. "Putin's Power Play in Syria." *Foreign Affairs*. 95/1: 106–113.

Stillman, Richard, II. 2004. *The American Bureaucracy: The Core of Modern Government*, Third Edition. Belmont, California: Thomson/Wadsworth.

Süddeutsche Zeitung. 2014a. "Gerichtsurteil Niederlande fur Tote von Srebrenica Mitverantwortlich." July 16. www.sueddeutsche.de.

—— 2015a. "Wer was erreichen will in Moskou." February 6. www.sueddeutsche.de.

—— 2015b. "US-Panzer fahren an Grenze zu Russland auf." February 25. www.sueddeutsche.de.

Terzuolo, Eric. 2006. *NATO and Weapons of Mass Destruction: Regional Alliance, Global Threat*. New York: Routledge/Taylor and Francis Group.

Thompson, Wayne C. 2004. "European-American Co-operation Through NATO and the European Union." In: *Redefining Transatlantic Security Relations: The Challenge of Change*, edited by Dieter Mahncke, Wyn Rees, and Wayne C. Thompson. New York: Manchester University Press, 93–131.

Trenin, Dmitri. 2016. "The Revival of the Russian Military." *Foreign Affairs*. 95/3: 23–29.

Tsygankov, Andrei P. 2013. "Foreign Policy." In: *Return to Putin's Russia: Past Imperfect, Future Uncertain*. New York: Rowman & Littlefield Publishers, Inc., 235–236.

—— 2014. "Review" *Political Science Quarterly* 129/3, 519–521.

Tucker, Robert C. 1987. *Political Culture and Leadership in Soviet Russia: From Lenin to Gorbachev*. New York: W.W. Norton & Company.

Ulam, Adam B. 1968. *Expansion and Coexistence: The History of Soviet Foreign Policy 1917–67*. New York: Praeger Publishers.

USA Today. 2008a. "Russian Warns Moldova over Separatist Region." August 27. www.usatoday.com.

—— 2008b. "Russia's Medvedev Adopts Tough Tone, Echoing Putin." September 4. www.usatoday.com.

—— 2008c. "Russian Defense Budget May Rise 25% in 2009." September 19. www.usatoday.com.

—— 2008d. "Russia Pushes Security Pact to Rival NATO." October 9. www.usatoday.com.

—— 2008e. "Reports: Russia Issues Warning over Missile Sites." September 10. www.usatoday.com.

—— 2014a. "Romania, Wary of Russia, Seeks Embrace of Washington." June 3. Accessed in www.usatoday.com.

—— 2014b. "Obama, NATO Chief Call for Afghan Security." July 8. Accessed in www.usatoday.com.

—— 2014c. "China Ends Drilling Operations in Disputed Sea." July 16. www.usatoday.com.

—— 2014d. "Obama to Speak with European Allies about Russia." June 2. www.usatoday.com.

—— 2015a. "NATO Returns Its Attention to an Old Foe, Russia." June 23. www.usatoday.com.

—— 2015b. "Putin Calls Turkey Downing Warplane 'A Stab in Back.'" November 24. Accessed in www.usatoday.com.

—— 2015c. "Kremlin Hits Turkey with Sanctions over Shoot Down of Russian Warplane." November 28. Accessed in www.usatoday.com.

—— 2015d. "Security Tight as Obama Arrives in Malaysia for ASEAN Summit." November 30. www.usatoday.com.

—— 2015e. "U.S. and Japan Train for 'High-End' Warfare on the High Seas." November 24. www.usatoday.com.

—— 2015f. "China Urges U.S. to Stop 'Provocative Actions' after B-52 flights." December 19. www.usatoday.com.

—— 2015g. "Relatives Told Buk Missile Downed Malaysia Airlines Flight 17." October 13. www.usatoday.com.

—— 2015h. "Ukraine Disputes Rebels' Weapons Pullback Claim." February 24. www.usatoday.com.

—— 2015i. "Ukraine Rebels Warn They Could Abandon Cease-Fire." March 18. www.usatoday.com.

—— 2015j. "Ukraine, Russia Trade Barbs amid Signs of New Offensive." June 4. www.usatoday.com.

—— 2015k. "Ukrainian Tatars Blockade Russian-Held Crimea." September 23. www.usatoday.com.

—— 2015l. "Resumed Violence Threatens Ukraine Cease-Fire." December 7. www.sme.sk.

—— 2015m. "Anger, Protests as Russia Destroys Tons of Banned Food." August 8. www.usatoday.com.

—— 2015n. "EU Will Stand Strong on Russian Sanctions." January 23. www.usatoday.com.

—— 2015o. "NATO Chief: Russia Is Behind Ukraine Rocket Attack." January 26. www.usatoday.com.

—— 2015p. "Hollande, Merkel Head to Ukraine with New Peace Plan." February 5. www.usatoday.com.

—— 2015q. "Leaders Agree to Ukraine Peace Deal after Marathon Talks." February 12. www.usatoday.com.

—— 2015r. "Officials: Ukraine Cease-Fire Largely Holding." February 15. www.usatoday.com.

—— 2015s. "Sweden Hopes Ukraine Truce Mends Russia–EU Relations." February 23. www.usatoday.com.

—— 2015t. "Kerry Arrives in Russia for Talks with Putin." May 12. www.usatoday.com.

—— 2015u. "Kerry, Russia Say Cease-Fire in Ukraine Must Continue." May 12. www.usatoday.com.

—— 2015v. "Biden Cracks Door to Lethal Aid to Ukraine." May 27. www.usatoday.com.

—— 2015w. "U.S. Protests Russian Jet Move on Air Force Plane." April 12. www.usatoday.com.

—— 2015x. "Survey: NATO COUNTRIES SEE AMERICA as Shield to Russian Thr"eat." June 10. www.usatoday.com.

—— 2015y. "Carter: U.S. to Put Military Equipment in 7 European Countries." June 23. www.usatoday.com.

—— 2015z. "Russia Appears to Extend Aid Hand to Greece." June 19. www.usatoday.com.

—— 2015aa. "Russia and Europe's Extremist Parties Find Common Cause." June 25. www.usatoday.com.

—— 2015bb. "Russian President Putin Pays a Visit to Iran Bearing Gifts." November 23. www.usatoday.com.

—— 2015cc. "UN: Death Toll from Syrian Civil War Tops 191,000." August 22. www.usatoday.com.

—— 2015dd. "Russia Offers More Aid for Syria's Assad, Could Worsen Europe's Migrant Crisis." September 10. www.usatoday.com.

—— 2015ee. "U.S., Russia Launch Military Talks on Syria." September 18. www.usatoday.com .

—— 2016a. "U.S. Stealth Jets Fly over S. Korea amid N. Korea Standoff." February 17. www.usatoday.com.

—— 2016b. "Navy Challenges China, others in South China Sea." January 30. www.usatoday.com.

—— 2016c. "At ASEAN summit, Obama calls for mutual prosperity." February 15. www.usatoday.com.

—— 2016d. "Obama, SE Asian Leaders Seek to Ease Maritime Tensions." February 17. www.usatoday.com.

—— 2016e. "Report: China Deploys Missiles to Disputed Island in South China Sea." February 17. www.usatoday.com.

—— 2016f. "Georgia Defense Minister Compares EU Integration to Soccer." February 13. www.usatoday.com.

—— 2016g. "Assad Forces Encircle Rebel-Held Aleppo." February 5. www.usatoday.com.

—— 2016h. "Russian War Planes Buzz U.S. Destroyer in Baltic." April 13. www.usatoday.com.

—— 2016i. "Defense Official: Russians Buzzed U.S. Plane in Baltic Sea." April 29. www.usatoday.com.

—— 2016j. "Threat from Russian and Chinese Warplanes Mounts." May 22. www.usatoday.com.

—— 2016k. "Russia Vows Response to U.S. Naval Ship's Entry into Black Sea." June 10. www.usatoday.com.

—— 2016l. "U.S. to Send 1,000 Rotating Troops to Poland, Obama says." July 8. www.usatoday.com.

—— 2016m. "Obama Applauds Halt to Decline in NATO Spending." July 9. www.usatoday.com.

—— 2016n. "U.S. Limits Training in Ukraine to Avoid Provoking Russia in the Region." April 11. www.usatoday.com.

—— 2016o. "Syrian Cease-Fire Set to Begin amid Doubts." September 12. www.usatoday.com.

—— 2016p. "Analysis: Syria Cease-Fire Deal with the U.S. Boosts Russia's Stature." September 14. www.usatoday.com.

"U.S. Covert Action in Chile (1963–1973)." 2005. In: *Major Problems in American Foreign Relations, Volume II: Since 1914*, Sixth Edition, edited by Dennis Merrill and Thomas G. Paterson. New York: Houghton Mifflin Company, 464–468.

Van Herpen, Marcel H. 2014. *Putin's Wars: The Rise of Russia's New Imperialism*. New York: Rowman & Littlefield.

Volgyes, Ivan. 1995. "The Legacies of Communism: An Introductory Essay." In: *The Legacies of Communism in Eastern Europe*, edited by Zoltan Barany and Ivan Volgyes. Baltimore, Maryland: The Johns Hopkins Press.

Walsh, Warren Bartlett. 1958. *Russia and the Soviet Union: A Modern History*. Ann Arbor: The University of Michigan Press.

Walt, Stephen M. 2007. "Taming American Power: The Problem of American Power. In: *American Foreign Policy: The Dynamics of Choice in the 21st Century*, Third Edition, edited by Bruce W. Jentleson. New York: W.W. Norton & Company, 571–572.

Warren, Keith, Cynthia Franklin, and Calvin L. Streeter. 1998. "New Directions in Systems Theory: Chaos and Complexity." *Social Work*. 43/4: 357–372.

Washington Post. 2008a. "Russian Relations in Doubt, Gates Says." August 15. www.washingtonpost.com.

—— 2008b. "Europe Gets Started on Quelling a Crisis." August 19. www.washingtonpost.com.

Webber, Mark. 2007. "Russia and the European Security Governance Debate." In: *Russia and Europe in the Twenty-First Century: An Uneasy Partnership*, edited by Jackie Gower and Graham Timmins. New York: Anthem Press, 267–288.

White, Jonathan R. 2002. Update. *Terrorism*, Fourth Edition. United States: Thomson/Wadsworth.

—— 2004. *Defending the Homeland: Domestic Intelligence, Law Enforcement, and Security*. United States: Thomson/Wadsworth.

—— 2009. *Terrorism and Homeland Security*, Sixth Edition. United States: Wadsworth/Cengage Learning.

White, Stephen. 2011. *Understanding Russian Politics*. New York: Cambridge University Press.

Williams, Nick. 1997. "Partnership for Peace: Permanent Fixture or Declining Asset," In: *NATO's Transformation: The Changing Shape of the Atlantic Alliance*, edited by Philip H. Gordon. New York: Rowman & Littlefield Publishers Inc., 221–233.

Index